RIVER *of* SPIRITS

RIVER *of* SPIRITS

A NATURAL HISTORY OF **NEW MEXICO'S LAS ANIMAS CREEK**

EDITED BY

HARLEY G. SHAW

PHOTOGRAPHS BY **MATILDE HOLZWARTH**

FOREWORD BY **TODD WILKINSON**

THE History PRESS

Published by The History Press
Charleston, SC
www.historypress.net

First published 2017

Manufactured in the United States

ISBN 9781625858603

Library of Congress Control Number: 2016956927

Dedicated to Joe C. Truett

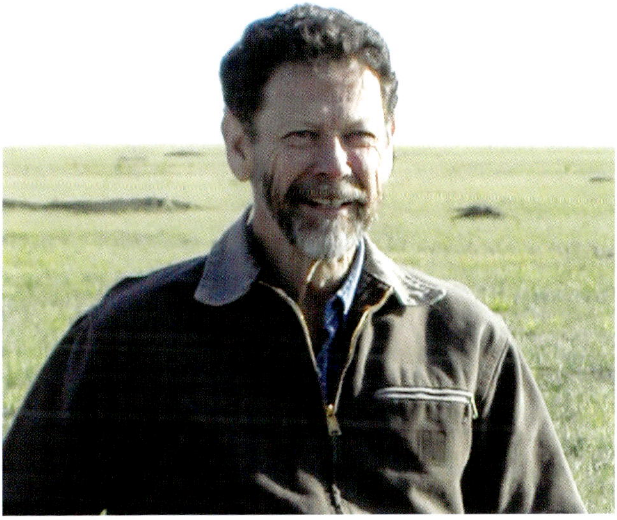

Joe C. Truett, distinguished wildlife biologist and author (1941–2011).

CONTENTS

FOREWORD

R*iver of Spirits* is a book eons in the making. Yet only recently did the cosmic forces conspire by bringing together such a group of distinguished, passionate biographers to take dictation from Mother Nature and share the story of a truly extraordinary stretch of American water.

Rio de Las Animas (River of Spirits), while not nearly as well known as other liquid life-ways, is, on so many different levels, a crucible for pondering our human relationship with the earth. More than a chronology of the people who have come to live by its banks over millennia, this book takes us on a humbling journey through time. From the "Ancient Ones," descended from those who crossed the Bering Strait and who first settled here, to those who followed in their wake long before the pyramids of Egypt were being built on another continent, to the more recent Puebloans, the arrival of conquistadors, the start of the cowboy era and onward to today with the presence of people like Ted Turner, the mosaic of human presence in River of Spirits is matched by the ecological natural history setting it apart.

Again, this is about far more than a creek in southwestern New Mexico. What Steve Dobrott, Harley Shaw and their colleagues have produced here is nothing short of momentous, and no matter where you live, whether you ever have the great delight of visiting Animas Creek or not, it will cause you to reflect on how much you actually know about your own backyard. Not many books hold the power to do that—to simultaneously entertain and cause you to muse long after the last page is turned.

I shall never forget a glorious autumn afternoon in the company of Dobrott and Shaw on the edge of a high butte in the middle of Ted Turner's Ladder Ranch. We had taken a group of Whitman College students with us as part of their "Semester in the West" program. Semester in the West is a novel course in which students travel the inner West experiencing firsthand its history, literature, cultural expressions and people. Here we were, at a place where pickup trucks could drive no farther for fear of falling off a precipice, and Dobrott invited a "Westie" to read from the writings of Aldo Leopold.

Steve, Harley and I choked back emotion, listening to Leopold's words of how the last grizzly bear and the last wolves were eliminated from the lands before us and a little farther beyond, in Arizona. Steve and Harley related how they had followed Animas Creek into the shadows of the Black Range to ground-truth the lore passed down in oral traditions, scrawled as indigenous pictographs, unearthed in archaeological digs, put down as ink on paper and shared over coffee in places like Hillsboro.

For a decade, I had heard how *River of Spirits* was coming together, each visit with Steve and Harley leaving my curiosity more piqued and inveigled. I had spent time with the late Joe Truett, who, too, regaled me with insights into native people who dwelled within the basin of Las Animas and how the clues they left behind are important harbingers as we confront climate change and loss of biological diversity.

Most of all, I came to greatly admire and respect Steve, Harley, Joe and others as I was researching my own book, *Last Stand: Ted Turner's Quest to Save a Troubled Planet.* Turner is globally renowned for founding CNN, for winning the America's Cup as a sailor, for becoming a forerunning environmentalist and second-largest private property owner in America. He is legend for hiring a lot of talented people to carry out his vision, and I remain convinced one of his greatest hires was Dobrott to oversee the Ladder Ranch.

I've had the good fortune over the course of more than three decades as a journalist to meet extraordinary people and visit extraordinary places, but this I can tell you: few other spots in the world intrigue me more than the wild, rugged flanks of Las Animas Creek because spirits really do roam its hinters—the haunting ghosts of people who came before, the wildlife that live large in the mythology of the West and as sentient beings in their own right, the constantly shape-shifting route of the river itself and even the geology that reaches back to time immemorial.

River of Spirits is an unforgettable collection of stories written by gifted storytellers. It is an important addition to the canon of place-based literature in the West. You will not only walk away with a greater appreciation for this corner of the American Southwest as a human crossroads, but you'll also be dreaming about this place. Let *River of Spirits* move you as much as it moves me.

Todd Wilkinson

Todd Wilkinson is an American writer and journalist who is the author of several books. His stories have appeared in a number of prominent newspapers and magazines, including *National Geographic*, the *Washington Post* and *Christian Science Monitor*.

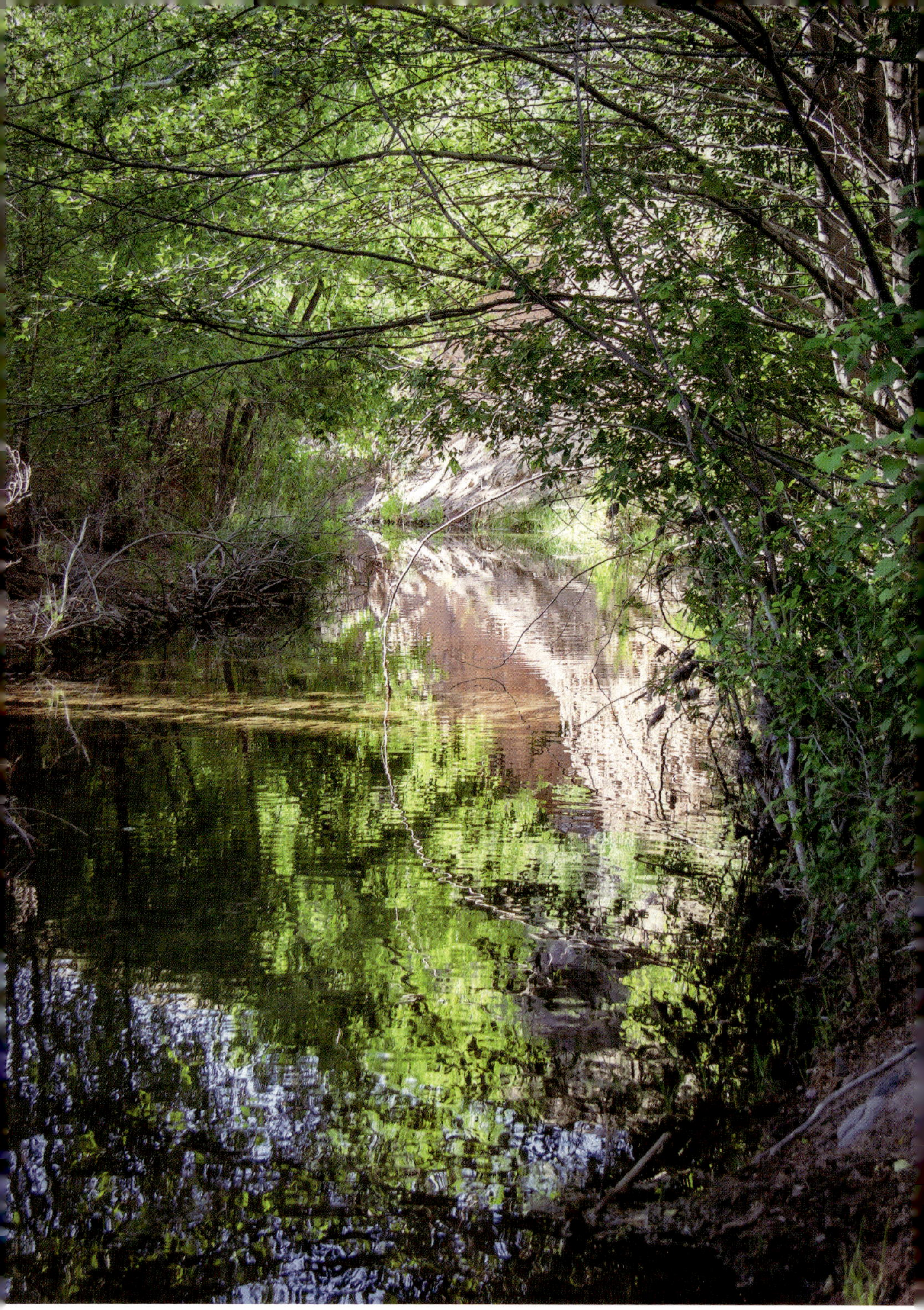

Mistletoe Pond. *M. Holzwarth, photographer.*

PREFACE

Harley Shaw and Steve Dobrott

I shall never forget that first sight of the Animas! We were on a bare and rocky ridge. No timber grew near to impede the vision. For weeks we had been picturing to ourselves this scene, but now, as we looked down over the maze of pinnacles, bluffs, rim-rock and boxes, the welter of formidable ridges and sharply cut canyons, we knew that nothing of our imagining approached this terrific fact in point of wildness or magnificence.
—William Pinkney Lawson, 1915

In 2010, Joe Truett, Turner Endangered Species biologist, and Steve Dobrott, manager of the Ladder Ranch, approached Mike Phillips, director of the Turner Endangered Species Fund, with plans for a popular book about Las Animas Creek. They felt that Las Animas was a worthy subject due to its unique history, its natural beauty and its importance as a riparian corridor. Joe and Steve envisioned a book that their boss, Ted Turner, would be proud to show his guests and that the general public would enjoy reading. They had barely begun compiling material when Joe died. He had contributed an outline and one chapter before his death.

Harley Shaw, retired wildlife biologist and longtime friend of Joe and Steve, offered to help complete the project and began investigating the history of the Rio de Las Animas as seen through the eyes of early homesteaders, goat herders, biologists and timber cruisers. We decided to try to write about the influences of the creek on the lives of humans down through time and the effects of humans on the creek, using this format to reveal its unique natural history. As we progressed, we realized we were dealing with two extremes in availability of information. On one hand, a variety of excellent texts were already available regarding certain aspects of Las Animas history; on the other, some subjects, such as geology, archaeology or post-settlement history, had never been covered, and neither Shaw nor Dobrott had the technical knowledge to create original materials on all of these subjects. We looked for outside help and ultimately reshaped the book into an anthology, with contributions by authors both living and dead. To us, this increased the diversity and readability of the book, but it also created unevenness in tone and chapter length. We haven't figured out how to make it otherwise.

Nonetheless, we hope to place in historic perspective the current visionary efforts set in motion by Ted Turner in his quest to restore lost or endangered ecosystems. We document protection or restoration of Chiricahua leopard frogs, Rio Grande suckers and chubs and Rio

Caballo Mountain sweep. *M. Holzwarth, photographer.*

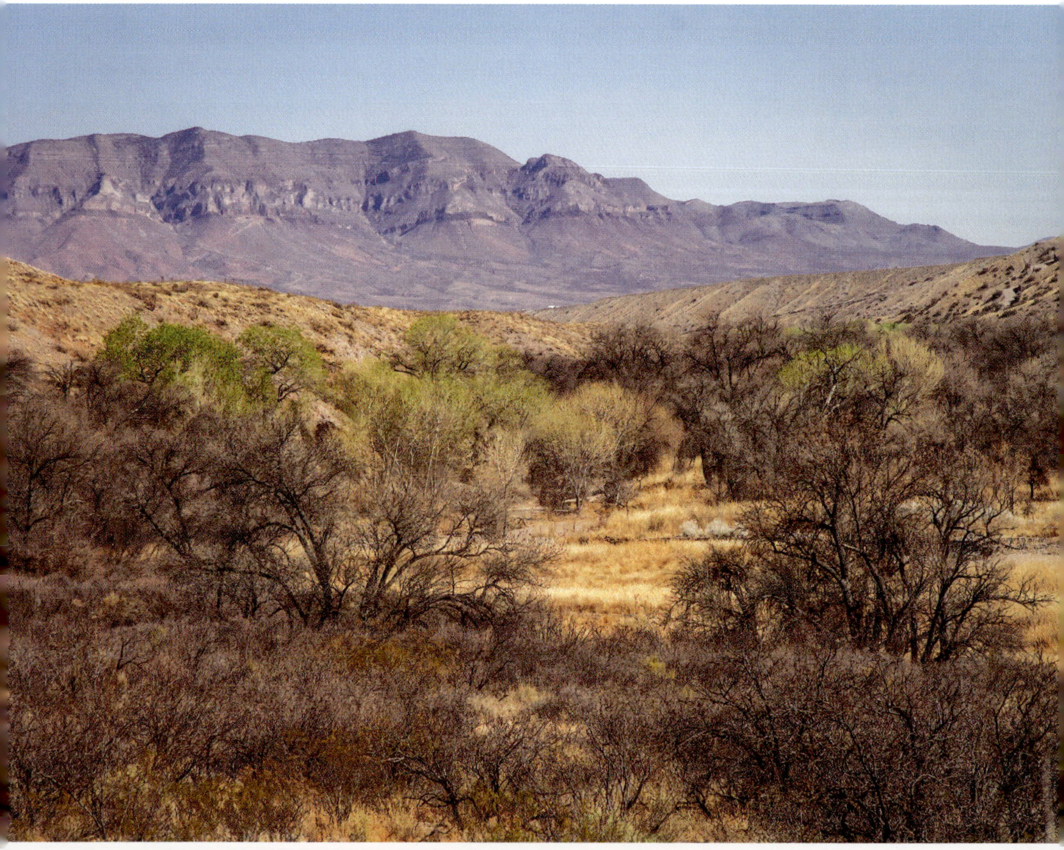

Grande cutthroat trout, along with habitat for a host of bird, mammal and reptile species.

Las Animas Creek is the least accessible watershed on the eastern slope of the Black Range. Originating high in the Aldo Leopold Wilderness, it flows almost due east for forty miles to the Rio Grande. Although flowing through an unquestionably western landscape, its waters ultimately join those of the Atlantic Ocean in the Gulf of Mexico, rendering the stream also a part of the ecosystem of the eastern United States. Except for its lowermost ten miles, the watershed has never been heavily settled. Prehistoric Western Mimbres cultures were scattered along it. Later, roving Apaches set up summer camps and gardens in its mid- and upper reaches and used it as a travel route between the Gila River watershed and the Rio Grande. Anglo and Mexican homesteaders eventually settled along it but seldom stayed. Its isolation, uncertain rainfall and ruggedness rendered it a poor place to homestead. It has never produced ore in abundance, so mines along its course remained small and as temporary as the homesteads. It is too remote and rugged for logging. Historically, the only economically viable use of the area has been goat and cattle ranching. Most of its watershed has now been incorporated into Turner Enterprises' Ladder Ranch, where sustaining wildness and ecological diversity, rather than producing meat or wool, are the guiding principles. Access to its upper reaches is difficult from any direction and possible by vehicle only from the east, with permission from the Ladder Ranch. Its uppermost tributaries lie within the Aldo Leopold Wilderness, where anything that runs on petroleum is disallowed.

Thus its inaccessibility, its history and its current status as wildlife habitat are enough to render Las Animas unique. But other features make it special. In its mid-reaches, it harbors magnificent stands of Arizona sycamores—the easternmost forest of this species and the only stand within the entire Rio Grande watershed. The massive and contorted trunks of these grand trees could occupy the creative efforts of a photographer or painter for a lifetime. Why only Animas Creek, of all the watersheds draining the Black Range, has sycamores remains a mystery. What unrecorded event brought this species so far east, and why does it not occur along other nearby streams?

Tiny upper tributaries of the Animas may have been the southernmost habitat for the threatened Rio Grande cutthroat trout, although the historic presence of this subspecies, or any trout for that matter, remains uncertain. Another threatened species, the Chiricahua leopard frog,

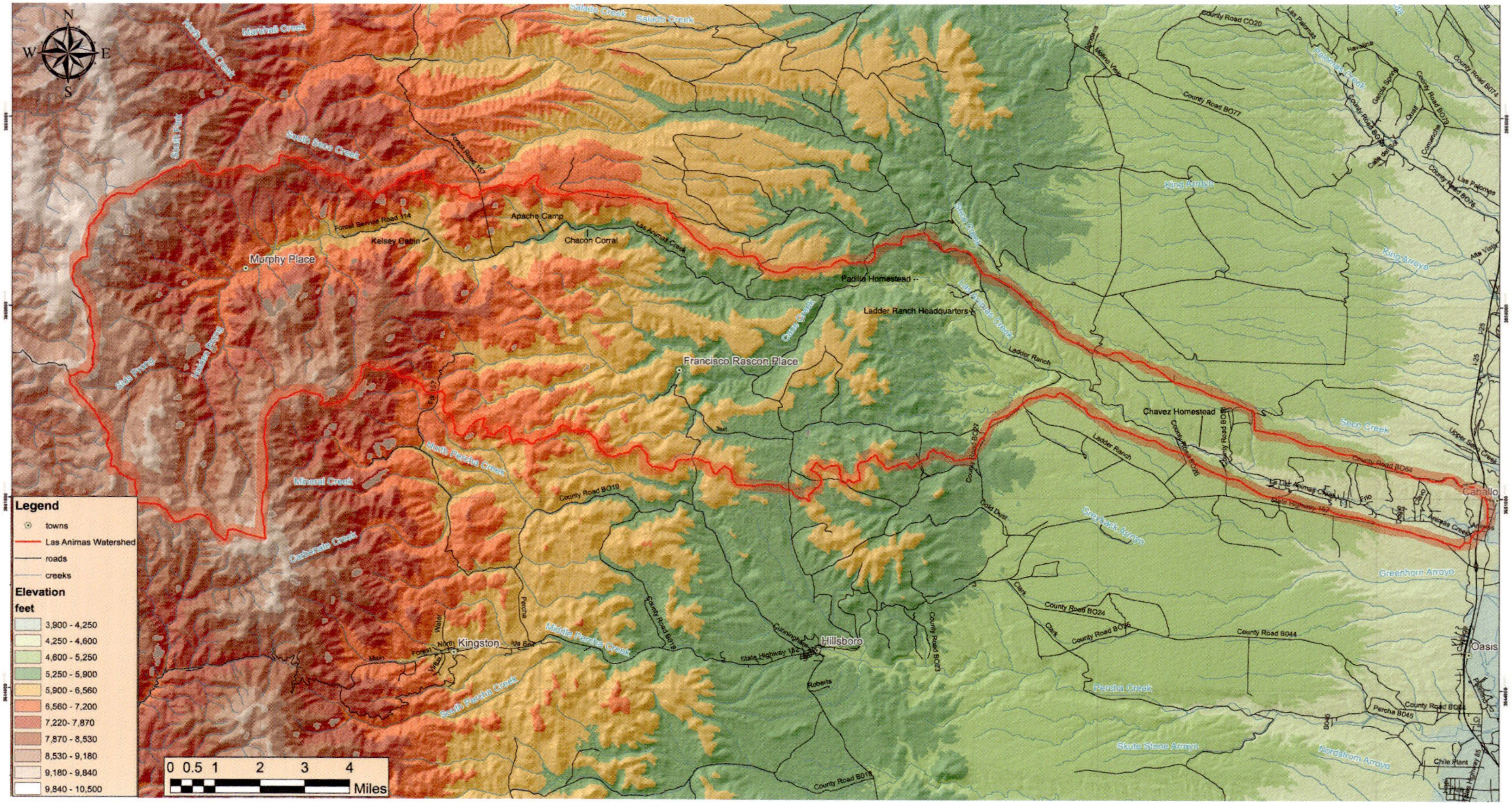

Legend
towns
Las Animas Watershed
roads
creeks
Elevation
feet
3,900 - 4,250
4,250 - 4,600
4,600 - 5,250
5,250 - 5,900
5,900 - 6,560
6,560 - 7,200
7,220- 7,870
7,870 - 8,530
8,530 - 9,180
9,180 - 9,840
9,840 - 10,500
0 0.5 1 2 3 4
Miles
N
S
E
W
Murphy Place
Apache Camp
Kelsey Cabin
Chacon Corral
Padilla Homestead
Ladder Ranch Headquarters
Francisco Rascon Place
Chavez Homestead
Kingston
Hillsboro
Caballo
Oasis

occurs along the Animas and is receiving special attention from the Turner Endangered Species Fund. White-tailed deer, mule deer, elk, mountain lion, black bear, wild turkey, javelina and bison all are abundant within its boundaries. Mexican black hawks and zone-tailed hawks are among its more interesting summer residents. Peregrine falcons nest in its cliffs, and Mexican spotted owls and northern goshawks live in the forests of its upper reaches. If efforts to restore the Mexican wolf to the Southwest are successful, Animas Creek will undoubtedly once again become part of its range. Wolves held in captivity to sustain the gene pool of this subspecies are periodically housed in large enclosures within the Animas drainage. Grizzlies once roamed the canyon. Their specters amid the ghostly sycamore trunks, lonely graves of buffalo soldiers and their Apache foes give mood and meaning to the name of the creek—Rio de Las Animas, or River of Spirits.

Opposite: Las Animas Creek Watershed map.

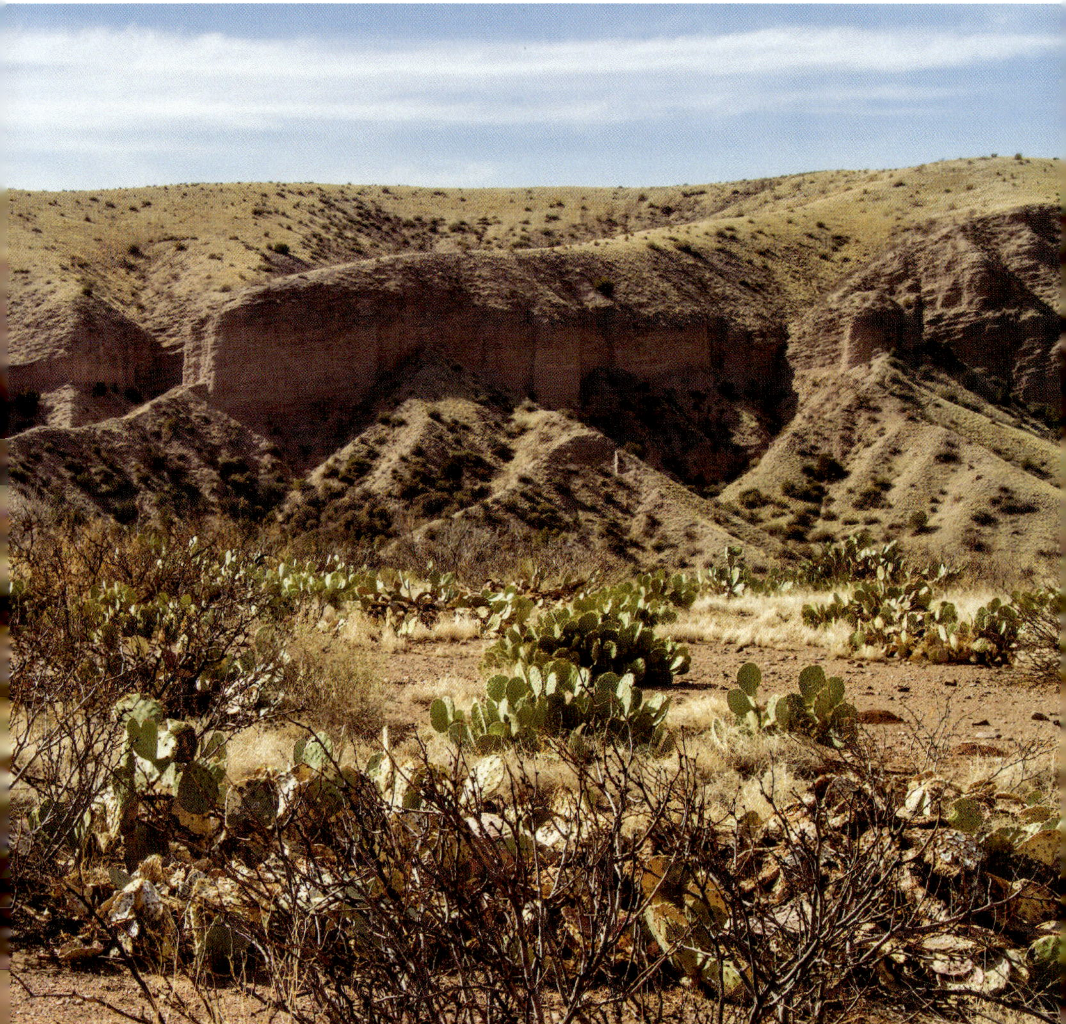

Prickly patch. *M. Holzwarth, photographer.*

ACKNOWLEDGEMENTS

First and foremost, we thank the individuals who have taken time to submit chapters for this manuscript. Their names appear on their respective chapters, and their biographical information is presented at the end of the book. The subjects covered here were too diverse to be handled by one or two people; we couldn't have done it without help.

Sally Antrobus of Houston, Texas, edited the book as it neared completion. Her suggestions regarding organization, questions on wording and encouragement helped us past a lull in our writing efforts. The following personnel of Turner Enterprises Inc. reviewed the book and offered helpful comments: Phillip Evans, chief PR/communications officer, and Baldwin Chambless and Kate Davis, editors. Mike Phillips, PhD, and Carter Kruse, PhD, both of the Turner Endangered Species Fund, also provided useful suggestions. In addition, we want to thank two anonymous reviewers who made useful suggestions.

We especially thank Helen (Dogie) Gordon Chavez, Josephine (Daisy) Faulkner Wilson and Leona and Harvey Chatfield for their insightful and entertaining stories. They made the homesteaders chapter come alive.

And, of course, we thank all the individuals, living or dead, who contributed chapters.

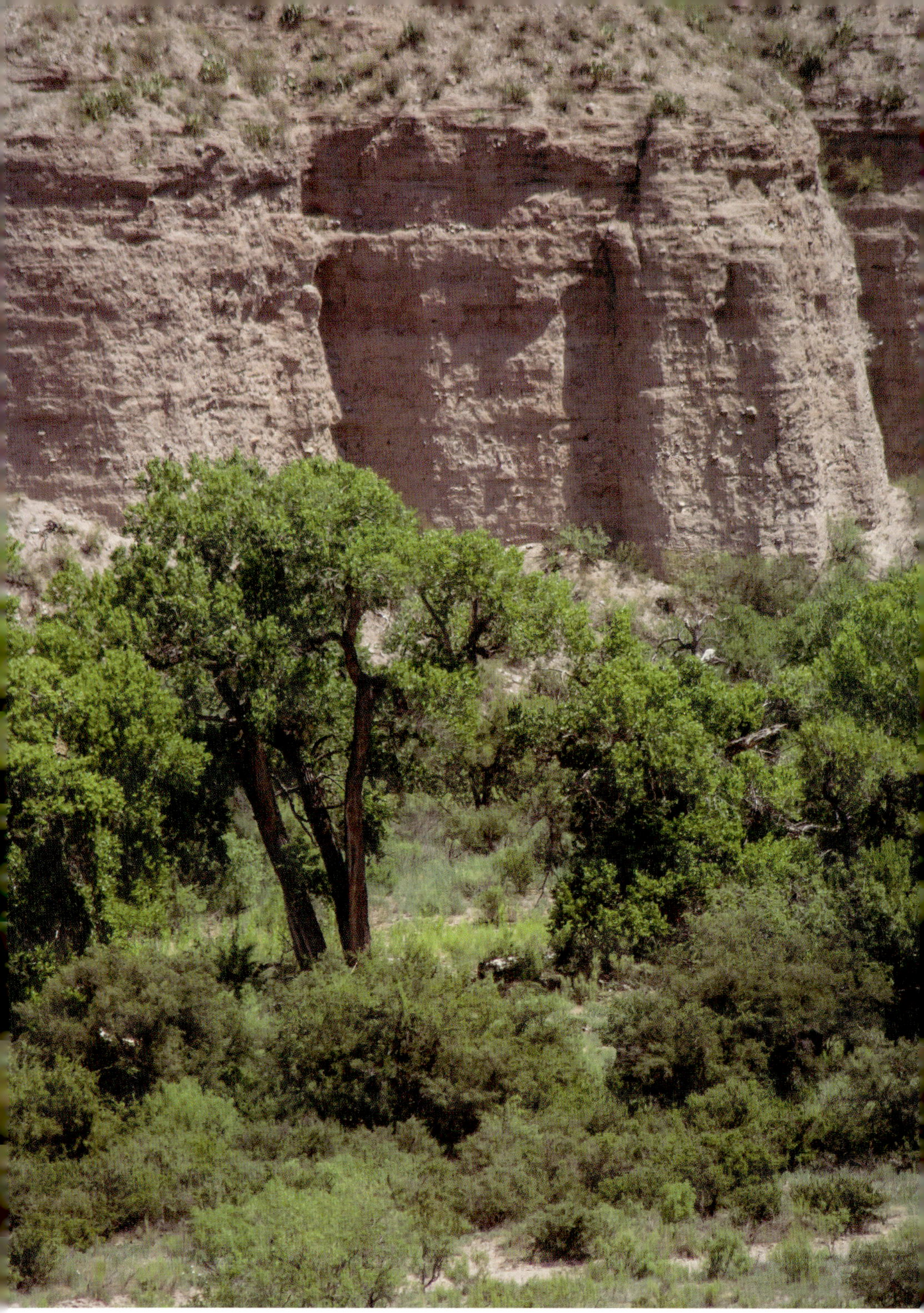

Cottonwood grove. *M. Holzwarth, photographer.*

INTRODUCTION

STEVE DOBROTT

Well, pal, you got the job.…Maybe you better go look at the ranch first." Ted indicated his approval of my brief interview with him in Bozeman. I was unprepared for such a quick decision. The next weekend, I visited the Ladder Ranch in south central New Mexico. My life was about to take an unexpected turn.

The call came in the spring of 1992. It was from Susan Anderson with the Tucson office of the Nature Conservancy. "How would you like to manage the Gray Ranch?" I was at my desk at the Buenos Aires National Wildlife Refuge—happily employed as the biologist responsible for the U.S. Fish and Wildlife Service's effort to restore the endangered masked bobwhite quail. The Gray Ranch in the "boot heel" of New Mexico wasn't new to me. I had worked there as a range and wildlife specialist from 1979 to 1985. The Conservancy had recently purchased the ranch in hopes that a conservation buyer could be found.

Somewhat stunned by her question, I replied, "Why? I spent seven years working there and am content where I am."

"Well, there is a person here that would like to speak with you. He said that if he bought the ranch, he would like a wildlife biologist to manage it, and your name came to my mind."

"Who is this person?" I asked.

"Ted Turner," she said.

"Ted Turner, Ted Turner…" I mumbled.

"You know, TBS, CNN…"

I knew who he was; I was just wondering what it would be like to work for the man. "Put him on."

The next voice I heard was loud, enthusiastic and somehow familiar: "Hi, pal, this is Ted." He explained that he was in New Mexico looking at the Gray Ranch and had just toured a portion of the 325,000-acre spread with Susan. "I like the ranch, and in addition to managing the quail, I want to restore species like the Mexican gray wolf, condors, prairie dogs and such. Would you be interested in the job as manager?"

I took a deep breath and then assured Ted that I would give it serious consideration.

"That's great, pal. I'll be in touch with you."

Susan took the phone and said she would be calling me back to explain further.

A bit dazed, I called my wife, Janie, and told her who had called. "You know, TBS, CNN…"

Several phone calls later, Ted revealed that he had decided not to purchase the Gray Ranch.

"Do you know anything about the Ladder Ranch in New Mexico?" he asked.

I told him that I was not familiar with that ranch but I would be happy to look into it for him. During one phone conversation, I revealed to Ted that I had done some ocean yacht racing while in my formative years in Southern California, that I rode horses and that my wife was also named Jane.

"That's great, pal. I would like to meet you and your wife," he said. "I'll send you some airline tickets."

Ted invited us to his Flying D Ranch outside Bozeman, Montana, to discuss my findings on the Ladder.

I suspected that this might be an interview. I was not really looking for another job, but I thought it would be fun to meet Ted and his new bride, Jane Fonda, so, equipped with maps and information on the Ladder and a one-page résumé, we flew to Montana. Knowing that Ted was interested in quail hunting as well as the bison-raising capability of the Ladder, I shared with him what I had learned regarding the biotic communities of the ranch. Based on the diversity of habitats and elevations from 4,500 to 10,000 feet, it was easy to predict that he would find three species of quail and lots of grama grass for grazing bison. What jumped out at me was the potential for the ranch to have running streams and the possibility for other unique habitats. I pledged to take a look and left Montana less sure of my future as a refuge biologist and more anxious about the possibility of taking a job with Ted. It was exciting and scary, but Ted had put his trust in me, and the notion of managing a ranch for him was intriguing.

Two weeks later, we visited the Ladder Ranch. I was not just amazed at the expanse and diversity of the four-hundred-square-mile ranch but was also impressed by the four semi-perennial drainages that emanate from the Black Range and drain into the lower Rio Grande. I was especially captivated by one, Animas Creek or the Rio Las Animas, as it was named by early Spanish explorers.

My experiences in Arizona taught me that any perennial stream in the desert Southwest is precious. I discovered that Animas Creek was still unspoiled and revealed little evidence of long-term cattle grazing, with the exception of localized impacts near headquarters. Such a pristine stream of this proportion is uncommon in New Mexico today and, sadly, only found on reserves that have excluded livestock for many years.

The Animas originates from the high reaches of Holden Prong, a beautiful but tiny stream that flows entirely within the Aldo Leopold Wilderness. It harbored a rich diversity of native plants and trees that my travels in the heavily grazed streams in Arizona had only revealed in comparative snippets. My initial impression of the ranch was one of wonder and intrigue. The wildlife biologist in me pondered what new and interesting species would be found in this fascinating place. I found petroglyphs made by prehistoric people depicting fish and turtles, suggesting the past occurrence of these species in the drainage. The fish looked like a trout with an adipose fin. Could this be a Rio Grande cutthroat? Could the turtle be an image of a tortoise? I encountered adobe homesteads melting back into the landscape along the creek, memorials to the efforts of Hispanic generations who scratched out meager livings within the narrow corridor of shallow soils and riparian vegetation. Named after still-traceable families like Padilla, Chavez and Zamora, these places bring to mind earlier days when life along the Animas was tough and unpredictable. Most families had small farm plots and raised Angora goats from which they harvested wool to send as far away as France and Germany prior to World War II.[1]

I noted that, compared to other places I had worked, few invasive plant species betrayed past abuses by these former inhabitants. The ubiquitous European perennial horehound had been introduced to the area in the wool of sheep and goats. Coastal Bermuda grass and weeping lovegrass had been planted during the Robert O. Anderson years to "improve" grazing capabilities. The inevitable Johnson grass existed near irrigated farms. A little Lehmann lovegrass occurred where a bag of seed had been spilled at

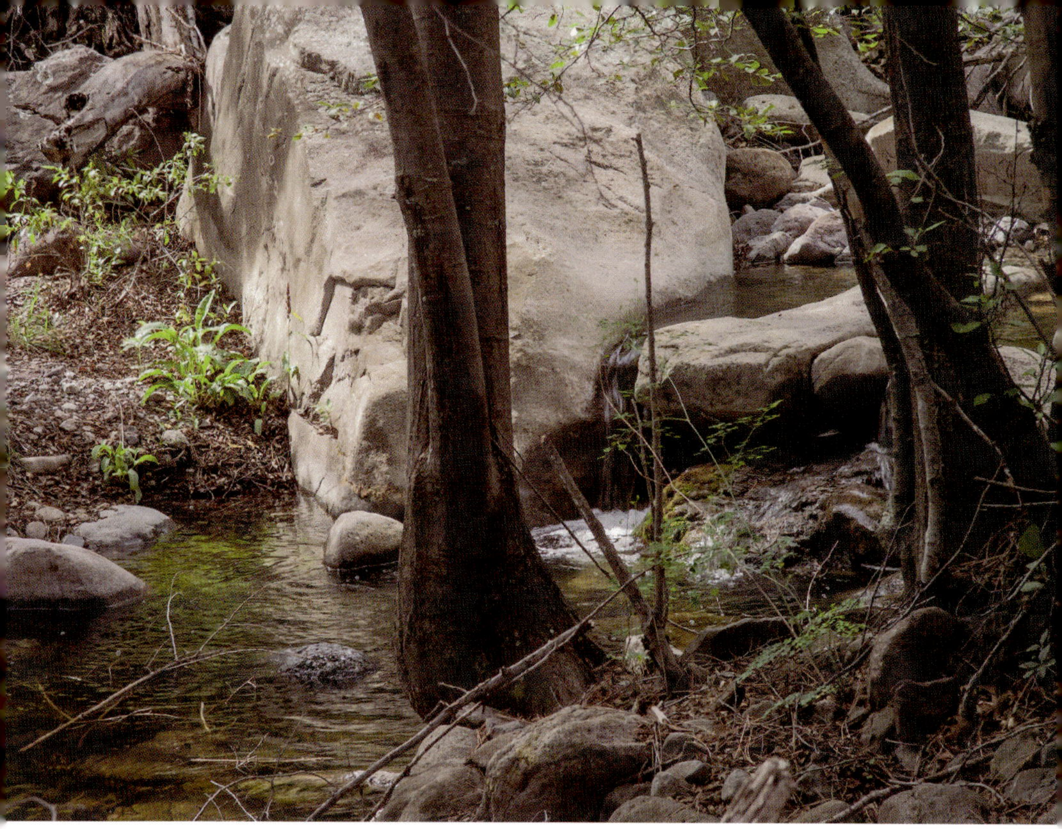

Headwaters. *M. Holzwarth, photographer.*

the Ladder headquarters. Animas Creek stood out as a jewel in the broader suite of remarkable Ladder Ranch landscapes. To think that one man could own or control such an immense amount of land—157,000 acres deeded, 20,000 acres state-lease land, 11,000 acres in Bureau of Land Management (BLM) and 100,000 acres in U.S. Forest Service allotments! That I was the prospective new steward of this colossal ranch was truly daunting.

I called Ted and accepted the job. I returned to the ranch, this time with Janie and all of my belongings, including an African grey parrot and some Spanish Barb horses. For weeks, I giddily explored, reminding myself that I was the manager responsible for the success or failure of its operation. Ted had given me a once-in-a-lifetime opportunity to bring to fruition his vision by putting into practice what I had learned as a range manager and wildlife biologist.

Twenty-five years later, I am still fascinated with the place and its vast and uncluttered spaces. My initial suspicions of what might live here were confirmed. During what seems but a turn of the page, I have participated in the discovery and protection of biological treasures while implementing

Ted's vision for quail, bison and rare species recovery. In April 2013, Todd Wilkinson's book *Last Stand: Ted Turner's Quest to Save a Troubled Planet* was published. Over the past two decades, I had become aware of the breadth of Turner's vision for wildlife conservation, but only after reading this book did I understand the magnitude of his concern for "planetary ecology." I was already proud to be part of the Turner operation, but I now feel that working on the Ladder Ranch has made me part of a new and far-reaching philosophy that I hope will spread throughout the private and public sectors of the world. The existence of our planet may depend on it.

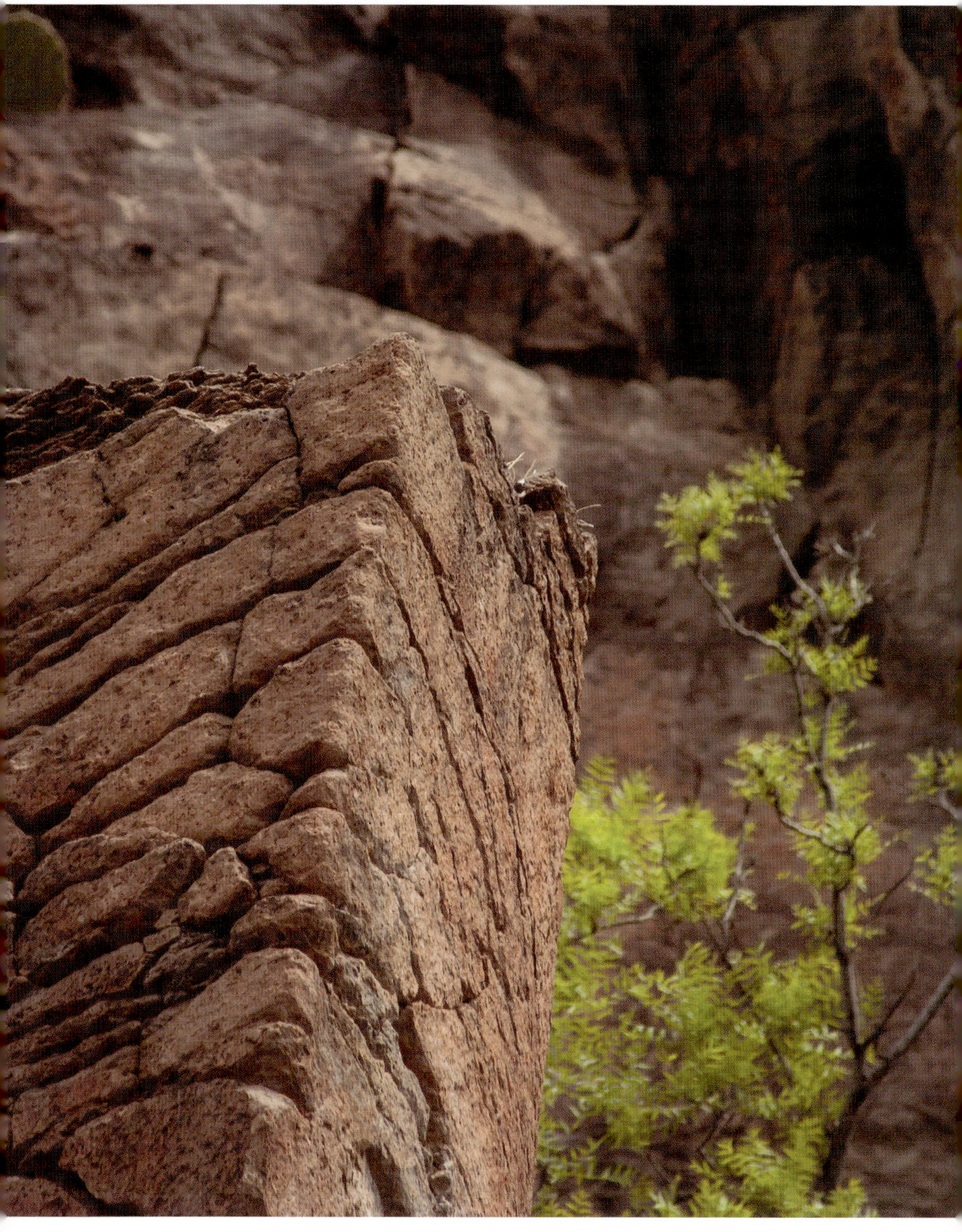

Canyon edge. *M. Holzwarth, photographer.*

Chapter 1

FORMING THE LANDSCAPE

DAVID COBLENTZ AND GRETCHEN KERR

While the development of Las Animas Canyon can be deduced from our understanding of regional tectonics and volcanic activity, no detailed geologic survey of the canyon has yet been completed. Rugged terrain and presence of hostile Apaches kept scientists and explorers from penetrating the mountain until the 1890s. Early geological interest in the Black Range was focused on ore-producing drainages to the north and south, and the Las Animas drainage seemingly lacked valuable mineral resources, so it was ignored. Once the Apaches were chased from the mountain, a wagon road was built connecting Hillsboro and Hermosa, resulting in an influx of people across the Las Animas Creek watershed. Well into the 1930s, ranchers, homesteaders, foresters, hikers, hunters and fishermen temporarily occupied the canyon's reaches. Prospectors undoubtedly explored the region. In fact, most of the travelers in the area between 1880 and 1930, regardless of their vocation, had an eye open for gold and silver. However, few mining claims were ever developed in the Las Animas watershed. George Townsend Harley's 1934 summary of Black Range geology and ore deposits made virtually no mention of Las Animas Creek, and his geologic profiles for the Black Range (Emory Caldera) are based on studies made north and south of Las Animas.[2] Ample opportunity remains for geologic studies of Las Animas drainage.

Las Animas Creek flows almost 40 miles from the head of Holden Prong to the Rio Grande at Caballo Reservoir. It is recognized as the longest, deepest, most rugged and least accessible of the canyons draining the Black Range. Its watershed drains 140 square miles of the eastern slopes of the Black Range and is made up of five principal sub-watersheds: Holden Prong, Headwaters, Cave Creek, Animas Gulch and Outlet Las Animas. Numerous smaller drainages feed the Animas, including Sand, Water, Pretty, Curtis, Massacre, Cave and Tank Canyons. Elevations along the creek range from more than 10,000 feet in the west headwaters to near 4,200 feet at its terminus in the Caballo Reservoir. Topographic relief along the Las Animas is extreme; slopes along the upper watershed typically exceed twenty degrees, and even along its lower reaches, the creek is deeply incised into the otherwise flat sedimentary strata that descend toward the Rio Grande.

The geology of the watershed is a complex assembly of rocks that represent more than 300 million years of alternating periods of quiet deposition and violent upheaval. The earliest rocks in the region are Paleozoic sandstones, deposited between 300 and 100 million years ago (Ma), when southwestern New Mexico was alternately tropical or covered by shallow seas. Las Animas lay within the large continent of Laurentia, which straddled the equator. Only a narrow band of these sandstones remains near the present Gila National Forest boundary. This was a geologically quiet period with a setting resembling the present-day Gulf of Mexico coast.

Starting about 80 Ma, the landscape became tectonically more violent, creating nearly 50 million years of active mountain building. Mountains rose above ten thousand feet, possibly to more than fifteen thousand feet. Volcanoes were common. The result of this geologic upheaval was a series of north–south trending mountains similar to the present-day Andean mountain range in South America.

Over the past 30 million years, further changes in the tectonic setting have resulted in the collapse of these once-mighty mountain ranges, producing the Basin and Range Province that characterizes much of the western United States. This period continued to be characterized by major volcanic activity throughout the Southwest. Hot magmas weakened the crust, and the mountains fragmented and then collapsed, as the abrasive movement between the Pacific and North American plates shifted from east–west to north–south orientation. Many volcanic calderas formed throughout the region, further jumbling the stratigraphy.

Two major geologic features of southern New Mexico developed during this time: the Rio Grande Rift and the Mogollon-Datil volcanic field. The Rio Grande Rift began forming between 35 and 29 Ma as tectonic forces fractured the North American plate. This spreading force triggered volcanism that formed the Mogollon-Datil volcanic field. The Black Range (Emory Caldera), which formed roughly 35 to 40 Ma, is at the southeastern edge of the volcanic field. Small eruptions continued until about 2.5 Ma, creating the numerous basaltic flows that cap the buttes and mesas throughout the Animas watershed. The result of this active geologic history is a complex mix of rocks from vastly differing ages and origins throughout the watershed. Currently, the region is undergoing extensional faulting, yielding the development of canyons along the eastern margin of the Black Range. These canyons, including Las Animas, cut through the jumbled rocks on the mountain slopes and the deep sediments farther out in the valley.

A journey up the Animas Creek is a journey through time. Along its lower reaches, the creek cuts through deep outflow sediments, called the Santa Fe Group, that are less than 2 million years old. Nearing the present Gila National Forest Boundary, the creek passes through a narrow belt of sediments that are more than 200 million years old, the remains of the original Laurentian seabeds. Like all of the other major streams coming off the east face of the Black Range, Las Animas and Seco Creeks pass through narrow canyons in outer foothills formed by a geologic event termed the Animas Uplift. This uplift mingles formerly deep crystalline plutonic and near-surface sedimentary deposits that constitute the extreme outer boundary of the Emory Caldera, the remnants of an old super-volcano that was perhaps as large as the present-day Yellowstone volcanic region. For some 15 million years, this part of southern New Mexico was the center of some of the most explosive and extensive areas of continuous volcanic activity in the world. About 35 million years ago, the caldera collapsed, spreading ash hundreds of feet thick over nearly one thousand square miles. This ash deposit, known as the Kneeling Nun tuff, is exposed near Silver City, New Mexico. In many locations along Animas Creek, the Kneeling Nun forms dramatic palisades and interesting solitary rock towers.

Geologic faults also play a major role in the character of Las Animas Creek. The narrow and rugged "box" that the creek flows through above the ranch headquarters is the result of two major fault lines that lie downstream from the mouth of Cave Canyon. These faults also mark the boundary of the Animas Uplift and have a role in the surface appearance of the very large spring upstream from headquarters. Once Las Animas departs this "box," it broadens and flows through the younger outwash sediments for the remainder of its way to the Rio Grande. This wider,

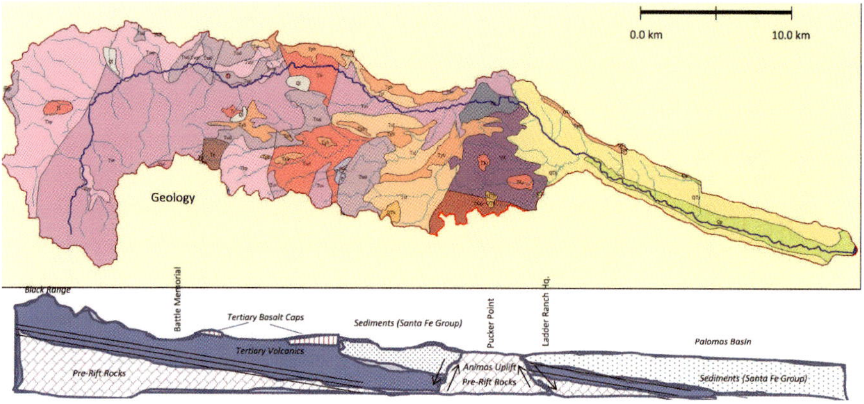

Geology: Las Animas Watershed map.

more level stretch of the canyon lends itself to farming and was the reach most homesteaded historically.

The stream flow of Las Animas comes mainly from precipitation at high elevations on the Black Range. Much of the rainfall infiltrates downward through permeable soils, rocks and crevices, being held as soil moisture or feeding the subsurface water table of the stream and moving to downstream aquifers. Snow from winter storms melts and infiltrates to feed springs and sustain perennial reaches of the upper tributaries, ultimately feeding into the downstream water table. Where faults and lava dams block subsurface flow, groundwater surfaces, becoming intermittent along mid- to lower reaches of the stream. The largest of these springs, mentioned above, comes to the surface where the canyon begins to widen, just upstream from the Ladder Ranch headquarters.

As a perennial stream in the Southwest desert, the Las Animas Creek is an elongated riparian oasis in an otherwise dry landscape. According to Davie and Spiegal, the Las Animas and Seco Creek aquifers are interconnected, with much of the groundwater from both streams directed into the Las Animas basin at the western edge of the Animas Uplift.[3] The Percha shale blocks water flow at this point, and ground and surface water combine to create perennial flow of Las Animas Creek downstream from the fault. A portion of this flow plus tailings from modern irrigation eventually sink back into the streambed alluvium downstream and once again become part of the water table.

The Las Animas water table has been exploited via wells and diversions over the past 140 years. Davie and Spiegal documented 146 wells within the influence area of Las Animas Creek. The Ladder Ranch is currently the main user of water, diverting the creek flow just below Warm Spring for irrigation of a series of pastures that are maintained as food for wildlife.

Because of the complex geologic history of the canyon, many types of rock contribute to the formation of creek bed sediments and flood plain soils. The Kneeling Nun and some of the sediment beds provide a source of abundant sand, gravel and cobbles. Other sediments, ash beds and basalts weather to clays. The subsurface geology of the streambed undoubtedly contributes to perched groundwater in some reaches of Animas Creek. In these areas, stream water held in the upper sediments by a hard subsurface layer remains available to sycamores and other riparian vegetation, even when surface water is not visible. Additionally, the varied rock types contain a broad array of chemical constituents, such as magnesium, iron, calcium, phosphorus and pH-buffering compounds that contribute to vegetation health and diversity.

The unique combination of topography, water and rock makes the creek a special place, with roots that extend many millions of years into the past. This long history has culminated in the Animas as we see it today—a wild and scientifically unexplored terrain that provides habitat for unique and threatened wildlife, relict plants and remains of earlier human cultures.

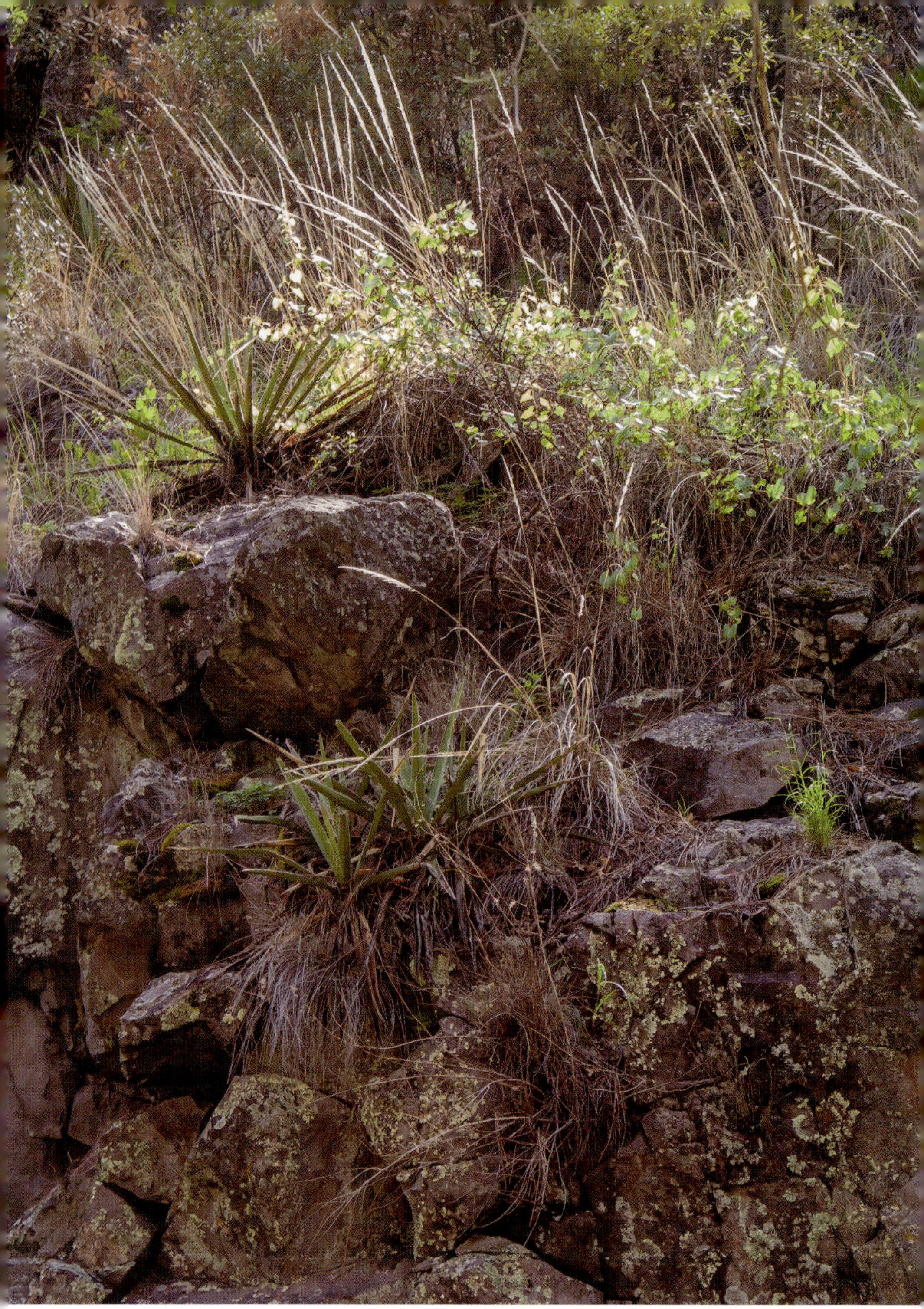

On the rocky wall. *M. Holzwarth, photographer*.

Chapter 2

BEFORE COLUMBUS AND CORONADO

THE MIMBRES

JOE TRUETT[4]

Traveling the roads and trails near Animas Creek gives a perspective of the surrounding landscape. Each traveler sees somewhat different things because perceptions are conditioned by prior experience. Botanists look at plants, geologists at rocks and hunters and birdwatchers at habitat and signs of their favorite animals. One vision remains obscure to nearly all: Animas Creek as it used to be. Living on land without understanding its past invites mistakes others have made. But the Animas country boasts a thin written history, most of it dating back little more than a century. Looking further into the past requires special skills and techniques applied to special sites. One such site sits on a high bench overlooking Animas Creek near Ladder Ranch headquarters.

Here on the north side of the creek, from an elongate flat one hundred feet or so higher than the flood plain, one can see the headquarters' buildings a short distance upstream. Irrigated acres stretch up and down the flood plain. Never-failing springs keep water near at hand, inviting human settlement.

The bench appears at first glance to be just a flatter-than-usual substrate for the shrubs, grasses and cacti that dominate the adjacent slopes. But closer inspection, particularly by a trained eye, discloses signs of past human occupancy—alignments of boulders on the surface or an occasional stone shaped and smoothed to fit a woman's hand. Archaeologists know these as markers of an ancient village, now largely beneath the land surface.

In the early 1990s, two well-known archaeologists gravitated to this site.[5] With approval and support from the Turner family, they and students from

Arizona State University commenced digging. They moved tons of soil by hand, unearthing collapsed roof supports, crumbled walls, stone tools, broken pottery, plant seeds and animal bones. With trowels and brushes, they exposed and mapped artifacts, developed calendars of human occupation and estimated the sizes of the village at various times in prehistory. On this basis, they explored the life-ways and the comings and goings of the people who lived here off and on for two millennia.

Drs. Margaret Nelson and Michelle Hegmon came armed with years of experience excavating abandoned villages of ancient southwesterners.[6] Such experience gave them intuitive understanding of hopes and fears of these early settlers, which translated their findings into images of past people living real lives. They called the people who had lived there in greatest abundance the Eastern Mimbres (*mimbres* is Spanish for willow). The Mimbres River thirty miles west of Las Animas had hosted the first studies of, and gave the name to, the Mimbres culture.

To artifact collectors, the word "Mimbres" elicits images of clay pots decorated with black-on-white designs including likenesses of animals. Such pottery comes from a region in southwestern New Mexico stretching from the Rio Grande west to about the Arizona state line and southward into northern Chihuahua. To some of European ancestry who settled and lived in this region after 1880, the term "Mimbres" brings to mind the excitement of excavating village sites with pick, shovel, bulldozer and backhoe to supply the artifact trade. To archaeologists, who call such digging "looting," it identifies as a distinctive culture the people who made the pottery. To history-minded ecologists, it suggests opportunities for understanding ancient ecosystems and human impacts on them as a basis for management and restoration.

Developing from a crude pithouse culture that began about 1,800 years ago, the so-called Classic Mimbres peoples rode a population wave that crested about 1,000 years ago.[7] They lived in large villages near dependable water and land that could be farmed—that is, along streams. At Las Animas, they probably cultivated some of the same flood plain sites the Ladder Ranch people farm now. Here, as elsewhere in Mimbres country, they ate primarily corn, beans, squash and other produce from irrigated fields. They harvested wild plants and animals to supplement crop production. Along about AD 1150, their numbers crashed. Signs of Mimbres culture—the distinctive pottery, the stone and mortar buildings—vanished from the archaeological record.

Nelson and Hegmon have spent much of their careers investigating the long-standing mystery: what happened to the Mimbres? Others have asked the same question about other prehistoric cultures that flourished in the Southwest during the same general period—the Anasazi, the Hohokam, the Mogollon. As with the Mimbres, these left only crumbling rock or adobe walls, potsherds and other relics of their one-time presence. All seemed to flourish for several generations and then vanish. What happened? Vacant cliff dwellings beg the question at Mesa Verde, Colorado, and on the upper Gila River thirty miles west of the head of Animas Creek. Open-air rock and mortar buildings ask it at Wupatki near Flagstaff, Arizona, and Chaco Canyon in northwestern New Mexico. Crumbled adobe structures ask it along the lower Gila, Salt and San Pedro Rivers in Arizona. What happened to the people who once lived here?

Similarities among these cultures suggest something about their disappearance. All farmed. All lived sedentary lifestyles near dependable water. All built their numbers on increasing acreages brought under cultivation. All probably became too populous to feed themselves without crops.

To better appreciate what happened, it helps to look further back, long before farming. The first New World people swept in from the Bering Land Bridge and Alaska twelve to thirteen thousand years ago. These so-called Paleoindians expanded southward and multiplied, feasting in the process on a plentitude of wild game—now-extinct mammoths, bison, ground sloths, horses, camels and others. Many scientists think the quest for food by these supreme predators caused many extinctions.[8]

New Mexico lays claim to the first two major discoveries linking Paleoindian hunters with their prey. The first discovery occurred in 1908 near Folsom, in the northeastern corner of the state. One spring morning in 1908, cowboy George McJunkin noticed bones of a large animal projecting from the eroded bank of an arroyo. Scientists who visited the site later found ten-thousand-year-old "Folsom" projectile points among the bones, which turned out to be those of an extinct bison, predecessor of the present-day form.

A more startling find came twenty-six years later near Clovis, in east-central New Mexico, about three hundred miles east of Animas Creek. Two amateur archaeologists found fluted projectile heads, later named Clovis points, among mammoth bones along the shoreline of a long-extinct lake. Later radiocarbon dating confirmed this mammoth kill as more than eleven thousand years old, fitting dates of other Clovis points subsequently discovered throughout North America.

Within a few thousand years after people entered the prairies and parklands of North America, the Pleistocene megafauna disappeared.

Only bison, elk and smaller mammals remained of the once-plentiful meat supply. Even these may have been whittled down to small numbers by meat-hungry bands of people. The cause of decline of the megafauna during this period is still a matter of contention among paleontologists. At the same time humans entered the Americas, the Pleistocene was ending and rapid change of climate occurred. The disappearance of the large Pleistocene species may have been brought about by climate change, human impacts or a combination of the two. Human numbers may have dropped in sync with the mass extinction of their prey, though that's hard to confirm so far back in time. In the Animas Creek region and throughout the Southwest for several millennia, people of this diminished culture left little sign—grindstones, mortars, the occasional stone scraper and arrowheads. Archaeologists often lump these little-known people into the catch-all Archaic tradition.

About three thousand years ago, knowledge of corn and cultivation arrived from southern Mexico, where farming had commenced a few thousand years earlier. Why it took so long to move north remains a mystery; perhaps new crop varieties had to be developed to withstand the different climates. In any case, archaeologists find the tiny cobs of three-thousand-year-old corn not far from Animas Creek, persisting in dry caves and other rock shelters. But sign of these earliest New Mexico farmers remains scanty. Indeed, farming seems to have been a marginal enterprise in the area for about one thousand years thereafter, and most archaeologists believe it added little to the diets or survival of people.

That all began to change some 1,600 years ago. Pottery, probably imported from cultures farther south, appeared about AD 400. People emerged from caves, started making pots and moved into more respectable quarters, all at about the same time. The first buildings, sunk into the ground and walled with rock and mortar, evoked the name "pithouse" to describe the architecture and the architects.

Over the next several hundred years, Pithouse peoples grew slowly in number, eventually giving rise to those we now call Mimbres. In the process, farming technologies and crop varieties expanded, and the people built their houses fully on the surface. They began making pottery that is praiseworthy even by modern standards. By the year AD 1000, the Classic Mimbres culture emerged in full bloom and peak numbers.

At Las Animas, as at other spots favorable for settlement throughout the world, new cultures built atop old ones. Hegmon and Nelson unearthed remains of Pithouse, Mimbres and post-Mimbres cultures—a sequence spanning almost two thousand years—on the flat overlooking Animas Creek.

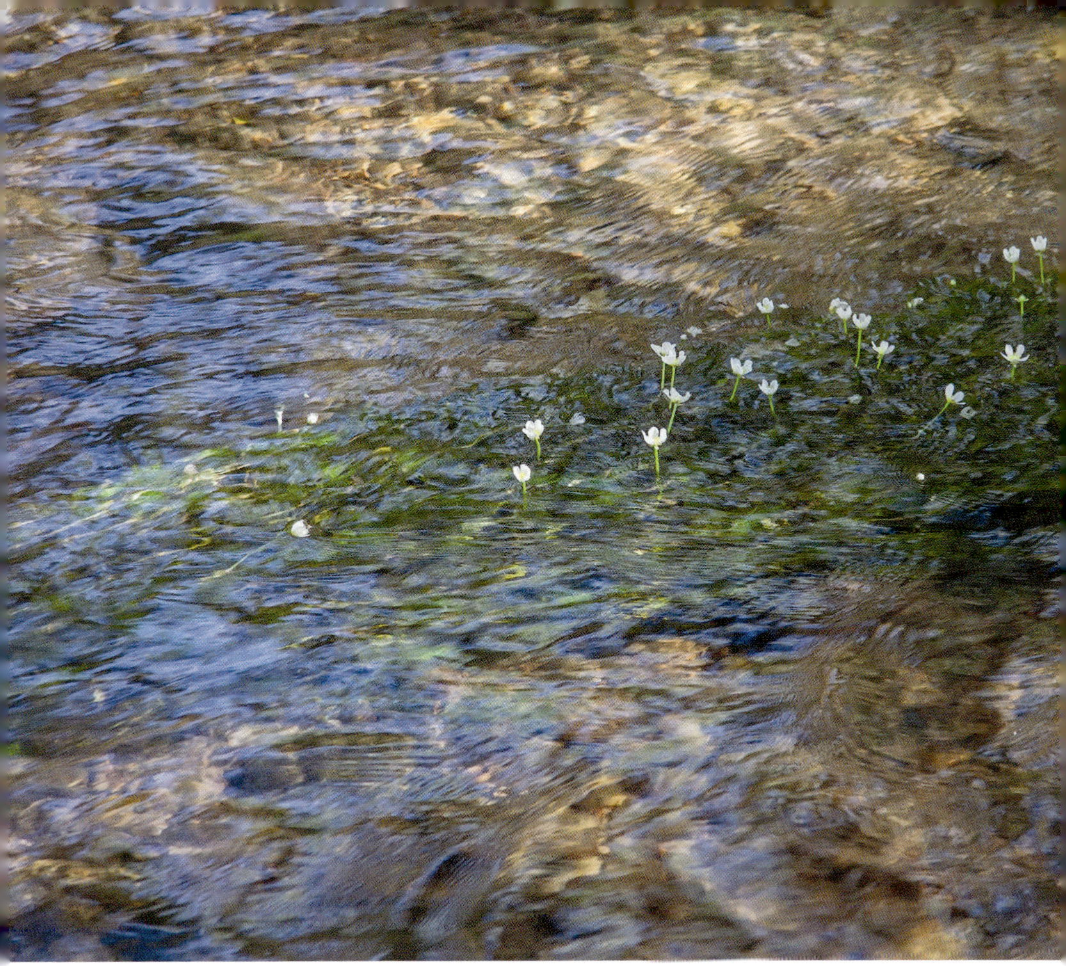

Emergent blooms. *M. Holzwarth, photographer.*

People from Paleoindian and Archaic times probably camped there in even earlier millennia, but they left little sign of their passage.

In early March 2001, a cadre of distinguished scientists gathered in the Ladder Ranch lodge to share ideas and knowledge about the Mimbres. Called together by Hegmon and Nelson under the banner "Mimbres Lives and Landscapes," these experts educated Turner managers and ecologists about how this and other southwestern farming cultures lived in and altered their surroundings. Turner biologists, predisposed to use pre-European or "aboriginal" conditions as a general guide for ecosystem management and restoration, were particularly interested in answers to two questions: What was the Animas country like in Mimbres times? Did prehistoric peoples impose important ecosystem impacts, and if so, what does this mean for restoration?

These scientists proved adept at describing the Mimbres as humans not much different from us in basic motivations. Like people everywhere, the Mimbres produced more children than needed for replacement, ultimately testing the limits of their agricultural technology and the landscape to produce food. They almost certainly produced crops and harvested wild foods to the limits of their abilities and immediate wants, with no appreciation for sustainability.

Jon Sandor, a soils specialist from Iowa State University, suggested one reason the Mimbres might have abandoned Las Animas. In the Mimbres Valley to the west, he had found that farm plots that had been abandoned nearly one thousand years ago were still depleted in nitrogen and phosphorus—testimony to the extractive practices of Mimbres farmers and the slow rate at which soil nutrients replenish themselves. Modern farmers know, but perhaps the Mimbres did not, that reduced crop production results from soil nutrient depletion.

Paul Minnis from the University of Oklahoma is an ethnobotanist. In past years, he combed the soils of prehistoric village sites along the Mimbres River, looking for thousand-year-old pieces of wood, plant fragments and seeds. Although the Mimbres Valley, the geographic core of Mimbres range, had more arable land and more people than Animas Creek, what Minnis found there complemented to some extent the less intensive plant analyses Nelson and associates did at Las Animas. Some plants, particularly aquatic species, thrived then but not now in the Mimbres Valley. Minnis found traces of cattails, bulrushes and reeds—indicative of a more dependable and slower stream in Mimbres times. As human numbers peaked, cottonwoods and other flood plain trees became scarce, presumably cut for firewood or removed to make way for expanding fields. Plant remains at Las Animas suggest less pervasive human impacts than in the Mimbres Valley, perhaps because farms were smaller and people fewer.

Recurrent fires probably killed trees and kept uplands along Animas Creek more open and grassy than they are now, said Minnis. But we can't tell that from clues left at villages. Evidence comes mostly from other sources—burning by later Indians, fire scars on old trees and known consequences of grazing and fire suppression introduced by Euro-Americans. Such evidence indicates a Mimbres watershed more amenable than now to occupation by large mammals. Native herbivores, including bison, elk, mule and white-tailed deer and pronghorn antelope, uniformly benefit from increased fire frequency in such habitats.

As the 2001 meeting progressed, a phenomenon that initially seemed insignificant began to take on more importance: the proportion of domestic foods in the Mimbres diet increased as villages grew. Because much more food per acre can be produced by farming than gleaned from the wild, people in larger villages not only ate more corn, but they also became highly dependent on it. Farming in those days meant plants—the Mimbres had little or no domestic meat.

As modern vegetarians could have predicted, a diet of mostly corn and little meat led to deficiencies of protein and nutrients. These deficiencies show up as bone abnormalities—in particular, porotic hyperostosis—in ancient skeletons. Porotic hyperostosis causes bone tissue to appear spongy and become soft. The disease is related to anemia due to malnutrition. The villagers needed, and probably craved, meat to correct for these deficiencies. Intensive hunting and eventually overhunting amplified the scarcity of meat as villages grew.

Meat scarcity shows up in prehistoric trash heaps in several ways. The proportion of large-mammal to small-mammal bone usually declines with increasing numbers and aggregations of people. The probable cause was escalating overharvest of the larger, less productive species. Remains of the largest mammals, and particularly those vulnerable to hunting, seldom or never appear in trash heaps of large villages. Probably these had been hunted to extinction long before. During the Classic Mimbres period, jackrabbits and cottontails formed the mainstay of animal refuse. Deer, pronghorn antelope and the occasional bighorn sheep came in a poor second.

How did the Mimbres interact with bison, elk and javelina, now abundant along Animas Creek? Most Mimbres sites have no evidence of bison; at Las Animas, only one bison foot bone, presumed to have come attached to a bison hide acquired in trade or war, showed up. From Classic Mimbres times onward at Las Animas, people left very few fragments of elk bone compared with those of deer and pronghorn. Analysts identified a few bones as javelina, but Hegmon and Nelson think they must have been mistaken—this species does not appear elsewhere in the archaeological record of the Southwest.

The experts convened in the Ladder lodge agreed that images of bison, elk and javelina do not appear on Mimbres pottery, suggesting unfamiliarity of the Mimbres with these species. In contrast, ceramics unearthed at Mimbres sites commonly depict rabbit, deer, pronghorn and bighorn sheep.

What could account for the near or complete absence of bison, elk and javelina in Mimbres times? Neither change in climate nor the present-day food subsidy (crops) near the Ladder headquarters seems a sufficient explanation for the abundance of these animals now compared with their scarcity then. Only one possibility makes a lot of sense: overhunting. Bison and elk provide a lot more meat per animal than deer and pronghorn, reproduce more slowly and under many circumstances are easier to kill. Javelina provide meat in modest parcels but fall easy prey to primitive weapons, as the modern bow hunter can attest.

But would hunters have ranged far enough from their villages to decimate these animals over broad regions? The Mimbres may have lain field to field along the favorable lowland streams, but large expanses of high elevation forest and meadow discouraged farming and settlement. Some high-country hinterlands suitable in particular for bison and elk lay far from major villages, perhaps a day or two by foot.

In the case of bison, the earliest Spaniards in the Southwest found none near villages but described villagers making long treks on foot to reach them in the distant hinterlands. In 1535, Cabeza de Vaca, the first European to cross the Southwest anywhere near the Ladder Ranch, found "many bison robes" as he passed through farming villages on the Rio Grande a few hundred miles downstream from Animas Creek.[9] Oviedo y Valdez, his companion, wrote that some of the villagers had "gone to eat the cows [bison], three days' travel from there at some plains between the Mountains."[10] Likewise, the agricultural Cochiti along the Rio Grande west of Santa Fe traveled to the Pecos River Valley one hundred miles or more to the east to hunt bison. Many southwestern tribes made pre-horse journeys even longer distances to the Great Plains to trade for bison meat and hides.

Extirpation of bison, if they ever existed in Mimbres country, seems a reasonable outcome. Indeed, Coronado and other early Europeans traveling through the Southwest found virtually no bison west of the Pecos River at the western edge of the Great Plains, two hundred miles east of Mimbres terrain. Scarcity of bison remains at southwestern archaeological sites less than one thousand years old and distant from the Great Plains suggest bison found little sanctuary anywhere aboriginal groups multiplied on the bounty of corn.

Elk, being smaller and more elusive than bison, fared better. The now-extinct Merriam's elk survived aboriginal hunting in southwestern New Mexico to fall finally before the settler's gun. But the infrequency of its remains alongside those of aboriginal farmers bespeaks its probable scarcity when southwestern tribes flourished. Only in the late twentieth century did elk, originating from Wyoming stock brought to fill the niche vacated by Merriam's elk, begin to expand into what had been Mimbres habitat. Now, released from persistent hunting, elk continue their expansion, far into low country never before thought suitable based on historic records.

James Ohio Pattie's company of trappers saw javelina along the San Pedro River in Arizona in the 1820s.[11] By that time, southwestern tribes, long afflicted by European diseases and persecution, probably were a mere remnant of their number prior to Coronado. Javelina, perhaps taking advantage of a three-century scarcity of aboriginal man, had expanded northward from previous refuges in Mexico. The species continues to expand today, having moved northward and into new areas well within our own lifetimes.

Among the smaller animals, even wild turkeys and prairie dogs may have been overhunted by the Mimbres. Nelson, Hegmon and students found only traces of turkey and prairie dog bones at Las Animas, despite both species thriving now nearby. Unlike rabbits, which are extremely common at Mimbres and other village sites in the prehistoric Southwest, both turkeys and prairie dogs probably would be easy to harvest in excess by a people ever on the watch for a piece of meat to spice the daily monotony of corn.

The vacant villages left by the Mimbres and other farming cultures in the Southwest bring to mind similar scenes in other arid landscapes. Farming as a novel human enterprise took root in the deserts of the Middle East and North Africa ten thousand years or more ago. Iraq, Egypt, Greece, Israel and other lands in these regions have supported farming much longer than lands in the American Southwest. Over time, human numbers grew as irrigation technologies improved and croplands expanded in area and productivity.

But also over time, most of these old-world villages and cities that built on the bounty of borrowed water succumbed. Desert winds and drifting sands swallowed them as rivers shifted courses, soils lost nutrients and gained toxic salts and meteorological and social climates changed. People periodically declined in number and moved, settling beside new river courses, on soils replenished annually by floodwaters or in new lands formed by new silt deposits on river flood plains and in deltas.

Once-bountiful Eden on the Tigris-Euphrates Delta in southern Iraq became the dusty outpost it is today not because the people disappeared from the face of the earth but because the rivers shifted course and the people moved to better places. All indications are that the fruit of the tree of knowledge shared by Adam and Eve failed to instruct their progeny in the fine art of sustainable farming in the desert. Ecological pressures, amplified by social ones, underlay the story of Moses's exodus to the Promised Land and many other relocations of biblical times.

So it was with the Mimbres. People in the large villages left because of soil depletion, water shortages, dwindling meat supplies, climate change, population stress or, more likely, a combination of factors. They reorganized in smaller hamlets along Seco and Palomas Creeks and elsewhere nearby or joined groups in better circumstances farther away. Freed from a century and a half of village-bound custom, women adopted new pottery styles and men began to build with adobe instead of rock. Like us, they changed when released from tradition—perhaps teenagers experimented with new hairstyles, body piercings and tattoos. As the old markers of their identity disappeared from their dwelling sites and trash heaps, the Mimbres became lost to us in the archaeological record.

And so abandonment is not as it seems, conclude Hegmon and Nelson. The Mimbres did not disappear; they just shifted residences and changed customs. The mystery stands resolved, at least in broad outline. It is the old, old story—dwindling resources could not support the populations and lifestyles generated by their depletion.

What does the story of the Mimbres suggest about management of the modern Animas Creek watershed? It indicates first of all that late prehistoric New Mexico may not be the best template for restoration. Instead of living in "harmony with nature," aboriginal farmers may well have depleted it, particularly of soil fertility, large animals and other qualities susceptible to exploitation.

Were pre-farming cultures easier on the land? The archaeological record of them is generally too lean to tell, although the suspicion that Paleoindians took out a wealth of large species at the end of the Pleistocene continues to grow in the collective scientific mind. Indeed, some scientists advocate an experimental Pleistocene Park, with old-world surrogates—elephants, rhinos, big antelopes and so on—to fill the vacant niches left by the end-of-Pleistocene extinctions. But for the present along Animas Creek, restoring and sustaining a rich complement of North American species may be challenge enough.

The Mimbres had no recorded history to warn them of the dangers of resource exploitation. Will we who have a history replete with catastrophic examples do any better? Escalating dependence on oil in the face of looming scarcity, famine-induced displacements of Africans that dwarf those of the Mimbres, pervasive soil and water depletion in America's farming regions—the signs are not comforting. Leaders, insulated from regional trauma by privilege and wealth, ignore the implications.

Can those living today along the Animas set a better example?

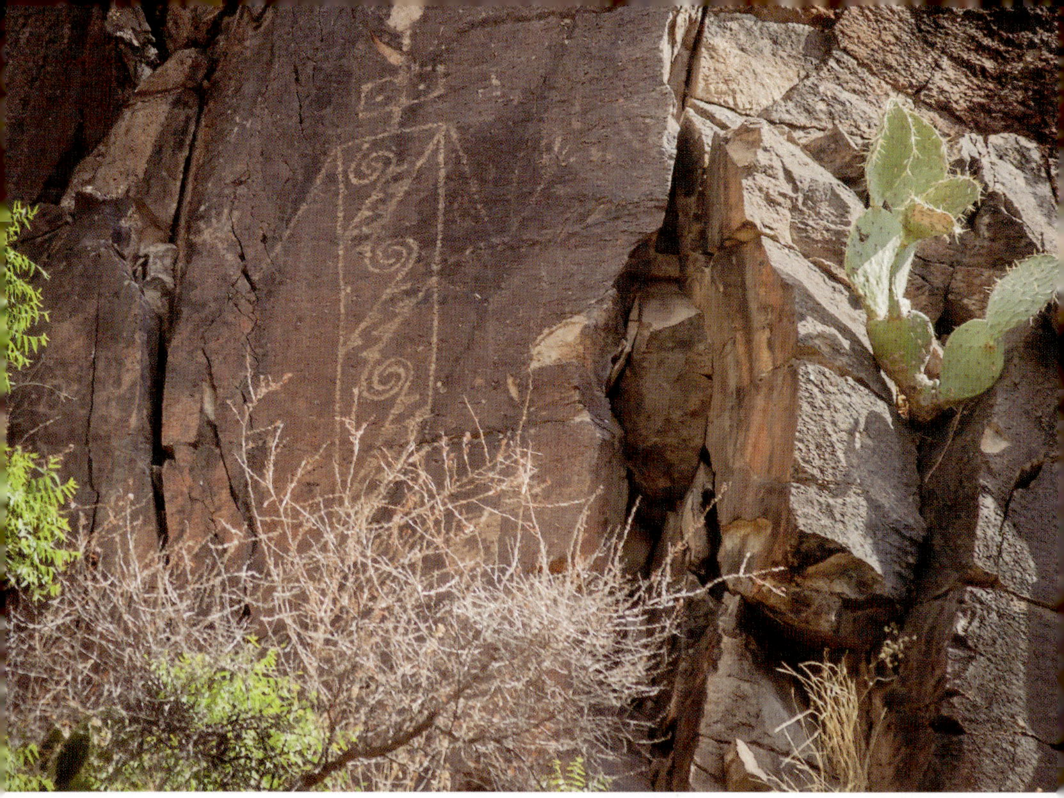

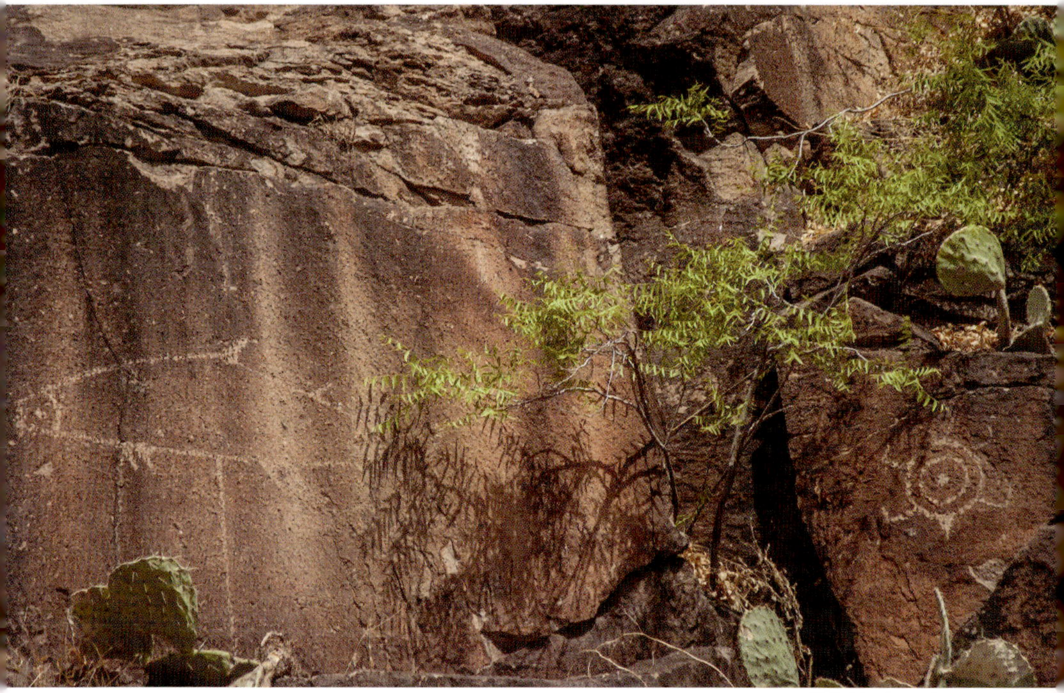

Art from the past. *M. Holzwarth, photographer.*

Chapter 3

THE ATHAPASCANS

HARLEY SHAW

No one knows precisely when the ancestors of Apaches and Navajos arrived in the Southwest. Current literature describes both tribes as nomadic when they came to the Rio Grande. They were hunters, gatherers and raiders. Historians seem unclear about the role these cultures played prior to the Spanish Entrada, and uncertainty exists regarding how early they arrived in the Black Range, hence Las Animas. Forbes notes, "It is very clear that the Western Apache were in the Little Colorado region in the twelfth century and gradually moved south to the Gila River watershed in the years from 1200 to 1400....We must not, however, think in terms of 'Navahos and Apaches' in that early period but rather in terms of numerous small groups or 'tribelets' who spoke various dialects or languages."[12] Forbes hypothesizes that the great drought of 1276–99 displaced Pueblo people southward, creating territorial conflicts between them and the already-present Athapascans.[13] Forbes states, "It is wrong...to picture the Navajos and Apaches simply as recent migrants from Canada to the Southwest. Biologically, we know that they are thoroughly intermixed with their neighbors of all languages, and this intermixture has included the absorption of bands, clans, or village units who were participants in ancient Puebloan or other Southwestern ways of life."

Not much is known regarding the pre-Entrada relationships between the Pueblo and Apache peoples. Undoubtedly some territoriality and antagonism existed, along with shifting alliances over time. Trade between the various groups also occurred. Considering the moderate climate of the Rio Grande Valley and its tributaries, as compared with the rugged and relatively sterile environment of the upper Black Range, it seems unlikely that the high-elevation portions of the mountains were permanently occupied by any of the tribes. From all indications, these groups moved their *rancherias* seasonally. Las Animas may have been a hunting ground for groups that inhabited the lower and mid reaches of Alamosa, Cuchillo Negro, Palomas, Animas, Percha and Trujillo Creeks in the eastern foothills of the Black Range. Of these, Alamosa and Animas undoubtedly had the most dependable water supply, and tribes using them may well have moved their camps to the upper, forested portions of the streams during summer.

Regarding the early relationships of Athapascans with the Spaniards, Forbes says:

> *A basic antagonism against the Spaniards had already developed in the area from Sonora to New Mexico by 1539, and this hostility cannot be entirely explained by the activities of Estevan alone. In all probability, the Indians of this area knew well enough the character of their would-be conquerors, because of reports from the south, for Spanish slavers had been raiding north from Culiacan for years.…Certainly the Indians of Sonora had received many reports of such outrages, and these accounts coupled with the memory of Nuño de Guzman's bloody entrance into southern Sonora in 1531, were probably enough to prejudice the natives against the Europeans.*

Most of the conflicts between Spaniards and Indians during the early sixteenth century involved Pueblos. The Athapascans seemingly stayed out of the way, but their presence undoubtedly restricted Latino or European occupation of the Black Range well after the first arrival of the Spanish. During the last half of the sixteenth century, two factors affected the relationship of the Spaniards with all the tribes: acquisition of horses by the Indians and the growing slave trade on the part of the Spanish.

By the mid-eighteenth century, Spanish troops, based mainly in Janos, were engaged in full-time efforts to permanently defeat the Gila, Chirichahua and Mescalero Apaches—a task in which they ultimately failed. The conflict between Spaniards and Apaches was not caused solely by Spanish aggression. Raiding had long been a way of life with the Apaches, for whom it provided proof of their warriors' valor and supplemented their supply of food and weapons. Conflict between the traditional Apache lifestyle and the Spanish, Mexicans and Americans was no doubt inevitable. Seemingly, the tribes "believed" in raiding for their livelihood. If so, they were destined to be subdued because the more settled societies could not endure such disruptive behavior. However, we know that the Apache also traded with other tribes and the Spanish at times.

Most of the easily accessible written history regarding the Apaches in the Black Range deals with nineteenth-century battles between them and Anglo settlers. A less well-publicized literature documents efforts of the Spaniards in the eighteenth and nineteenth centuries to subdue the Apache raiders.[14] During the late nineteenth century, Anza's efforts were focused on southwestern New Mexico, and expedition correspondence and diaries tell of several attempts to follow the Apaches into the Black Range. In general, operating from Janos or Chihuahua City, the Spaniards' horses were exhausted and their supplies were running out by the time they reached this region. Those Apaches, so pursued, must have had frequently used camps in upper Animas Creek because they consistently retreated to it. We know nothing of their lifestyle during periods of relative peace, if such periods existed.

Pre-American occupation of Las Animas by Apaches is poorly documented. Wilson concluded that the east face of the Black Range between Cuchillo Creek and Trujillo Creek was not permanently inhabited by the Gila, Warm Springs or Mescalero Apaches.[15] He noted that references to Apaches in the area were very scarce prior to 1850 and that the country was virtually unknown through the first 150 years of Spanish occupation. Juan Bautista de Anza may have led troops up Animas Creek in 1780 but mentioned no evidence of Apaches there, even though he had seen abandoned rancherias in the Fra Cristobal Mountains. Anza assigned no name to Animas. Colonel Fernando de la Concha pursued Apaches into Las Animas in 1788, and Captain Antonio Cordero wrote that he entered the "Cajon de las Animas" in 1789. We have no record of any actual battle occurring between Apaches and Spaniards in Las Animas.

Explorers during the mid-1800s found little evidence of Apaches along the east face of the Black Range, almost invariably first encountering them nearer the Mimbres Valley. Wilson suggested that the eastern face of the Black Range did not provide suitable natural foods, especially agave, to allow permanent residence, but he also mentions Cuchillo Negro's tribe farming the upper Animas in 1855. Rancherias were found along Alamosa Canyon and along Trujillo Creek prior to the 1870s, and Apaches farmed on Palomas Creek by 1858.

Victorio's most damaging victory over American troops occurred in the upper Animas—one of the last places he felt secure. Although his warriors won the battle at Massacre Canyon, they abandoned this final hideout. Victorio knew there would be more American troops to come and headed for Mexico, where his band was destroyed by the Mexican army.

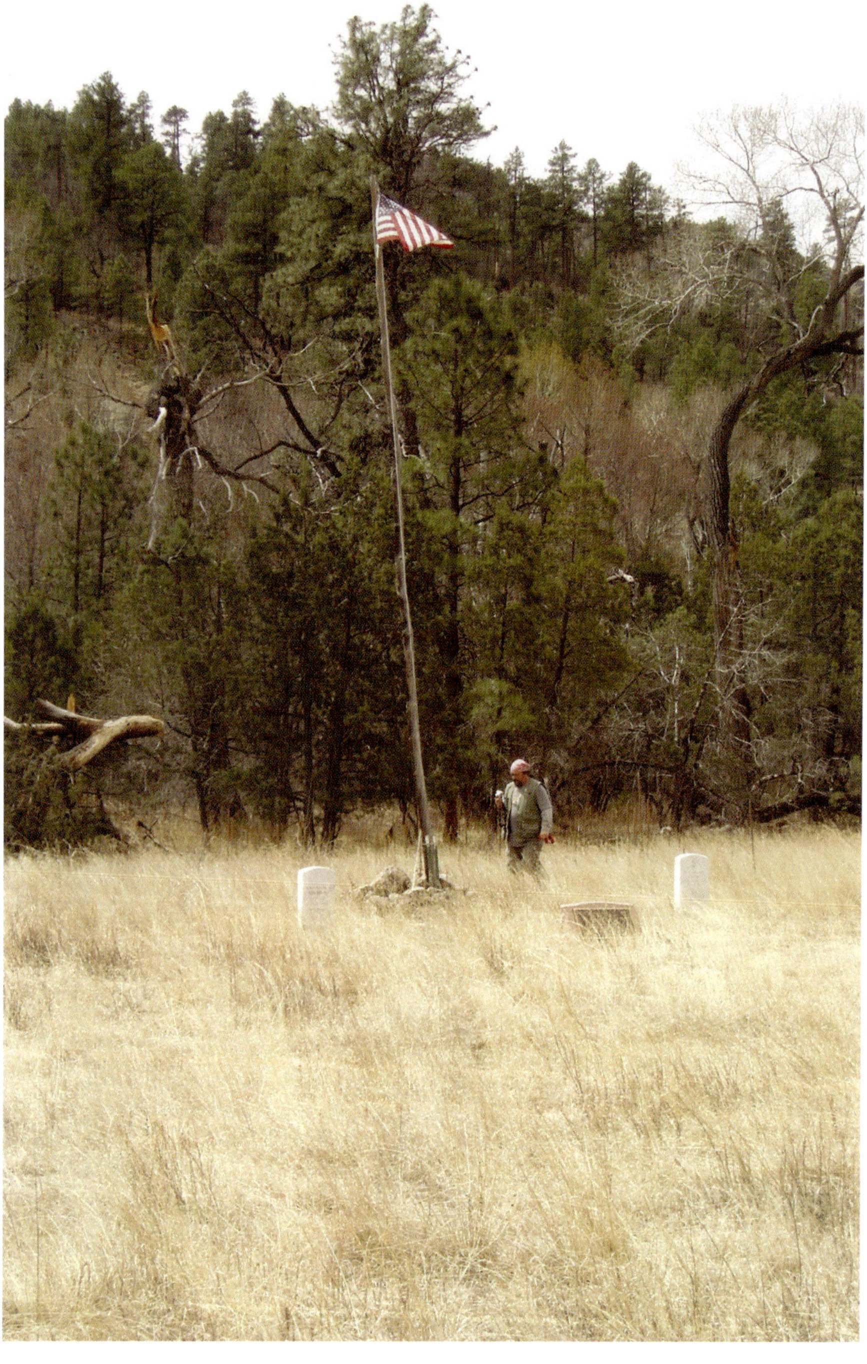

Buffalo soldier graves, Animas Creek. *H. Shaw, photographer*.

Chapter 4

THE BATTLE OF MASSACRE CANYON

Kenneth A. Dusenberry

During August 1879, the U.S. Army decided to disarm the Warm Springs Apache people at the Mescalero Reservation to prevent their leaving. The Apaches immediately resisted. Interviews with the women and children left behind revealed that the Apache men believed that after their guns were taken away, they would be arrested and hanged. A telegram from Colonel Edward Hatch to Washington, D.C., announced that "sixty-five warriors and some of their chiefs made a desperate attempt to escape our fort. So far ten are reported killed—thirty have escaped." The army started seeking the escapees.

The leader of the escaped band was Victorio. On September 4, 1879, he and his warriors attacked the unarmed soldiers guarding the horse herd of Company E, Ninth U.S. Cavalry, at Ojo Caliente, about forty-five miles north of Hillsboro. *Ojo Caliente* translates as "warm spring" and was the source of the name for this band of Apaches. Five troopers and three civilians were killed in the attack, and the Apaches captured sixty-eight horses and mules. The entire Ninth Cavalry was ordered to the field.

On September 17, 1879, a party of citizens searching for Victorio found him and about one hundred warriors near Hillsboro. The civilians were overmatched. At least nine of them were killed and several wounded. The Apaches took all of their stock. Victorio also attacked several isolated ranches around Hillsboro. Troops from Company B, supplemented by troops from Company A and possibly E Company of the Ninth Cavalry, were soon on the trail.

On the morning of September 18, 1879, Captain Dawson found Victorio near the headwaters of Las Animas Creek, about thirteen miles north of Kingston. According to oral tradition as related by the late journalist Gene Ballinger, lead elements of Dawson's battalion, perhaps his Navajo scouts, spotted an Apache woman near the creek. The woman fled up a side canyon toward Victorio Park, the camping spot of the Apaches. The Navajo scouts supposedly told the soldiers not to follow this woman, as the scouts expected a trap. The soldiers ignored this advice. At about 9:00 a.m., when the troops had advanced into a rugged canyon between high cliffs, Victorio sprang his ambush. This battalion was immediately pinned down, and many of their horses were killed. The ambush was well planned, and the soldiers could not retreat. At some point during the day, Second Lieutenant Mathias Day tried to push forward through the ambush, but he and his troops only made it about six hundred feet before they were stopped. They then retired to the rest of the battalion. Late in the day, when the order to withdraw was given, Day returned alone to this advanced position to retrieve a wounded soldier left behind.[16]

Meanwhile, Captain Charles Beyer with Companies C and G was searching nearby. These troops heard the gunfire and rode to the aid of the first battalion. They were engaged in the morning, but they were unable to join up with the trapped soldiers. Companies C and G made repeated flank attacks but were repulsed with loss. The Apaches continued to attack the trapped companies.

Second Lieutenant Robert Emmet noticed a long spur of mountains in the rear of the Apaches' position. Captain Beyer ordered Emmet, Lieutenant Hugo and about thirty-five men to attack this position to get above them and drive them out of the cliffs. They succeeded in getting to this position after a desperately hard climb with the loss of two men, but the Indians retired to some heights above them. Emmet describes their location as a very rough place where the Indians could slip up close on all sides. The troops were in an area of very dense scrub oak, and the Indians had camouflaged their bodies with garlands of oak leaves.

Emmet and his party forced an easing of pressure on the trapped battalion. Under the cover of twilight and three volleys from Beyer's companies, the trapped soldiers retreated about four hundred yards to a rock-crested hill. This retreat was under fire from the rocky crest of the ridge. Private Freeland, wounded in the thigh, was attempting to walk when Sergeant John Denny picked him up and carried him to the shelter of the hill held by the troops.

With the release of the troops held in the cliffs, Emmet and his party decided to withdraw. Emmet and five men served as a rear guard to cover the withdrawal of the rest of his party. They remained in place until some horses tied below were recovered and were subsequently able to escape, without being fired upon.

In the night, the Apaches escaped, and the next day, the Ninth Cavalry withdrew to McEvers Ranch, about thirty-five miles south, where Private Jerrymiah Crump died of his wounds.

Five days later, on September 26, 1879, Major A.P. Morrow arrived at the battle site with 191 men and 6 officers of the Sixth Cavalry, along with 36 Indian scouts. The Apache camp had been abandoned for at least three days. Morrow reported that it took him an hour and twenty minutes to walk from the ambush site to the Indian camp. He said that "under fire it would have been an absolute impossibility for any number of men to have taken the position by storm as it was as much as my command could do to take it, without having anybody on top to shoot at us."

Insofar as anyone could determine, the Apaches suffered no casualties. Two American casualties were recorded by name: Private Jerrymiah Crump, mentioned previously, and Peter Haines. By some accounts, an additional three troopers died, but these are unnamed in reports. Either two or three scouts (Navajo) died, and one civilian doctor was killed.

Victorio continued to lead his band until he was killed on October 15, 1880, by Mexican soldiers ninety-two miles north of Chihuahua City. General Terrazas reported that he killed sixty warriors with Victorio.[17]

On June 14, 1997, the New Mexico Home Town Heroes Committee for the National Medal of Honor Society, with the assistance of the New Mexico Army National Guard, placed a small monument and several headstones at the cemetery on the Kelsey property to commemorate the engagement. The ceremony was attended by descendants of Victorio's band, soldiers from the modern Ninth U.S. Cavalry, three recipients of the Medal of Honor, descendants of Charles Beyer and Robert Temple Emmet and many others. Emmet's descendant Chris Emmet brought his grandfather's Medal of Honor, awarded for this action, to the site.

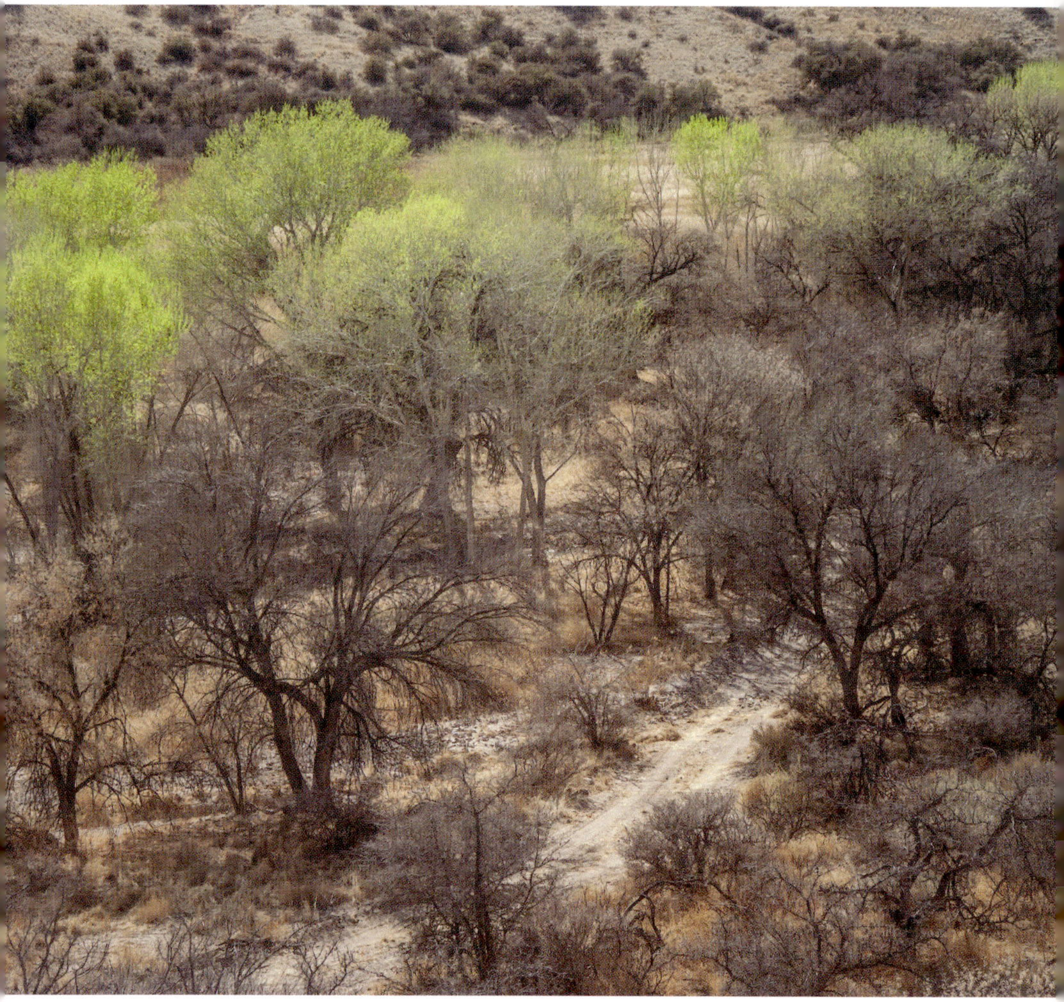

Spring blush. *M. Holzwarth, photographer.*

Chapter 5

AFTER THE APACHES

HARLEY SHAW

Although the upper reaches of Animas Creek lie within the Aldo Leopold Wilderness, the rugged and isolated nature of the creek, rather than its official designation, has kept it wild. The source of the name Rio de las Animas has been lost to history. A map of the "Southern Apache Indian Reservation" in Wilson shows that the current names of the major canyons, including Las Animas, were in place by 1875.[18] Because most of the Spanish-era travel, as well as later travel, followed the Jornada del Muerto to the east of the Caballo Mountains, Animas Creek was infrequently traversed by early expeditions. The Rodriquez-Chamuscado expedition traveled up the Rio Grande and crossed the mouth of the Animas in 1581, but reports from this expedition provided no descriptions of the area, noting only that it was unsettled.[19] Antonio de Espejo, traveling northward for fifteen days from the approximate current location of El Paso in 1583, described the region as empty of humans and having vegetation made up of mesquite groves and prickly pears in the lower elevations, with pine, pinyon, "sabines" and cedars higher up. Sabine is a Spanish name for cypress, which was probably not present along their route. Espejo undoubtedly applied this name to the alligator-barked juniper.

Espejo did not mention crossing the mouth of the Animas or other drainages from the Black Range, although he probably did so. According to Crouch, after Juan de Onate established the route across the Jornada del Muerto in 1598, Spanish travel along the river route almost ceased.[20]

De Anza may have chased Apaches into the Animas drainage in 1780, but he assigned it no name. Colonel Don Fernando de la Concha led troops against Apaches across Las Animas in 1788 and did not name the stream.[21] He noted existence of a marsh, perhaps in the area where the Ladder Ranch farms now exist.

Mark Santiago, director of the New Mexico Farm and Ranch Museum, discovered an apparent penetration into the upper Animas by Cordero in 1789. Citing AGN Provincias Internas, vol. 193, "*Copias que contiene los partes Justificados del Capitán Dn Antonio Cordero sobre efectos de su campaña y varias ordenes comunicadas a este oficial*," he notes, "In an October 4, 1789 correspondence between Captain Antonio Cordero, commander of Janos and Commandant General Jacobo Ugarte y Loyola concerning several campaigns made in pursuit of Apaches, Cordero writes that on the 25th of September with 250 men he entered the Cajon de las Animas the roughest and most elevated of the Sierra Mimbres (*…el Cajon de las Animas, lo mas aspero y elevado de las Sierra Mimbres…*)." This is the earliest usage of the name that we have found and almost certainly applies to Las Animas Creek.

In 1809, the Spanish party escorting Zebulon Pike, under arrest as a spy, followed the river route southward rather than crossing the Jornada del Muerto.[22] Other than noting that the country was mountainous on both sides of the river, Pike provided no description of the landscape. He did mention sign of Apaches and their Spanish pursuers in the area.

During the Spanish and Mexican reigns in New Mexico, the Animas was hardly explored by Europeans. The few travelers following the river route stayed near the Rio Grande, where Las Animas and the other Black Range drainages are broad, indistinguishable desert valleys. This changed little during the exploration phase of American occupation. James Ohio Pattie and a body of Taos trappers purportedly crossed the Black Range in 1825, but Pattie devotes only a single sentence to the event.[23] Lieutenant W.H. Emory and Henry Smith Turner, traveling with Kearny's Army of the West, acknowledged crossing Las Animas and camping in Percha Creek on October 15, 1846, but neither assigned names to these drainages.[24] Water in both of these was found to be good and grama grass abundant. Philip St. George Cooke's Mormon Volunteers also crossed the stream's mouth in 1846, and several of the men keeping diaries noted the roughness of the terrain, but none singled out the Animas drainage.[25]

The American military began entering the Black Range more frequently once forts in the region had been established. An 1855 map showing a trail along the east face of the Black Range does not name Animas or any of the other creeks. The names of canyons from the east side of the Black Range do not show up on 1853 or 1859 military maps, although Rio de las Animas appears by that name on an 1864 military map of New Mexico Territory. It is also labeled Rio de las Animas on an 1875 District of New Mexico map in the U.S. National Archives and on an 1881–82 "Trial Sheet" map, also in the National Archives.[26]

General H.H. Sibley's ill-fated Confederate army, in its effort to take New Mexico for the South, marched up the river route from Mesilla in 1862 but left little record about the landscape or terrain. Some of his bedraggled troops, after their defeat at Glorieta Pass, spent one night camped at the mouth of Seco Creek and passed by Las Animas the next day but did not note it or call it by name.[27]

Joseph Walker led a party along the east face of the Black Range in the winter of 1862–63 en route to newly found gold fields in northern Arizona. His expedition was documented by Connor, although the dates they passed specific locations are not recorded.[28] Walker led his men into the Black Range from a point somewhere near Val Verde, hoping to find a short route to the Santa Rita Mines. Ultimately, discouraged by rough and brushy terrain and the constant Apache harassment, Walker gave up the direct passage and took the established southerly route around the mountains, via Cooke's Spring.

Perhaps one of the most interesting and least-heralded expeditions passing through the vicinity of lower Las Animas was the private railroad survey sponsored and promoted by William Jackson Palmer. This survey fielded parties that explored a variety of potential railroad routes between the thirty-second and thirty-fifth parallels in 1867 and 1868, shortly after the end of the Civil War. English physician and geographer William A. Bell recorded and photographed the southern route. The observations made during the expedition were published by Bell in a scholarly work titled *New Tracks in North America*.[29] This book was reprinted in 1965 by Horn and Wallace Publishers of Albuquerque. This later printing carries a foreword written by industrialist Robert O. Anderson, who, only five years earlier, had purchased the Ladder Ranch and thereby owned the land through which Las Animas flows.

Bell himself accompanied the segment of the expedition that traveled down the river route and crossed Las Animas. Like earlier chroniclers, he failed to name or single out the Animas, but he gives an excellent description of conditions in the landscape between Fort Craig and the upper Mesilla Valley. Entering the Rio Grande Valley by way of the Tijeras Valley and Albuquerque, Bell and his fellow travelers traveled down the Rio Grande to Fort Craig. Above Fort Craig, they described the Rio Grande Valley as varying in width from five miles to a few hundred yards, with bluffs on either side. Atop the bluffs was a level, grass-covered and dry plain sloping gradually toward the mountains, which were some distance from the river. Below Fort Craig, the eastern ranges crowded the stream and reduced the bottomland to a narrow strip. To the west, the slopes were longer and the mountains more distant. While the party noted the roughness of the terrain, unsuitable for a railroad route, they provided little information regarding vegetation or wildlife. According to the map accompanying the book, Bell's group ultimately crossed into the Mimbres Valley through the saddle between the Black Range and Cooke's Peak.

The last "expedition" to explore the vicinity of Las Animas was a part of the G.M. Wheeler surveys of the 1870s. According to party member Nell, the larger streams passed through deep canyons that were severe obstructions to road building. He notes:

> *The most important are Palomas, Arroyo Seco, Animas, Perchas, and Apache. At the mouth of the Palomas is a Mexican town of the same name. The recently-established mining town of Hillsboro is on the Perchas, in the foothills. Except this, only a few settlers are found away from the River; a little mining camp is on the Animas, about ten miles above its mouth* [shown on the Wheeler map as Ellis], *while near the road leading from Hillsboro to Mule Spring, four settlers are established. The foothills of the Mimbres are rocky and steep; a slide seems to have occurred* [this is probably the ancient rim of the Emory Caldera], *which has left a valley between the main ridge and the foothills, through which later the streams cut in narrow rocky canyons. Good grazing is to be had, which has heretofore been principally devoted to sheep.*[30]

Regarding the mines around Hillsboro, Nell wrote:

> *There is abundance of grazing and plenty of water. Timber is abundant ten miles from the town. There are about 300 inhabitants, including Mexicans. There are 20,000 head of livestock in the vicinity, including sheep, cattle, and horses—principally sheep. The country roads are very poor. The route in use follows up the bed of the Animas River, and is subject to "wash outs." Freight costs 3 to 4 cents; stage fare from railroad, $80. Deer, antelope, bear, rabbits, turkeys, ducks, and geese are found.*

Thus, by 1878, settlers had begun to expand into the Animas and surrounding landscapes, and considerable grazing, mainly by sheep, was underway. An early eyewitness account by a journalist from a Las Cruces newspaper who visited Las Palomas in December 1883 observed, "The road follows the course of the river, and there is splendid meadow land, covered at intervals with a thick growth of cottonwood. Many ranches are passed that are still inhabited, and many more ranches, and in some places even small villages, are entirely deserted."[31]

The outbreaks of Victorio, followed by Nana, Geronimo and Johanna, slowed expansion of settlers for at least another five years. Until Geronimo's surrender on September 5, 1886, prospectors and ranchers avoided the higher reaches of the Animas. By the 1890s, prospectors and homesteaders again began to explore and settle the upper Animas, but they left little written description.

Battles between Apaches and settlers didn't end with Victorio's death, but more and more the raiders retreated to Mexico when pursued rather than seeking refuge in the rough and isolated terrain of the southwestern mountains. Over time, the U.S. Army, under the guidance of General George Crook and others, adapted to the Apache method of warfare. Using pack animals and hardened soldiers, they allowed the warrior groups no rest and reduced their opportunities to acquire supplies. They killed them during battles and starved them between encounters. The Mexican army learned how to fight them as well, so they received no rest on either side of the border. Geronimo's well-publicized surrender effectively ended the Apache wars.

American and Hispanic settlers were moving into the Black Range before the Apaches were subdued, but Animas Creek was one of the last drainages to be settled. Its rough upper tributaries were unsuitable for irrigated farming. With cold winter air coming down from ten-thousand-foot Hillsboro Peak, perhaps the growing season was too short. For some reason, Animas does not hold the valuable minerals that surrounding areas contained, so mining did not become a major use. No doubt prospectors probed it, but gold, silver and copper were found elsewhere, bringing about the development of Lake Valley, Hillsboro and Kingston. For much of its upper terrain, seasonal grazing by livestock was the only economic use. The cattle industry arrived early, and the Animas was incorporated into large ranches (see chapter 8, "Becoming the Ladder Ranch"). Near Kingston, the Armer-Reid goat ranch was established by 1892, and over time, portions of the Animas watershed became part of its operation (see chapter 7, "Goat Ranching"). Amidst these

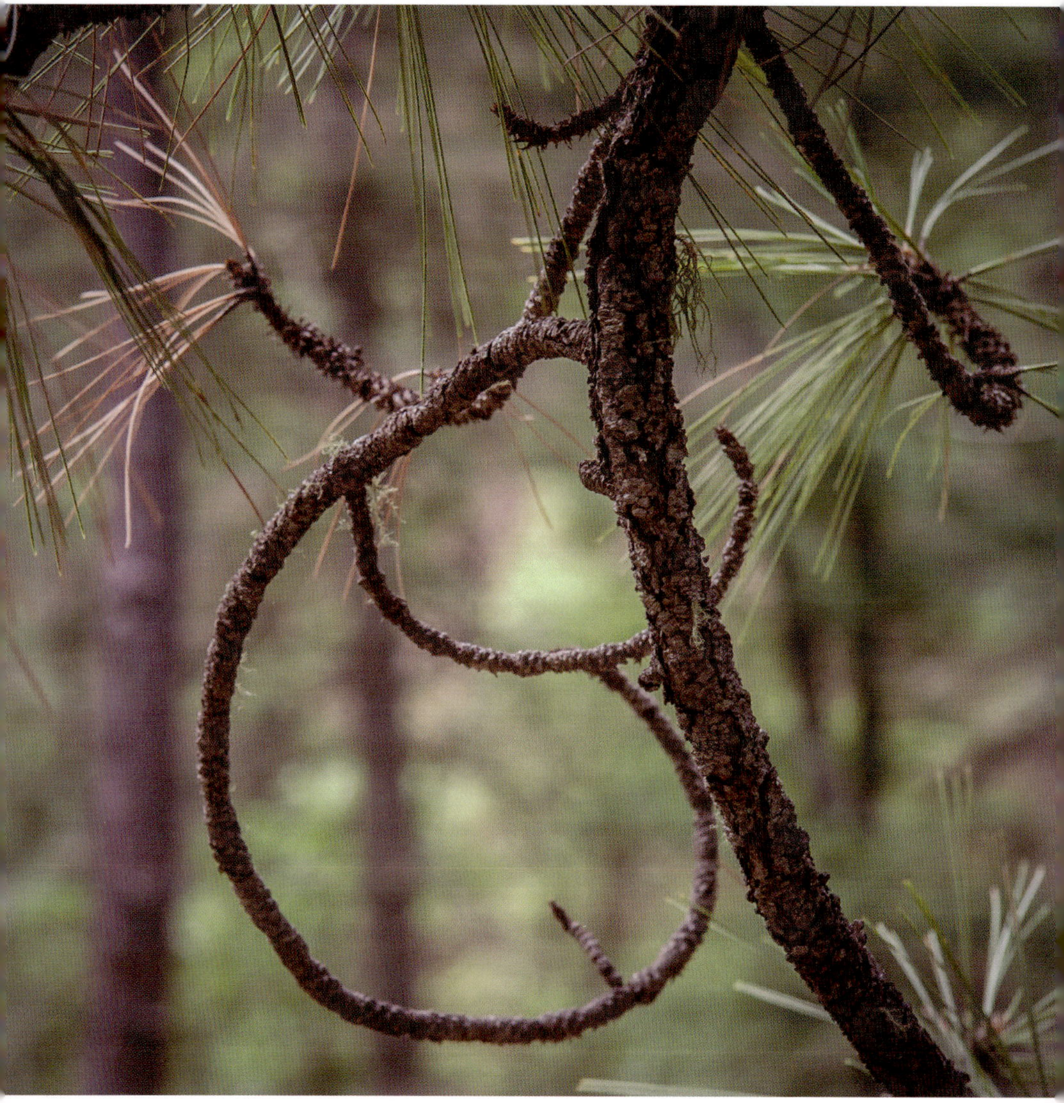

Arabesque. *M. Holzwarth, photographer.*

larger ranches, smaller holdings by both Hispanic and Anglo struggled to survive by farming and raising livestock. Settlers along the upper reaches of the creek built log or frame houses and barns at sites such as Apache Camp, Dunn, Kelsey and Murphy. We know very little about the families for whom these cabins were named, and most of them became seasonally used line camps for the larger ranches by the middle of the twentieth century. Of these, only Apache Camp survived the fire of 2013.

In the middle reaches of the canyon and below, homestead buildings were largely adobe and stone (see chapter 6, "Homesteading Las Animas"). Because people still live whose parents and grandparents owned these holdings, we know a little more of how they lived. Ultimately, the U.S. Forest Service and larger cattle ranches bought these smaller holdings, and the families moved away. The first to leave any detailed record of the area were goat ranchers and employees of the U.S. Forest Service, and this did not occur until after the beginning of the twentieth century. Their writings appear in later sections of this book. Only when the Ladder Ranch came under the ownership of Turner Enterprises did in-depth, baseline botanical, zoological, archaeological or geological surveys begin. Much opportunity for research in the watershed remains.

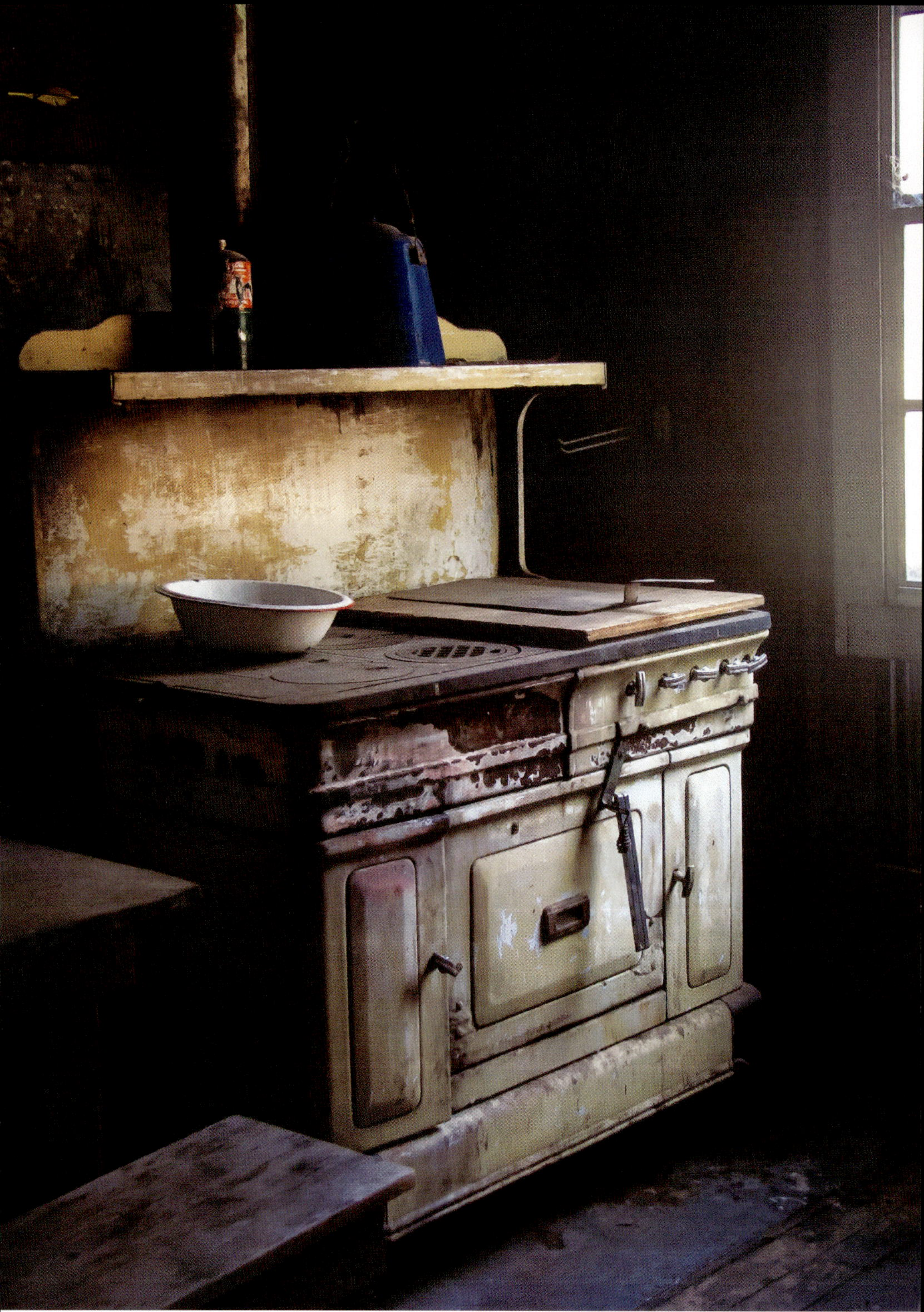

Remembrances. *M. Holzwarth, photographer.*

Chapter 6

HOMESTEADING LAS ANIMAS

MARGIE GIBSON

Imagine early spring 1880 on the Rio de Las Animas. On the lower creek, cottonwoods were a haze of bright green as leaves began to unfurl. In a few weeks, tom turkeys would begin puffing up like feathered cannonballs and strutting around; occasionally, a fight would break out. Hens seemed indifferent to these performances as they searched for food. The abundant quail scattered into the grass when the turkeys got close. Water and the life it supported seemed to hold the promise of a better future for the people coming to settle along the Las Animas.

It was still wild country. Grizzly bears and wolves roamed the upper Animas. It was also part of the traditional lands of the Chihene Nde Apaches, the Red Paint People, who fought to hold on to it. The discovery of gold near Hillsboro in 1877 and silver the following year at Lake Valley brought a rush of miners and other settlers into the area. Conflicts increased. The military worked to confine the Apaches to harsh reservations. The death of Victorio in 1881, the capture of Nana in 1885 and the final surrender by Geronimo in 1886 ended these conflicts.

The boomtowns of Hillsboro and Kingston were full of hell-raising miners and the men who would like to steal their claims. Gangs of cattle rustlers plagued the region, including John Kinney, who sent bands of a half dozen armed men from his Lake Valley ranch to the large ranches in the Black Range. Although the settlers may not have been targets, they must have felt relief when Kinney and other rustlers were arrested in a campaign led by Colonel Albert Fountain in 1883.[32]

Homesteading was made possible under the Homestead Act of 1862, signed by President Abraham Lincoln. Any citizen, or anyone declaring his intent to become one, could own up to 160 acres of "free" government land. Originally, the law required an applicant to be over twenty-one or the head of a family and to live on the land for five years. The government then granted title in the form of a patent. At first, these were actually signed by the president of the United States but later by officials on the president's behalf.

THE FIRST HOMESTEADS

The first written record of a settler in the Animas is from 1875.[33] Another undocumented account notes that there were three cabins in 1877,[34] but the earliest federal records are in 1885, with patents granted for six homesteads and one cash sale of 158 acres. Under the conditions of the act, this would have put homesteaders here by at least 1880. Three of these first homesteads on the lower Animas were contiguous. The lowest of these, about three miles above present-day I-25, belonged to Jose Chavez. His adjacent upstream neighbors were Veneaslao Chavez; his wife, Publita Candelaria; and their children. Next to them were Blas Chavez; his wife, Olympia Apodaca; and their children—in later years, the sons Robinson and Alvaro would also homestead on the Animas. Veneaslao, Publita, Blas and Olympia were born in the Territory of New Mexico, as were their parents, so they already had well-established roots here.[35]

Half a mile upstream of Blas was Albert Johnson, from Texas. He would later move to the Luna Valley to raise horses with his two sons but returned to this area, and his oldest son Asa homesteaded. Upstream of Albert was Edward Montgomery from Ohio, whose homestead is now part of the Ladder Ranch. A little over a mile upstream of him was Judson Strong. The last in the group of the earliest settlers was William F. Mckenzie, who was about a mile and a half above where Cave Creek enters the Las Animas; he was roughly seven miles upstream of Judson Strong. Unlike the other settlers, he purchased federal land rather than homesteading.

In late May 1885, sixteen-year-old Eugene Manlove Rhodes, who during his life became a popular writer known as the "cowboy chronicler," worked with two other boys his age building a stone house for an Animas Creek homesteader. When they finished, Eugene rode east, and the other two,

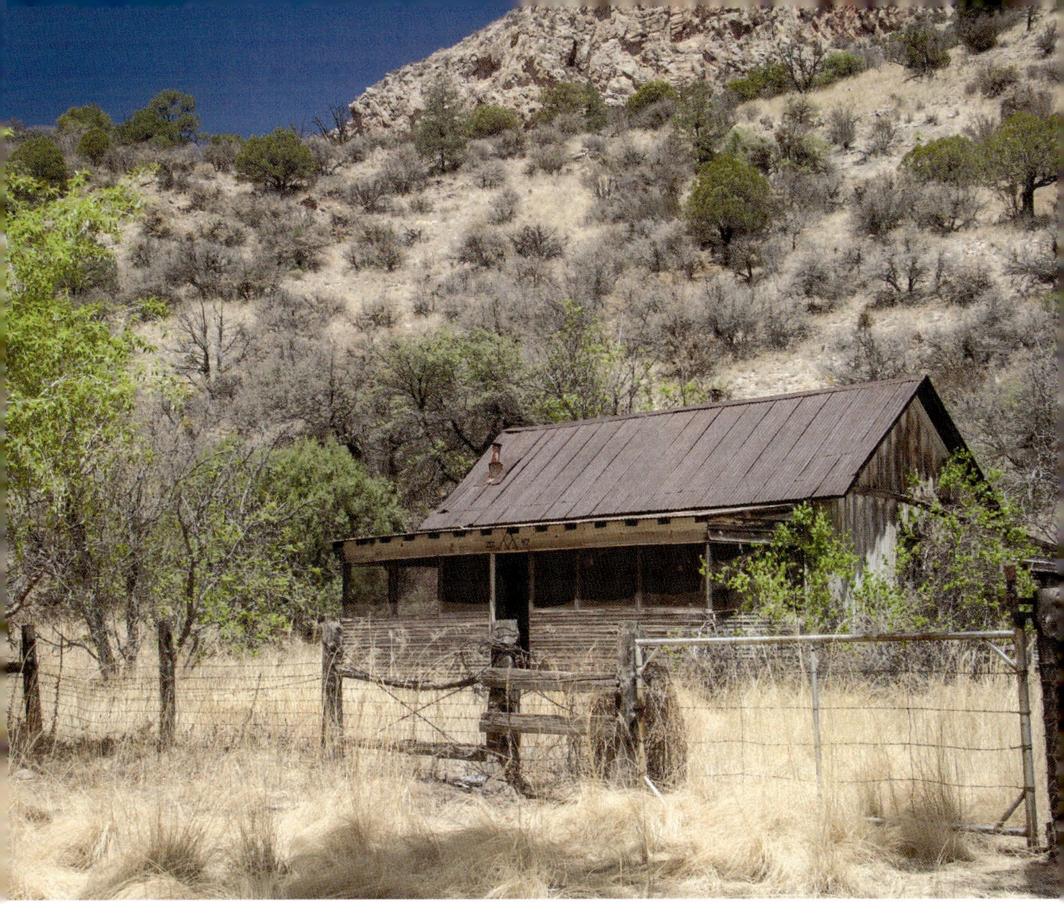

Apache Cabin. *M. Holzwarth, photographer.*

Harvey Moreland and Fred Adams, rode west.[36] The next day, Harvey and Fred were killed by Apaches while working on a fence for a ranch about six miles north of Grafton.[37]

The federal government granted fifteen additional patents and several cash sales by the close of the century: six to Hispanic settlers, one using Sioux scrip and the remainder to Anglos. The Sioux scrip is a story in itself. Land had been set aside in 1830 in what is now Wisconsin for mixed-race Dakota Sioux. The land was illegally settled by whites, who refused to leave. In exchange for their land, in 1857 "Dacotah or Sioux half breed" certificates, or scrip, were issued to mixed-race Sioux that could be used to buy unsurveyed federal land anywhere.[38] This homestead was bought using scrip in the name of Josette Moutre Bush by her heirs. Her land on the Animas was very remote, near what is now called Massacre Canyon in the Aldo Leopold Wilderness of Gila National Forest. Very little is recorded about most of these settlers. Jose Chacon, who purchased land

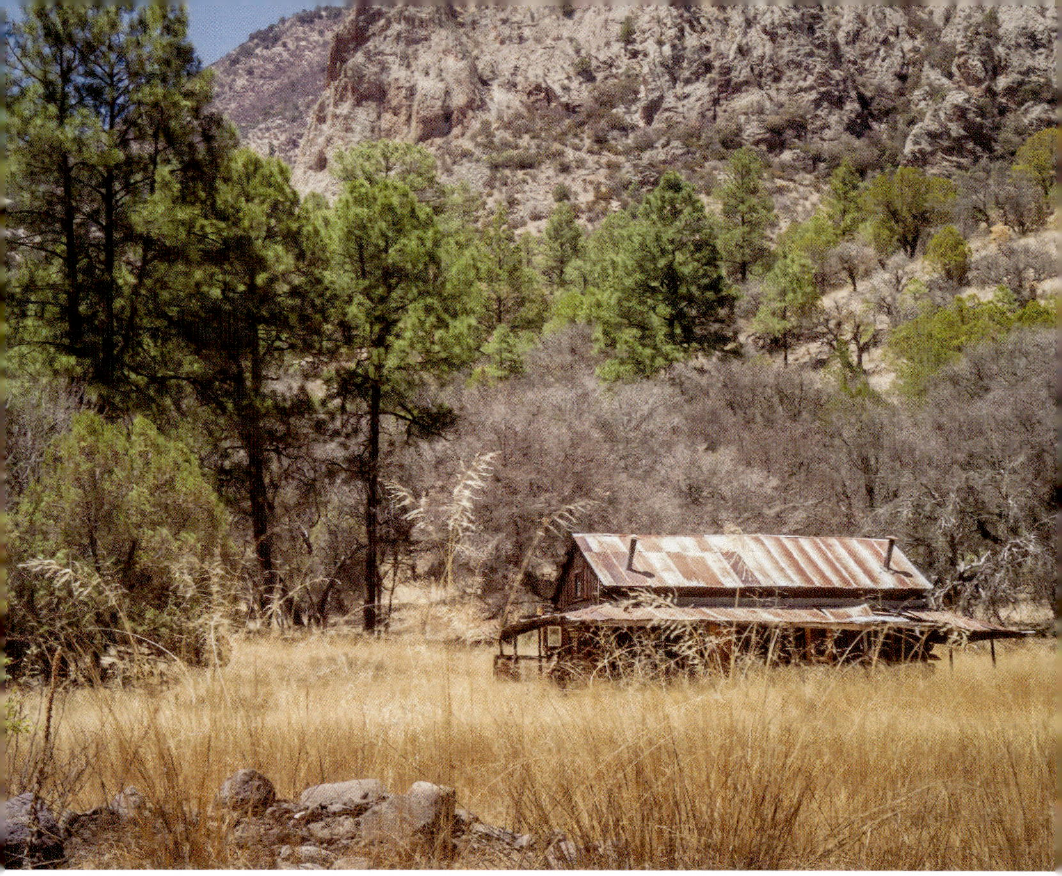

Kelsey Cabin. *M. Holzwarth, photographer.*

in 1891 and 1893, lives on in name—Chacon Park near the Gila National Forest boundary.

Other settlers in this period were Gregorio Chavez, who with his wife, Sabina, came by covered wagon to Las Animas. Their son Lasaro homesteaded the adjacent 160 acres. Both homesteads were on what is now the Ladder Ranch. Gregorio and Sabina's granddaughter remembers them farming and having horses, cattle, sheep, hogs and chickens.[39]

A Methodist missionary, Reverend Thomas Harwood, first met Gregorio in Palomas in 1873. On the same trip, he met Blas Chavez at San Marcial near Fort Craig. Harwood later made several visits to

> *the beautiful orchards of Don Gregorio Chavez and his nephew, Julian Chavez.... They have a large orchard of first class, eastern fruit. I was at this place, in 1875, before they had set out a tree.... I was there again when the trees were quite young. The Apache Indians had made a raid*

> *over the country and killed quite a number of people; run off stock and had cut down and destroyed a good many of the choice fruit trees. Brother Gregorio showed me a tree that the famous Geronimo tied his pony to. The tree was badly twisted, but it had grown in spite of it all and bore fine, delicious apples.*[40]

The family had experience with Apache raids. Gregorio, Sabina and their three toddlers—Lasaro, the middle child, was two at the time—lived in San Ygnacio de la Alamosa, a farming community also known simply as Alamosa, the site of which is now in Elephant Butte Lake. The town was established in 1859 but abandoned by early 1867 due to frequent Apache raids, and they moved to Palomas.[41] One of the Anglo homesteaders was Willard S. Hopewell, who would go on to manage and then own the Las Animas Land and Cattle Company and become a county commissioner with the establishment of Sierra County in 1894. The new county was formed primarily from Socorro but also portions of Dona Ana and Grant Counties. Hillsboro was the county seat. The commissioners declared a number of

Rosendo Chavez's grave marker. *M. Holzwarth, photographer.*

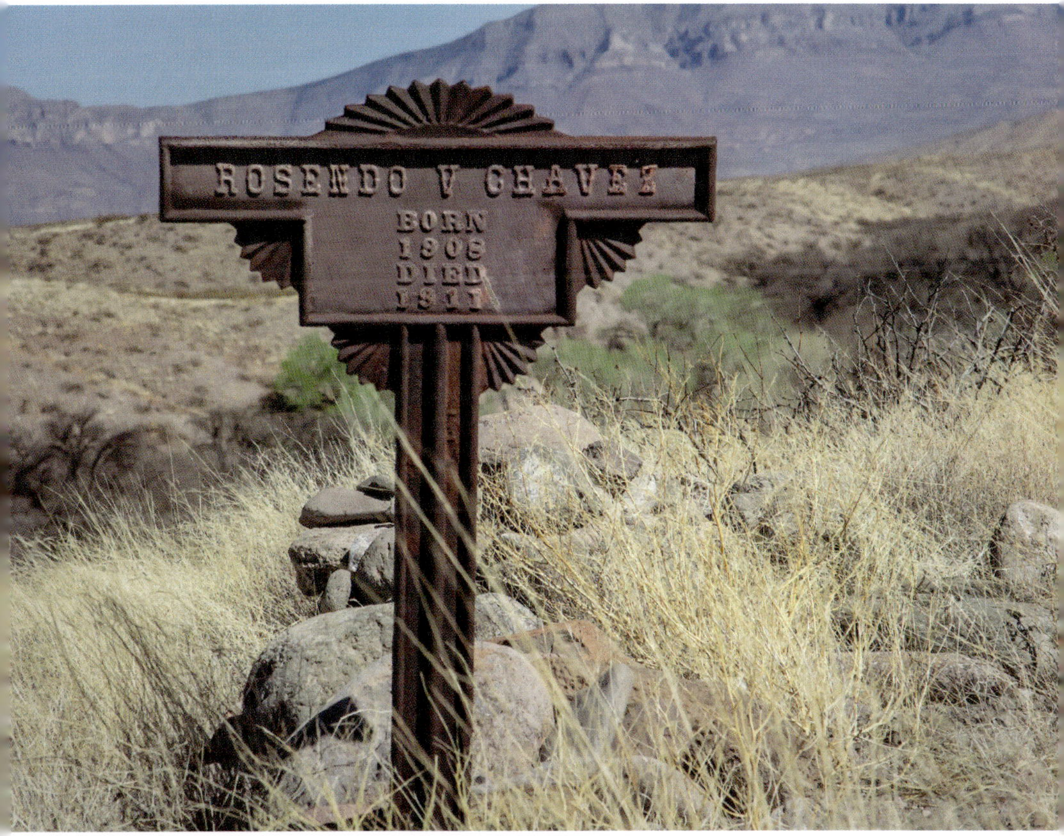

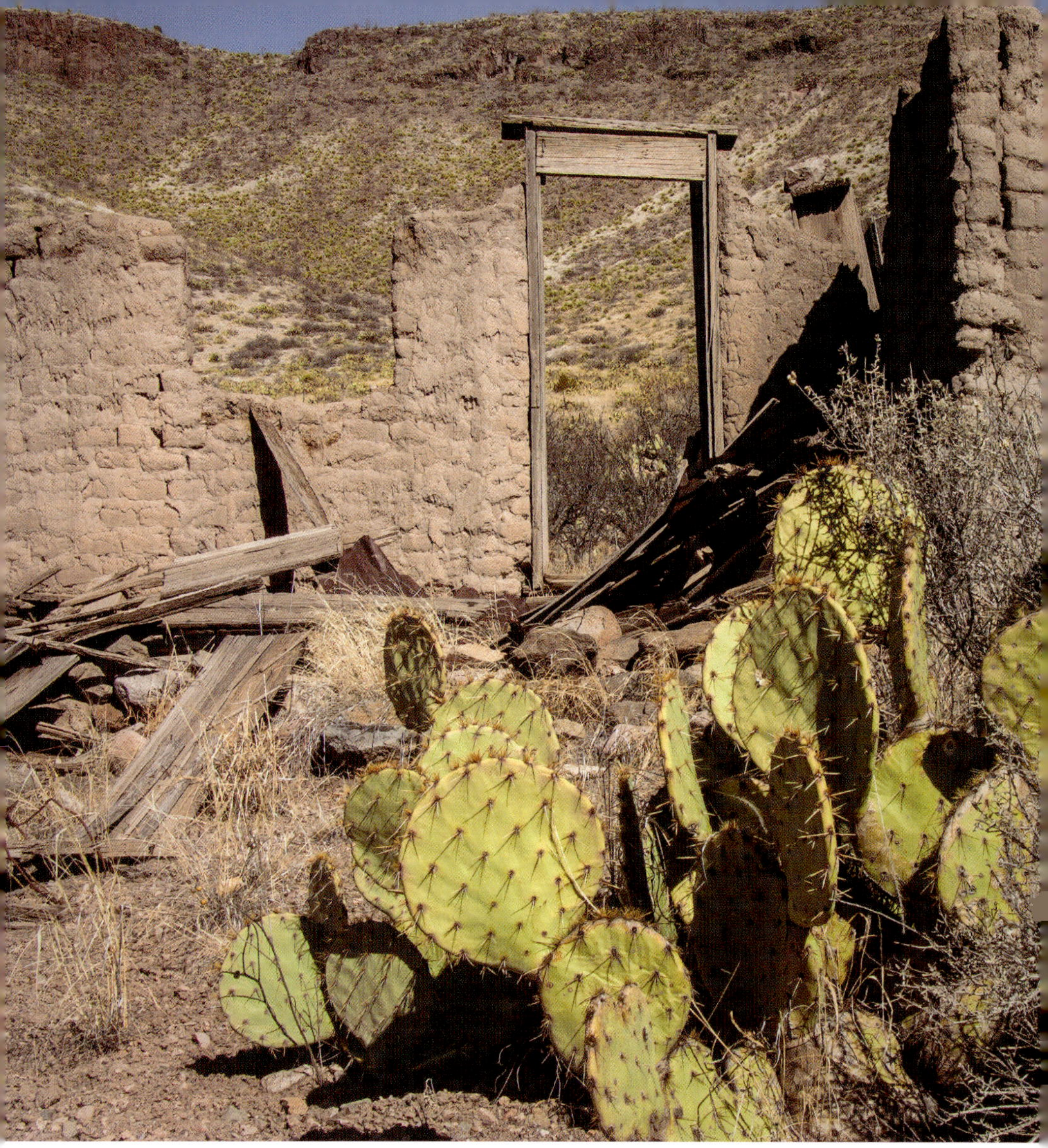

Padilla homestead ruins. *M. Holzwarth, photographer.*

roads to be public, including one from the Rio Grande to the mouth of the Box Canyon on the Animas, below present-day Ladder Ranch headquarters.

These early settlers needed to be very self-reliant. The winter of 1885–86 was more severe than any in over thirty years, with a resulting loss of crops and livestock. The following winter was equally harsh. Rangeland also declined due to overstocking, and in 1889, the New Mexico Territorial Assembly passed an act to prevent this. Severe drought followed in 1891–

92, with less-than-normal rainfall continuing into 1894.[42] But things were looking up by 1898, when the *Weekly Crop Bulletin* for April 28 reported alfalfa ten inches high and noted that "the prospects are good for an abundant fruit crop from the mountains of the Rio Grande along the valleys of the Percha and Animas creeks."[43]

Only two homesteads were patented along Las Animas in the ten years following Hopewell's patent in 1899. One was for Antonio Majalca; he and his wife, Lazarita, had a prosperous farm.[44] The other homesteader was Antonio Padilla.

In March 1899, the Gila River Forest Reserve was established and included a portion of the headwaters of Las Animas near the continental divide. Later, the reserve became part of land managed by the newly created U.S. Forest Service, and "river" was dropped from its name. It became a national forest in 1907.

1900–1919

Animas Creek and its tributary, Cave Creek, were in a news report by the *Albuquerque Daily Citizen* on May 24, 1902. A Cave Creek rancher reported an exceptionally good calf crop, but the calves were falling prey to wild animals. The same story reported that two brothers, Charles and Jean Rouse, on their return from a hunting and prospecting trip, "report many dead cattle on the Animas killed by lobo wolves." In December, two American men robbed the Sierra County Bank in Hillsboro and were later seen on the Animas.

In 1909, Congress passed the Enlarged Homestead Act, which recognized that much of the West required larger areas to eke out a living dry land farming and allowed a homesteader to acquire 320 acres. This did not appear to have any impact along Animas Creek until 1923. From the passage of the act until 1912 was another dry period in New Mexico.

In 1912, New Mexico became a state.

Thirteen homesteads were granted from 1910 through 1919, and there were two federal land sales. The majority of the settlers were farmers, a few cattlemen and two goat ranchers. One goat ranch belonged to Francisco Rascon, who bred milk goats with an Angora buck bought from Bob Reid, who raised goats upstream on the national forest.[45] The second belonged to the son of Gregorio and Sabina Chavez, Robinson, and his wife, Everista, and is described by their daughter Elizabeth in *History of Sierra County*:

> *Dad took a homestead after the gold rush. We lived in Cave Creek 50* [sic] *miles above the Ladder Ranch. He had over a thousand Angora goats and sold milk, cheese, meat, hides and wool….*
>
> *Everyone washed on Mondays. All came and brought tubs, lye soap, washboards and buckets. The men cooked deer meat for lunch and watched the burros to keep them from eating the clothes.*

Elizabeth wrote that it took all day to get from the ranch to Las Palomas to shop. Her brother Albert also homesteaded in Las Animas. "He and my dad built a road to Hillsboro so they could sell vegetables and buy food. We built a home for Albert of adobes using dishwater for water. It is there yet." Elizabeth attended Harwood School in Albuquerque, begun by Reverend Harwood, who met first her grandfather Gregorio in 1873.[46]

A number of farmers brought produce to sell in Hillsboro and perhaps to the mining town of Faulkner. Faulkner was on the Animas on what is now the Ladder Ranch, but all that remains is broken glass. The town had postmasters from 1883 to 1898.[47] Many of the Las Animas homesteaders appear in the 1900, 1910 and 1920 federal census surveys for Faulkner.

In 1914, Mrs. Fanny Chatfield started a forty-acre homestead on Animas Creek, where her brother Robert Rouse had already received a patent on eighty acres. They were both adjacent to Blas Chavez. She had two downstream residents, Cleto Fuentes and Isidoro Tapia, build a two-room adobe home. Cleto Fuentes received a patent in 1911. Isidoro married Fuentes's daughter Teresita, and Cleto gave them a portion of his homestead.

The Chatfields grew vegetables and livestock food, and the older boys took care of cattle, horses, sheep and goats. In 1918, one of her sons, Harvey, died of influenza in the worldwide epidemic that became the deadliest plague in recorded history.[48] Fanny received her patent in 1919.

Mrs. Chatfield's former husband, Alfred, and his family had lived in the Alamogordo area with another family, the Gordons, who would also become Animas Creek settlers. John N. Gordon and his wife, Mallie, settled in the bosque near the Rio Grande in what is now Caballo Lake. Two married daughters and their husbands came with them.[49] Their daughter Jesse and Jefferson Milton Holden settled along the Animas and received a patent for eighty acres in 1915. Later, the Gordons' son John would become a settler.

With more people along Las Animas, in 1916 the first post office opened in Caballo. It was housed in a general store belonging to Bill Green at the mouth of Animas Creek. Just north of the Greens' store was a store run by Mannie Benson.[50]

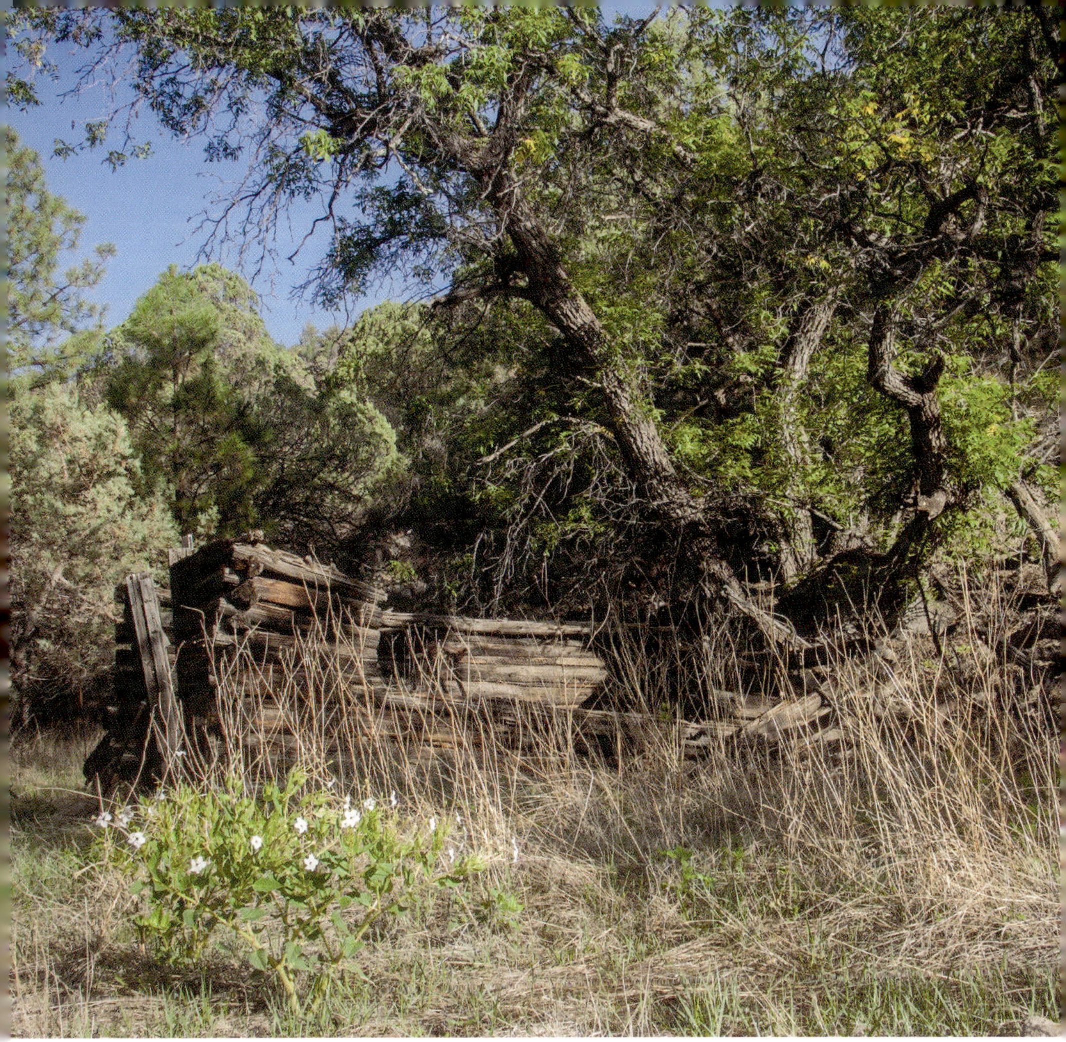

Murphy's cabin. *M. Holzwarth, photographer.*

A severe drought hit in 1918. Cattlemen struggled to save their stock by cutting down cottonwoods, chopping sotol and burning off the spines of prickly pear.[51]

The 1920s

In 1916, Congress passed the Stock Raising Homestead Act, allowing settlers to claim 640 acres of land, but that is reflected in patents to only one homesteader along the Animas in the 1920s: in two 320-acre patents to William J. Fergusson, who sold cattle and horses. An additional eleven new homesteaders received patents in the 1920s, and the goat ranchers Francisco Rascon and Robinson Chavez increased their holdings. By the 1920s, there was little open land left along the creek except for the upper reaches.

Two of the eleven new homesteads were in the rugged and wild headwaters of the Animas in what is now the Aldo Leopold Wilderness. One of these belonged to Asa A. Johnson, who had forty acres in Victorio Park Canyon. He appears in draft records for World War I in September 1918 at age thirty-nine. In 1918, the draft, in the previous year registering men ages twenty-one to thirty, was amended to include men ages eighteen to forty-five. The war ended in November. Johnson received a patent in 1920. The other homesteader was Lester Dumm, whose ninety-acre homestead was on the boundary, half in and half out of the wilderness area.

Many of the other homesteaders in this period were relatives of earlier settlers. One of these was Gregorio Majalca, eight miles downstream from his younger brother Antonio. Gregorio and his wife, Terecita, had a daughter, Refugia, born in Las Animas in 1898, but they did not receive title to land until 1920. Refugia married Albert Chavez, who was a neighboring homesteader. Another daughter, Filomena, married Ruben R. Chavez.[52]

THE DEPRESSION: A FIRSTHAND GLIMPSE OF LIFE ON LAS ANIMAS

The end of the era of homesteading on Las Animas coincided with the years of the Great Depression. Many of the homesteaders sought title to the 640 acres allowed under the Stock Raising Act—if they could find that much available land. The majority of these homesteaders were Anglos with cattle, such as John and Mary Cunningham, but a few raised goats. Some patents went to people already living here, such as Gregorio Majalca and Fanny Chatfield. There were also two 40-acre patents in this time frame, one to Fanny's son-in-law Hubert Bryant in 1935 and the other to her son Jack in 1939. The latter was the second-to-last patent granted along the Animas and the home of Jack and his wife, Leoma.

Leoma Baker (later Chatfield) first came to Animas on May 11, 1931, to stay with her aunt and uncle. She met Jack a few weeks later on lower

Animas Creek when she and her aunt went to pick up the mail. Jack and Night Rouse were going to move a bunch of sheep to the other side of Hot Springs (now Truth or Consequences). "When I met them he had the sheep bedded down and was fixing to cook supper on a campfire for him and Night."

Early on, Leoma also met the Gordons. In the early '30s, John R. Gordon, youngest son of John and Mallie, moved with his wife, Leona, and their family of four daughters and one son to be close to the Caballo school. One of their daughters was Helen Lorraine, nicknamed "Dogie" by her dad. Leoma tells the story of the first Sunday she went to church: "I saw this lady a struggling, she had a baby in her arms, and she was trying to fix a button on her other little girl's dress....She was having a time. I just walked over there and stuck my arms out, and she laid that baby in my arms. That was Dogie. I think she was about seven months old."[53]

Helen "Dogie" Gordon became best friends with Josephine Daisy Faulkner. Daisy's father, Monroe McGee Faulkner, had been a cowboy with John Gordon, but in 1926, he sold his cattle, and he and his wife bought Green's general store.[54] The store, as described by Daisy (later Wilson), had everything, including hardware, horseshoes, sewing notions, canned goods, candy, potatoes and onions. Ice was delivered by bus and stored in a big icebox. There was a hitching post for horses. Later, they put in a gas pump and had one of the first telephones.

Homes were small, with no indoor plumbing. As Daisy described, "You just packed your water from the well into the house....There were four of us kids and beside the store, there were just two rooms. So my sister and I, we slept in the kitchen—that was our bedroom, in the kitchen. My two brothers, they slept in the bedroom with my folks. But everybody then had a little house, there'd be six kids in a two-room house, and everybody did that. We were just used to little houses; everybody had little houses."[55]

Dogie related a visit to the Tapias, who lived nearby: "I can remember when I was a kid, we went in there for something, because you know I was a Depression kid, everyone had trouble finding enough to eat. Teresa Tapia she used to take in any kid that somebody else didn't want. I went in there and they slept on sheepskins. She'd take them out, and just shake them, and roll them up and stack them in the corner."[56]

Daisy told of the arrival of her brother Leo in 1933. Hot Springs was growing and had a doctor, and he came to their home. Her aunt was there to help, with all her kids.

> *So my Dad said, "Okay all you kids, we're going rabbit hunting." And it's in the afternoon. "It's too hot to go rabbit hunting." It was in April, so it wasn't too hot, but none of us wanted to go rabbit hunting.*
>
> *"Yes, we're all going rabbit hunting. Come on." He got his gun. So we're all going rabbit hunting…We walk down around, down toward the river and* [we're] *messin' around. We kept saying "Daddy can we go back to the house?" "No, no, we haven't seen a rabbit yet we got to find a rabbit." We're going on and on, complaining all the time.*
>
> *When we get back to the house, here's this big baby. And so I asked Daddy, "Where'd that baby come from?" And he said, "Oh, the doctor came and brought the baby." And here the doctor had one of those little black suitcases that they don't carry any more, they used to carry. And I'm looking at that and I'm thinking, how did they, they had to squash that baby to get him in that little suitcase. "Are you sure, Daddy?" "Yah, yah, I'm sure."*
>
> *But Leo, I guess he probably weighed about nine pounds. I don't know how much he weighed. But he was big! That just worried me, that they had mashed him inside that little suitcase and brought him down there. Now the kids know everything. But when I was growing up we didn't know anything about a baby.*[57]

Jack Chatfield married Leoma in Reserve in 1934, and shortly after their marriage, they returned to Animas Creek.[58] Jack's mother, Fanny, had told the family she would poison anyone whom Jack married—she expected him to be around to take care of her. Jack had almost forgotten her threat. Leoma tells a story about the first time they stayed with her new mother-in-law: "The next morning she got up and made coffee. We got up and went in there, and she poured Jack a cup of coffee, and herself a cup of coffee."

Fanny said she didn't have another cup, but there was one in the bedroom. Jack told her:

> *"Don't you drink out of that cup when she brings it back." He said, "Get over here." He grabbed me and pulled me over in his lap, and said, "Drink some coffee here with me." And when she came through the door, he said "Momma, don't pour her any coffee, we have to go now. I promised Ollie—that was his brother—that I would be down early this morning to help him."*
>
> *I figured right then there was something drastically wrong. So when we got out the door—she just kept after him—"Well, let her drink a little of*

> *it. Let her drink a little of it." Jack said, "No, she hasn't got time." And he just grabbed me almost running with me. And he said, "You watch, and see if she don't pour that coffee out. I'll tell you, its not like Momma to waste good coffee." She would put it back, and drink it herself because she drank coffee all day.*
>
> *We got in the car, and he said, "Watch and see if she don't dash it out." Sure enough, out the door, I saw her dash the coffee out the door.*

When they decided to homestead, at first they lived in a tin shed that Jack built. Leoma said, "When we moved up here, we didn't even have a tent.… We didn't have any front of the shed at all. And he put a roof on that old leaky tin.…We had planned to dig a dugout in the hill here, before we built a house, and then build onto the dugout. We called it a cellar."[59]

Jack had a job, but when he was home he would loosen the dirt with a pick. Leoma would shovel it into an iron-wheeled wheelbarrow and move it out to make a level spot where they would eventually build. They cleared some land nearby for a garden and orchard, and Jack hand dug a well. When the cellar was big enough, they moved in. Sometime after their first son Harvey was born in 1936, they built a room out in front of it.[60]

Leoma tells a story that describes not only how little cash people had but what it was worth as well. Jack needed some vaccines for the calves, and he'd left them at his sister's house, where they were living when Harvey was born. The house was locked, but Jack told her there was a window that would not lock, and she could crawl through it. She said, "So away I went. Went down there, and I pushed that window up and lo and behold, if there wasn't fifty cents there.…We had run out of money and were about out of food." With fifty cents, Jack bought flour, baking powder, coffee and a sack of Bull Durham tobacco. She went on to say, "We've had hard times but we never went hungry."

Back then, Leoma said, "a man had to work for a dollar a day. He got top wages if he got a dollar a day." Jack was offered five dollars to dig a well for someone along the creek. When it only took him a few hours, the man wasn't going to pay. "Jack said, 'Okay, I'll just fill 'er back up.' 'Oh no, don't do that, don't do that.' He said, 'Well give me my five dollars.' And he did. He got his five dollars. He said, 'I'd of filled it up as sure as the world.'"[61]

People were very self-sufficient. As Dogie described, "Everybody had milk cows and chickens, pigs, raised their own beef.…We always raised a garden. Dad always butchered.…In the spring he would buy a couple of pigs and we'd feed them out. As soon as it got cold, we'd butcher them. Mama would make bacon and ham with Morton's Sugar Cure."[62]

It was similar for the Chatfields. Harvey said, "We always had a big garden and Mother canned stuff out of the garden, and then we had a big orchard there too, with a lot of fruit trees, peaches and everything. Mother canned peaches and whatever we had, made apple butter....We always raised a hog or two, and Daddy'd kill a deer or two, and grind that meat up together, so it wouldn't be quite so gamey."[63]

Dogie explained, "We used to pick fruit on the halves. Mama would can it. Whoever's fruit it was, they'd get half and we'd get half. There were a lot of small orchards. I remember we'd go to Alvaro's [Chavez]. He had a whole bunch of cherry trees that we would pick. If she had any money, she would buy some."

Other neighbors were the Crouches. "The Crouches had a real nice farm, a good orchard, I mean good with big old trees. That's how they made their living, selling vegetables and fruit."[64]

Dogie and Daisy both spoke of a huge grove of native walnut trees near the river. Daisy explained that they used to go in a wagon with Dogie's mother to pick walnuts. "We did that every year, I can remember, picking up those walnuts. We'd put them in cakes. It was the only nut we had, so we put them in everything."[65]

Children had chores, but they had time to play too—but for the most part they had to entertain themselves. Dogie told a story of a day when the creek was roaring. She and her sisters and brother were watching when a big tree washed by, and her brother roped a branch that was sticking up. "Man, us four girls were helping him pull. Finally that branch broke off. I said, 'You dummy!' He said, 'Man, I wasn't going to let loose of that, that's my brand new rope.'"[66]

Harvey told what a treat it was when his grandma Fanny would read to him, particularly when he spent the night and was getting a little homesick. She had a monthly magazine with the continuing story of Peter Painter, a little rabbit. "She'd sit down in the evening and read that story about that little rabbit to me, and then it'd be continued in the next edition." Then one day an aunt arrived and decided the place needed cleaning up. She tossed the magazines in the fire. "That was devastation for a kid, cause we didn't have any TV, we didn't have any radio, we didn't have any anything."[67]

Children attended the Caballo school, across the road from the Faulkners' store. It had two rooms, one for first through fourth grade and the other for fifth through eighth grade. Daisy recalled, "Back then, so many kids quit school when they were fifteen and went to work, and so there weren't too many in that room. But we all had recess at the same time, so we all played together with the big kids."[68]

In addition to the two small stores in Caballo, there were two stores in Las Palomas. Dogie relates, "Hot Springs wasn't very big, and Hillsboro at that time was the county seat. That old Hillsboro road was just like corduroy. It was a dirt road." People had very little cash and would bring things to the stores to trade.[69]

In 1936, the county seat moved to Hot Springs and construction of Caballo Dam began. Workmen for the Bureau of Reclamation cut down all the native trees and brush, including the grove of walnuts. The rising waters of the dam would flood the school, stores and homes of Caballo in 1938, and the residents were forced to move. Many moved up Animas Creek, but the Faulkners moved to Hot Springs. The Crouches moved up Animas Creek and hired Jack Chatfield to move their fruit trees, too. He dug them up by hand and was paid in trees, as Harvey explained: "Daddy got so many of the trees for digging." He said there were a lot of fruit trees along Animas Creek when he was a little kid.[70]

The end of homesteading on Las Animas was the end of a way of life as people became less self-sufficient and more reliant on a cash economy. Cars became increasingly common and roads improved, so people were more mobile. The days when it was possible to make a living off the land ended, but some of the original families live on. Helen "Dogie" Gordon later married Ruben Chavez, whose great-grandfather was Blas Chavez, one of the first homesteaders. Dogie and her sons Adam and Matthew still live here. Matt is the current bison manager for the Ladder Ranch. Leoma Chatfield lived in the home she and Jack built until a few months before her death on February 12, 2016. Her son Harvey lives on Animas Creek, as do several of her grandchildren.

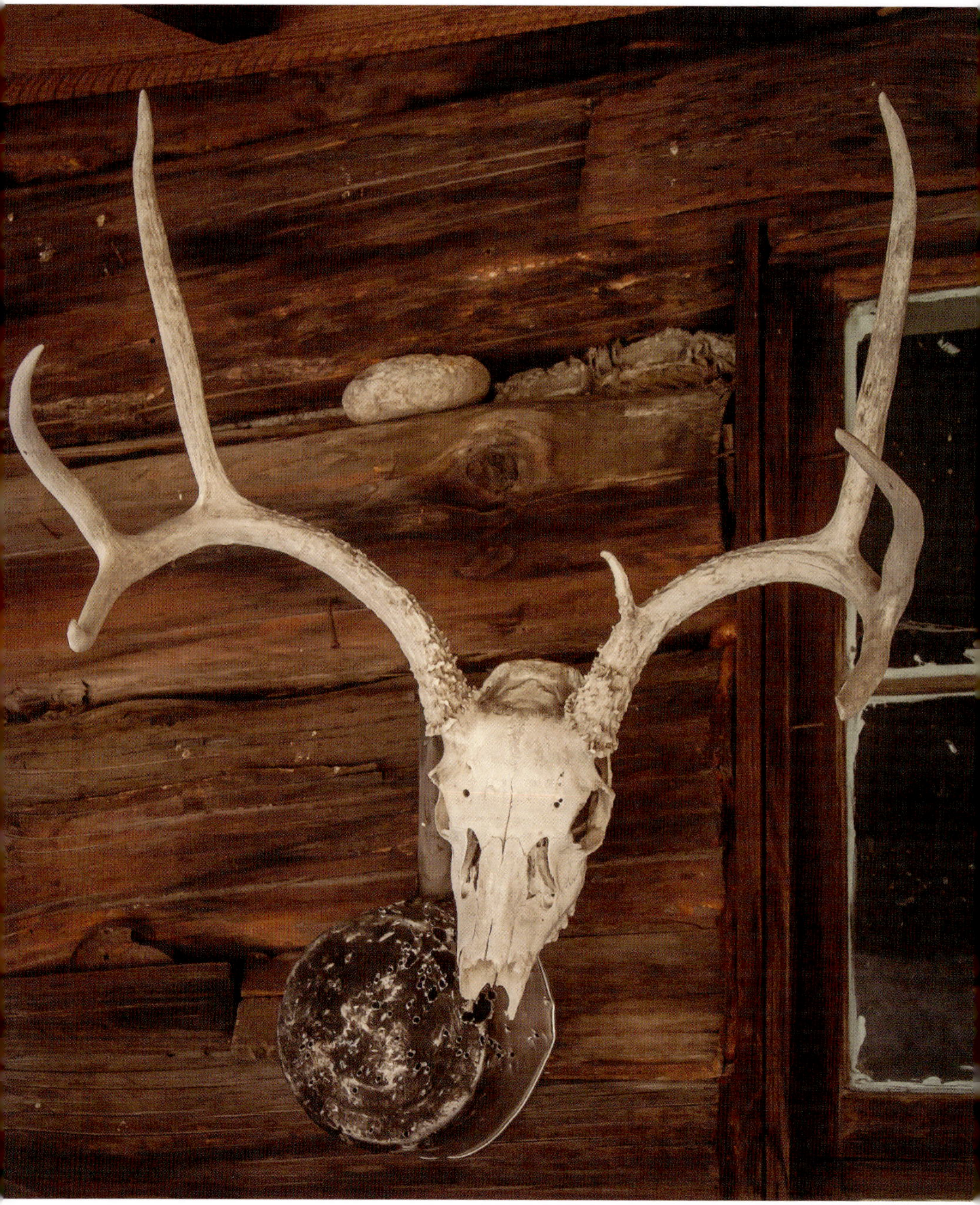

Trophies. *M. Holzwarth, photographer.*

Chapter 7

GOAT RANCHING

HARLEY SHAW

Some of the most detailed records we have found of an early livestock operation were written by two generations of the Armer-Reid family.[71] Only a portion of their Angora goat ranch extended into the Las Animas watershed, taking in upper Cave Creek and a small part of Las Animas itself. However, the firsthand story of their operation provides insights into the details of the business, as well as the day-to-day life of goat ranching families. According to Joseph W. Reid, his mother, Margaret (McIlvoy) Armer-Reid, devoted forty-five years of her life to raising goats and producing mohair. Her first husband, Simpson Percy Reid, had served in the Civil War as a drummer boy. After the war, he went west during the boom mining days of Virginia City, Nevada. From there, he went to California, where he met and married Margaret. They moved to Lake Valley, New Mexico, where high-grade silver ore was being extracted. Soon after their first son, Bob, was born, the couple took up a homestead on the Rio Grande and put out an orchard, but in 1887, the river flooded their land. They then moved to Sawpit Canyon, two miles north of Kingston. The ruins of the Sawpit ranch are still visible, and the trail the Armer-Reid children traveled to attend school in Kingston can still be followed. While on the Rio Grande, they had acquired a few goats. Kingston at that time also was a thriving mining town, and Reid returned to mining, which he followed until his death in 1892. Margaret then married Ed F. Armer, who did not remain with the family.

Margaret had acquired a few milk and meat goats in 1884, but she quickly became interested in Angoras. She was convinced that they were adapted to the Black Range habitats. She bought an Angora buck from C.P. Bailey's bloodlines in 1887, and by the time Reid died, she was fully committed to the Angora mohair business. A single mother with six children, she was confronted during the 1890s by one of the worst droughts to hit the Southwest. Cattle were dying by the thousands and cattlemen were going broke, yet her goats remained thrifty. The range at that time was unregulated public domain, and livestock of all classes were crowded onto it as long as there was any feed. Federal supervision of range management within the national forests came as a blessing. Leases of state lands and homesteads granting 640 acres for stock-raising allowed ranchers to control large enough acreages to make a decent living. At that time, one goat per 5 acres was considered a suitable stocking rate, with a portion of the land being rested while the other was grazed.

Margaret expanded her herd by taking goats onto her range on shares, looking after them and raising the kids for one-half the mohair and one-half the young. By getting the best bucks possible, she built up a herd that was unequaled in these regions. She sold the meat to the mining camps, packing it and all ranch supplies on burros. In 1900, when the American Angora Goat Breeders Association was organized, Margaret became a charter member. This marked the beginning of registered goats in the United States. She was later elected president of this association and served throughout her life as an honorary vice-president and one of its directors. She exhibited her goats at two world fairs and at major shows in Kansas, California, Oregon, Arizona, New Mexico and Texas.

By 1928, she was selling an average of three hundred registered bucks each year, ranging in price from $35 to $100 per head. Registered does were bringing from $25 to $50 per head. Unregistered does brought from $7.50 to $10 per head. She was selling more than twenty-five thousand pounds of mohair each year at $0.55 to $0.85 per pound. Chevons (meat goats) brought from $5 to $7 per head.

The elevation of the Armer goat range varied from 5,000 feet at the lowest points to the extreme elevation of 10,000 feet at the highest points. The goats were herded during the summer in the lower grass, brush and weedy areas. They were moved high up in the timbers, where more browse existed, during the winter. Between growing season and winter, they were kept in the middle elevations or brush-covered areas between 6,000 and 7,500 feet. The temperature varied from zero in the winter to ninety-five degrees in the summer and rarely exceeded these extremes. Snows of more than 2 feet were rare. The annual precipitation ranged from ten to sixteen inches, mostly falling during the months of July and August.

In the early days, the principal goat losses were to mountain lions, bobcats and bears. A single lion might get into an enclosure with the goats and kill as many as twenty-five during one night. The goats were kept under herd during the day and within enclosures at night. Predatory animals were trapped or hunted with dogs. "Lobo" wolves drifted in at one time and did a great deal of damage before they were exterminated. Once the larger predators—lions, wolves and bears—were reduced—the coyote became the greatest pest, drifting seasonally from the open country in the lower altitudes into the brush and timber of the highest elevations.

Shadows. *M. Holzwarth, photographer.*

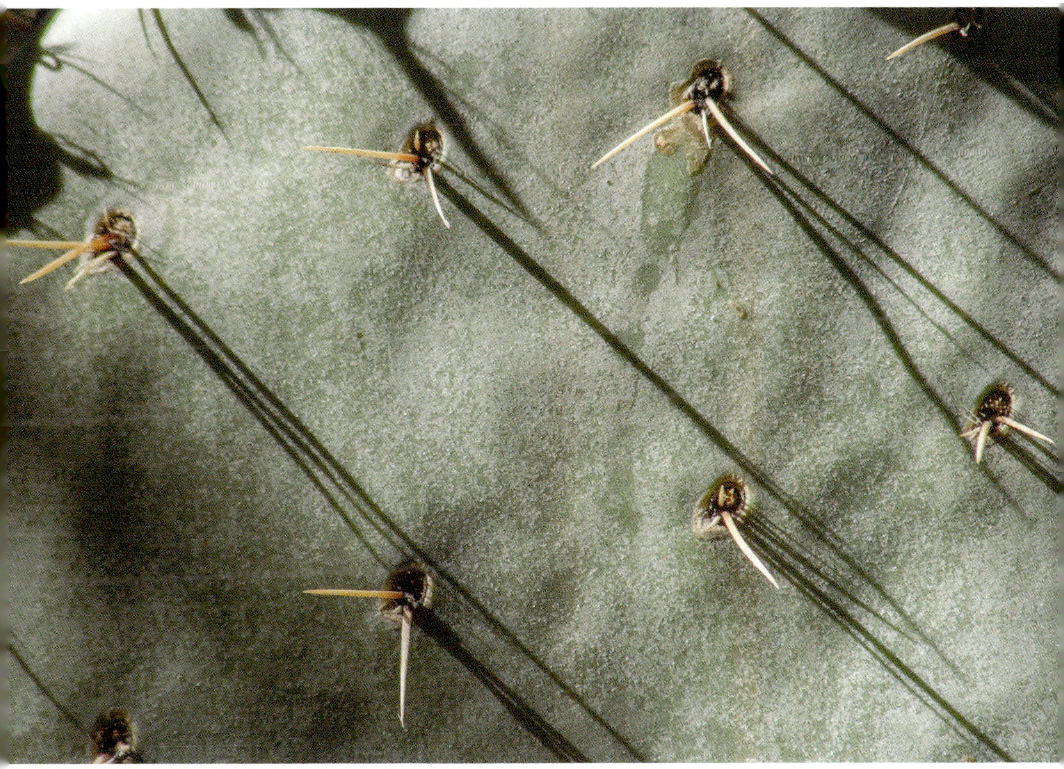

Margaret's oldest son, Robert W. Reid, was born on February 6, 1884, in Lake Valley, New Mexico. Bob, as well as his brothers and sisters, attended public school by walking two miles over the hills from Sawpit Canyon to Kingston. He attended Northern University at Ada, Ohio, graduating in 1904. Between 1908 and 1916, he worked as a ranger for the U.S. Forest Service. In 1916, Bob's mother became sick and had a serious operation, so Bob moved his family to the Saw Pit Ranch. Bob, his mother and two brothers, Percy and Sim, became partners. Bob gave most of his attention to the breeding and care of the goats. In 1920, Sim moved with part of the goats to Texas, leaving Bob and Percy on the home ranch.

During World War I, stock raisers were asked by the government to keep all possible breeding animals, as they would be needed to win the war. If their ranges were not fully stocked, they were encouraged to borrow money from the war finance board to buy more animals. Many of the stockmen accepted this easy money, but at the end of the war, they were notified that 50 percent of their loans must be repaid within four months. The only means they had to pay was to sell their stock. So many cattle being sold swamped the market. To further complicate matters, a severe drought set in on the already-depleted ranges.

In 1924, the banks closed their doors. The Reid family could not pay a goat herder, so Bob and Mary Reid, with all three thousand head of their goats and one horse, moved to a run-down log house in the mountains several miles from Saw Pit. They had no corrals, and the goats bedded near the cabin at night. Predators were bad, and if any goats were left out, some of them might be killed. Bob's wife ran a line of traps for coyotes and foxes to protect their herd and take pelts to sell as fur. The couple kept the goats at this high-elevation camp from January to April, when the does commenced to kid.

By 1928, the Armer-Reids were running more than three thousand head of registered purebred Angora goats, between one and two thousand head of high-grade unregistered Angoras and a herd of Hereford cattle. They held grazing privileges on 22,400 acres of the Gila National Forest and 13,000 acres of private and state land, or 35,000 acres in all.

During the Depression in the winter of 1931, Bob and Mary again took all the goats to a small cabin in the mountains and herded them. The cabin was just large enough for a bunk, a small table and a stove. They kept two horses at this camp and used them to break trail through the snow so the goats could get to the feed on the south slopes. The snow became so deep on the north sides of ridges that the goats could not be seen on the trails.

Margaret Armer-Reid died in 1933. In 1936, Bob and his brother Percy decided to split the ranch. Percy took the cattle, and Bob took the goats and stayed at the Saw Pit headquarters. In 1937, the family bought the Pitchfork Ranch from the Cunninghams, with a twelve-room adobe house. This ranch lies in a tributary of Las Animas Creek. Bob, like his mother, continued to be influential in the Angora goat association and other livestock affairs until his retirement in the 1950s.

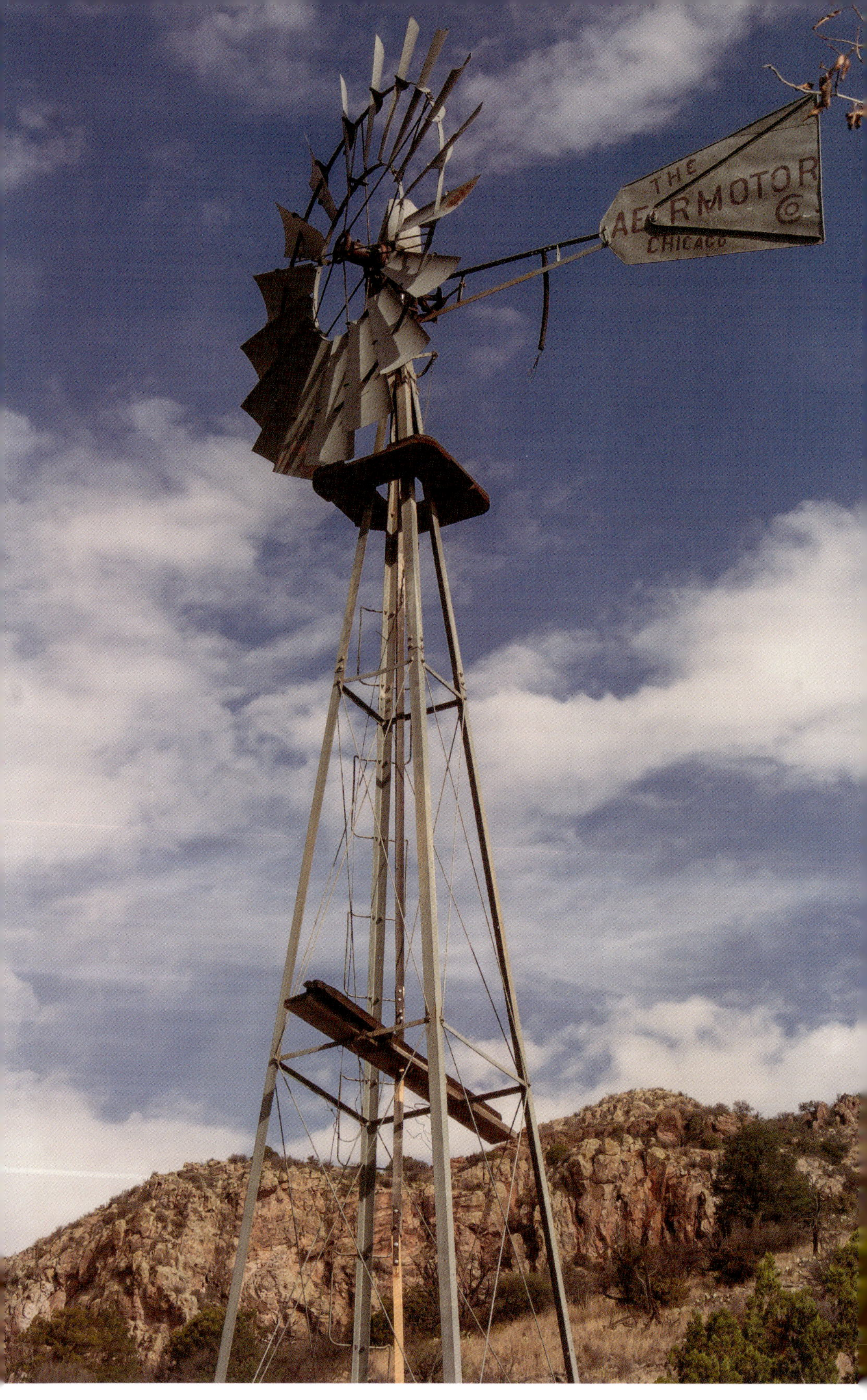
THE
AERMOTOR
CO
CHICAGO

Chapter 8

BECOMING THE LADDER RANCH

CHARLES BRITTON, ART EVANS,
STEVE DOBROTT AND MARGIE GIBSON

In the beginning, large cattle ranches in the Southwest were owned and operated mainly by men who brought their wealth with them. These men dabbled in mining and ranching concurrently, reveling in unbridled entrepreneurship on the one hand and the wildness of the West on the other.

The immense unoccupied public lands of the New Mexico Territory attracted such men, particularly after the end of the Indian wars. Cattle were grazed on open range, where they had to fend for themselves. This system started to disappear with the increase of competing uses or claims on the land.

Around 1880, the Atchison, Topeka and Santa Fe Railroad built a station at Engle, which became a major shipping point for livestock, ore and supplies in what a few years later would become Sierra County.

Willard S. Hopewell arrived here at about the same time. In addition to mining, he started some of the earliest large-scale ranching in the area. Sometime in the 1880s, he organized the Las Animas Land and Cattle Company and eventually became the sole owner. Part of the company's lands would in time become the Ladder Ranch. Hopewell would go on to be a part of the history of statehood.

Early land and ranch dealings are difficult to trace. Many of the records kept by early ranchers have disappeared; in addition, legal records such as deeds, tax collections and brand registrations were often recorded by

Opposite: Aeromotor. *M. Holzwarth, photographer.*

individual owner names rather than ranch or company names. In newspaper accounts from August 1883 to June 1884, Hopewell had a partner, C.M. Brooks. A story in the February 1, 1884 issue of the *Black Range* reports them as having "4,300 head of cattle ranging in the Salados and on Monument and Palomas creeks, and that another thousand are expected in a few days. They have a range to which there is practically no limit."

The first ranch headquarters was about two miles south of Las Palomas at a place called Vega Blanca. By 1884, nearly one hundred men were employed on the ranch, erecting buildings and caring for stock. The headquarters consisted of a new residence, a large corral, housing for the men, a blacksmith shop and a storeroom. The ranch used the J-Half Circle Cross brand, known to locals by the cowboy description John Cross, a name also applied to the ranch itself. It was also called the Animas Ranch in 1885 and 1886 newspapers.

Rustling and diseases from other herds were both problems on the open range. Local papers reported that Hopewell and thirty mounted men arrested sixteen cattle thieves in Kingston in June 1884. In July, he paid a $1,000 reward for the exposure of cattle thieves. In October of that year, Hopewell pursued rustlers all the way to Rincon. The next year, the ranch lost fifty head of cattle to "Texas fever" when a herd from there was settled adjacent to it.

It is challenging attempting to unravel Hopewell's early business partnerships. Newspaper accounts have Brooks as his partner in June 1884, but by July, Hopewell is part of Grayson and Company. At about this time, Nathan Grayson lived in Hillsboro. His brother George W. Grayson was a well-known Californian involved in the mining industry and cattle business. The *Daily Los Angeles Herald* of May 18, 1881, described him as "the engineer of many a skillfully concocted deal." George was partners with another Californian, Archibald Borland, with similar interests and skills. The July 27, 1883 issue of the *Black Range* reported that the two of them spent a week with Hopewell and Brooks.

In August 1884, Hopewell loaned money to one of the first homesteaders on the lower Animas, with the land as collateral. The following February, the two Californians bought the land a month before the homestead patent was granted. Big ranches commonly bought out smaller homesteads throughout the state.[72]

On May 10, 1889, the Las Animas Land and Cattle Company filed articles of incorporation in California with the two Californians as major shareholders and Nathan Grayson and Hopewell as minor ones; Hopewell

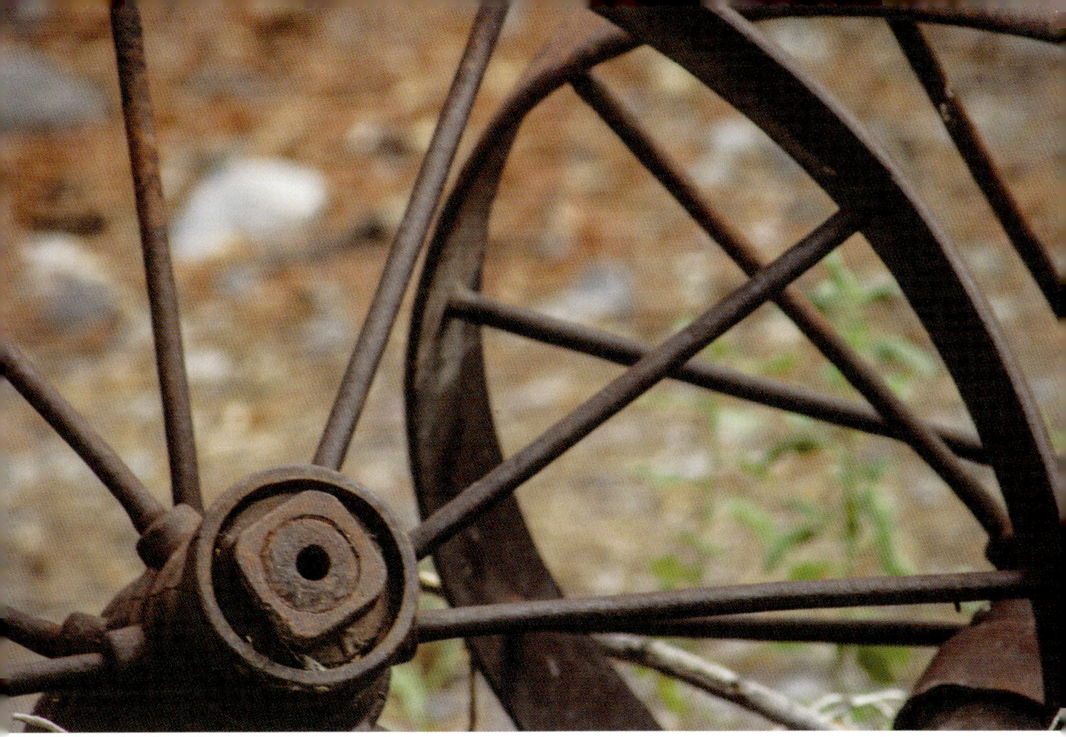

Rust at rest. *M. Holzwarth, photographer.*

was named manager. The company was valued at $2 million. George Grayson and Borland deeded land they had previously purchased to the company. Borland died in February 1890, and the company applied for dissolution in California the following September. It continued in New Mexico with Hopewell at the helm.

Hopewell held on to the Las Animas Land and Cattle Company through some tough times. During a severe drought in 1891 and 1892, 60 percent of the company's fifty thousand head of cattle died. Below-normal precipitation continued for two more years, and much of the remaining stock was shipped out by rail. During 1892–93, Hopewell served in the House of Representatives for the territory. In 1899, under the Homestead Act, he received title to almost 160 acres of federal lands north and east of the present-day Ladder Ranch headquarters buildings.

In 1902, Hopewell resigned as manager of Las Animas Land and Cattle Company in order to manage the Santa Fe Central Railroad.[73] William J. Borland, son of Archibald, took over management of the ranch.

In 1904, Hopewell drafted a petition on behalf of the residents of Sierra County asking the secretary of the interior to include lands along Cuchillo, Palomas, Seco and Las Animas Creeks as part of the Gila Forest Reserve, citing damage to the watersheds by goats and sheep. The reserve, established in 1899, became the Gila National Forest in 1907, and the townships named in the petition are part of it.

The Ladder brand was first recorded as the ladder-slash by Thomas J. Ross in 1899 and morphed over time into simply a horizontal ladder, eliminating the slash. Between 1902 and 1906, first Ross, Hopewell and Ross and then Ross and W.H. Bucher were listed as owners of the brand.

In 1910, the Ladder brand was registered to the Hermosa Land and Cattle Company, and the ranch headquarters were moved to the mining town of Hermosa, where the Hopewells built a large summerhouse. The entire Hopewell family reached this vacation paradise from Albuquerque by rail to Rincon, thence to Lake Valley via Nutt, then by stagecoach to Hillsboro, where they would spend the night. From there, they proceeded to Hermosa by stagecoach some thirty miles across the precipitous canyons of Las Animas, South Seco and North Seco Creeks.

Hopewell was involved in the ranch until his death in 1919, by which time he was apparently the sole owner. His family then sold the ranch to J.A. Wigmore of Cincinnati, Ohio, who was involved in the munitions business during World War I.[74] Dick Kendrick, the new manager, eventually obtained the allotments for the portion of the ranch on national forest lands.

Wigmore moved the ranch headquarters to its present location on Las Animas Creek. He developed over one hundred acres of farmland with an underground concrete pipe irrigation system. He was a horse fancier and built a trotting horse track and polo field, along with two large barns, a two-story bunkhouse, silos, a large shop, a large main house, a small guest house and three duplex and one single-family worker houses. Most of these structures are still present. Wigmore sold the ranch in 1928.

Mr. Pettefield of Los Angeles appears as the next owner of the ranch, but his name does not show up in the federal census for that period or in any news items for California or New Mexico. Wigmore shipped polo ponies from the ranch as late as 1930, which suggests that Pettefield was an absentee owner and the ranch remained in Wigmore's control. However, Art Evans relates a tale told to him by Earl Coalson, whom Pettefield hired to drive for him on a visit to the ranch. Between headquarters and Hermosa, they kept seeing herds of cattle, and Pettefield would ask whose cattle they were. "Yours, Mr. Pettefield," was Coalson's inevitable answer. By the time they reached Hermosa, Pettefield said, "My God, Earl, there is no way we can keep track of all of my cattle. Start gathering these cattle and sell them." According to Evans, they did just that.

In 1930, Pettefield sold the ranch to Sam Lard of Fort Worth, Texas. Two members of the family shared this name. The elder was a prominent businessman in Fort Worth. The younger Sam lived at the ranch and seemingly had a rich social life. He and his wife appeared frequently at events in El Paso and even Santa Fe. They often hosted family and dignitaries at the ranch. A son of the younger Sam, Bob Lard, also spent time at the ranch. During these years, Burton Roach was the ranch manager. Roach was a larger-than-life figure in many ways. Before coming to the Ladder Ranch, he was the Potter County sheriff out of Amarillo, Texas, for a decade and a past president of the Texas Sheriff's Association. In 1940, while still managing the ranch, Roach was elected to the New Mexico State Senate, serving through 1951. He unsuccessfully ran for governor at least twice during that period.

In 1953, the Lards sold the Ladder Ranch to Tovrea Land and Cattle Company of Phoenix, Arizona. Tovrea owned and traded in ranchlands throughout the Southwest. Tovrea held the ranch five years and imported Art Evans of New River, Arizona, as ranch foreman.

In 1958, a group from Albuquerque and Roswell, New Mexico, bought the ranch from Tovrea. J.P. White, one of the owners, became manager, and Art Evans continued as foreman.

The Ladder Ranch Company was incorporated on January 9, 1958, for one hundred years with an initial stock of $1,500,000. Although the Ladder brand had been in existence for over fifty years, this appears to be the earliest legal document calling the ranch by this name.

About 1960, Robert O. Anderson, founder of the Atlantic Richfield Oil Company, bought the Ladder Ranch. At the time, he was said to be the biggest landowner in the United States.[75] Art Evans remained as foreman. Anderson, a legendary figure in the oil industry, also owned and operated the Diamond A Cattle Company. He was a philanthropist who supported the arts and many environmental causes, although his principal source of wealth came from developing the Prudhoe Bay oil fields in Alaska.

Gerald Lyda, organizer of the largest construction company in Texas, purchased the Ladder Ranch in 1985. He performed a land exchange with Ted Turner in 1992, rounding up five thousand cattle and relocating them to a new ranch near Fort Stockton, Texas. Rather than rebranding the five thousand Ladder Ranch cattle, Lyda registered the same brand in Texas under the Spanish name for "ladder," and the Escalera Ranch was born.

Ted Turner acquired the Ladder Ranch in 1992 and still owns it. The ranch contains about 290,000 acres, of which some 160,000 are deeded and the rest is leased public lands.[76] Art Evans ran the ranch for twenty-eight years and stayed on as a mentor to Turner's new manager, Steve Dobrott. Art passed away in 2013.

The history of ranching on the national forest portions of the Las Animas watershed is more complex than on the private lands. Cattle and sheep were both in the area by 1880, but the remoteness of the Las Animas drainage may have postponed its use for grazing. Margaret Armer-Reid was running goats near Kingston by 1892 and apparently expanded into the Animas. Over time, feral horses and burros, released by prospectors and ranchers, grew in number.

A report on the Cave Creek allotment, written about 1969, provided a glimpse of grazing history on the watershed. By that time, five older and smaller allotments—Vic's Park, Holden Prong, Sid's Prong, Cave Creek and Mineral Creek—had been combined to form the Cave Creek allotment. With the exception of Mineral Creek, all of these were part of the Las Animas watershed. Bob Reid estimated that three thousand goats and five hundred cattle used the area during the 1920s, and most of these belonged to the Reids. This level of use probably existed until about 1957. At that time, the Reids held the combined allotment, although most of the

River of Spirits. *M. Holzwarth, photographer.*

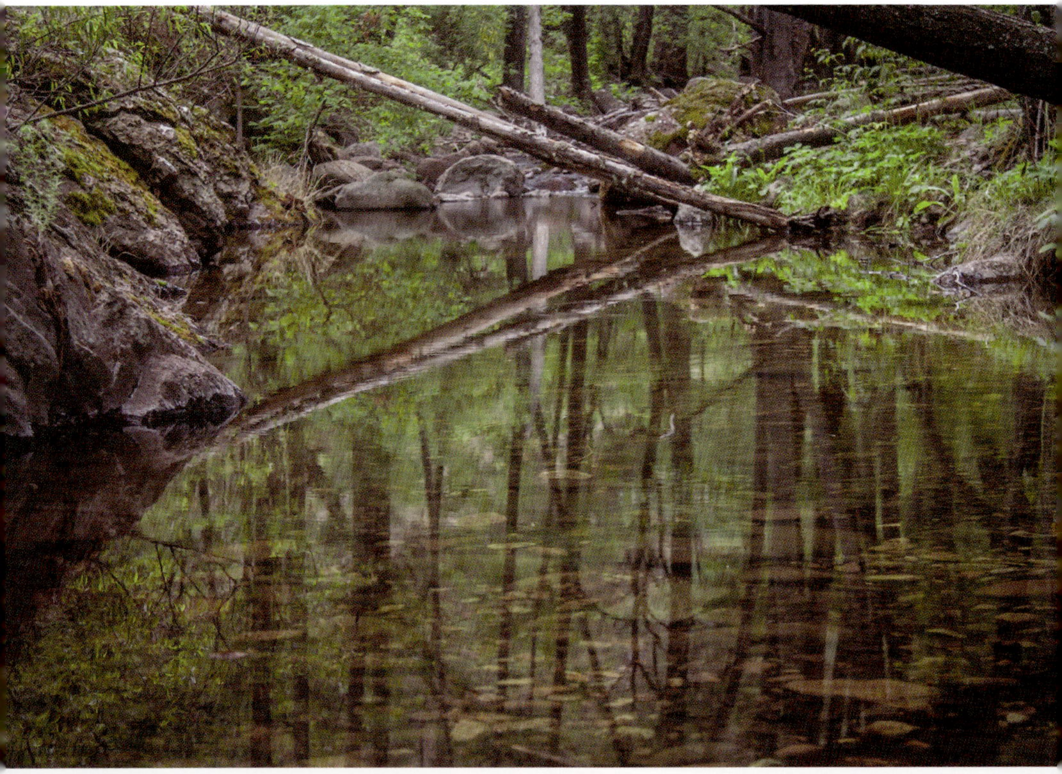

goats had been removed by 1949. The McKnight fire burned two-thirds of this allotment in 1951, and livestock numbers were reduced voluntarily by the permittees. Grazing levels then increased until three hundred head of cattle were present yearlong. The national forest permit was transferred in 1962 to Thomas Miller and then to Robert O. Anderson two years later. Between 1962 and 1964, fifty-six head of wild horses and fifty head of wild cattle were removed. No Ladder Ranch livestock were on the allotment during those years. By 1969, the allotment effectively included all of upper Las Animas Creek and was held by the Ladder Ranch Company. Trails were generally in poor condition, and work was started to reconstruct most of the trails, but due to the rough terrain, it was not considered a good livestock prospect.

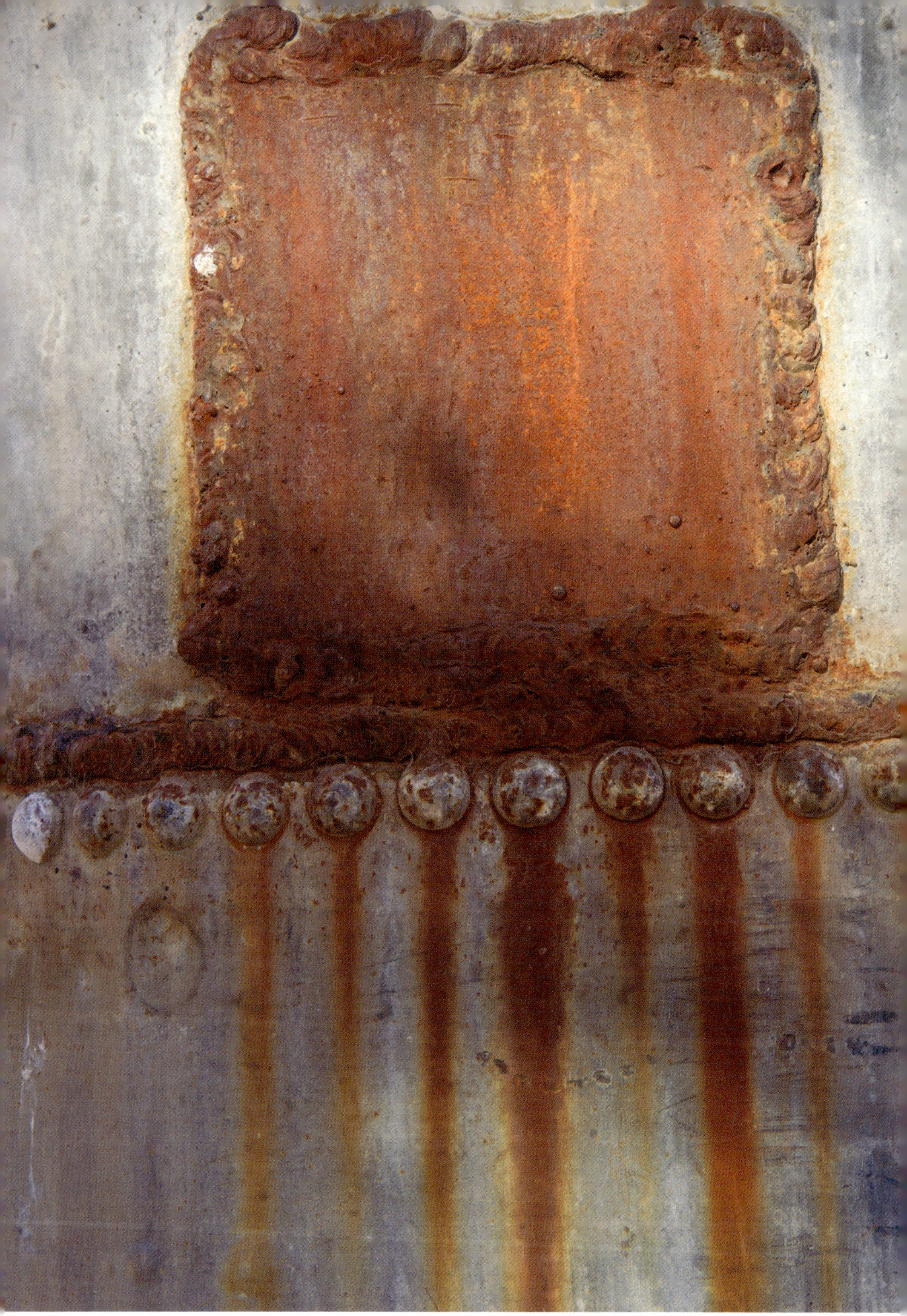

Patched. *M. Holzwarth, photographer.*

Chapter 9

CONSERVATION RANCHING

Steve Dobrott

To this day, the Animas captivates those privileged to venture up from headquarters through the ancient Arizona sycamores. Located on the east side of the Black Range, it is one of a few perennial streams that flow toward the Rio Grande. Upstream from the ranch lie the Gila National Forest and the Aldo Leopold Wilderness. Downstream from the ranch are numerous private landholdings, including old family ranches, small farms and residences.

Draining some 40 miles of primary creek (140 square miles of watershed) with innumerable tributaries, the Animas can flood during heavy snowmelt or monsoon rains. Its gentle nature can change with one August microburst, stranding downstream residents for days. A few folks who have tried to cross during such flows have been swept away and perished. These dynamic flows affect the vegetation within the flood zone. Such flooding can carve a new stream course, injecting new life into an old flood plain. The creek is constantly changing from the same natural forces that carved it into existence.

> *It's not the years, it's not miles; it's the corners you've been drug around that age you.*
>
> —*Art Evans*

In the beginning, I had a steep but short learning curve aided by a past Ladder Ranch manager, Art Evans, who spent four years as my mentor. Ted Turner had great foresight in hiring Art to get me started. A bonus for me in many ways, Art assisted in every aspect of the ranch. He had spent twenty-eight years managing it. From Art, I learned the history, grazing capacity and logistics of running the ranch. One of Art's favorite places was Animas Creek, where he and his family often went to picnic, cut a Christmas tree or just hang out. He loved to tell of the homesteaders who tried to scratch out a living by diverting water onto small farm plots that he had later "rehabilitated" into rangeland during his time as the Ladder boss.

By his stories and recollections, Art gave me a good understanding of places. Art was well liked by everyone, and though the local sentiment about Ted buying the ranch was mixed, Art did his best to get me acquainted with people in nearby communities. With Art's patient support and advice, we readied the ranch for bison, with an equal emphasis on wildlife management. Roads were reworked with heavy equipment. Water systems were repaired or upgraded. All nonfunctioning windmills were gradually replaced with solar-powered pumps. Fences were removed or modified. Art wasted no time turning me into a ranch manager. Even though neither Art nor I knew how to manage bison, within three months of acquiring the ranch, we received our first shipment of calves. We had one thousand head by the end of the first year.

> *Give me land, lots of land, under starry skies above. Don't fence me in.*
> —*Cole Porter and Robert Fletcher*

Little did we know that within a month of the purchase of the ranch, we would decide to remove all the sheep fences that Art had proudly built. We realized that these net-wire barriers were a detriment to movements of deer, elk, pronghorn, javelina and wild turkeys. They were also an abomination to Ted. The gruesome evidence of deer leg bones twisted into the top wires was enough to convince us that these fences had to go. Within three years, we removed 250 miles of net-wire that had been installed in the early 1960s for a short-lived experiment with free-ranging sheep. The results favored an army of predators that, although pursued by traps, poisons and guns by ground and air, nixed any hope that a wool business could be profitable on the ranch without day-herding.

After initially cutting game passages in pasture corners, we removed fence from the middle of the ranch outward. With the help of Apache crews, the job took three years. We decreased the number of pastures from forty-five to six, the latter being surrounded by "wildlife-friendly" high-tensile smooth bison wire with pipe wildlife crossings. This had an immediate effect on the pronghorn, mule deer and elk herds. No more was wildlife fenced in or limited in range. No more did we find the entangled bones of deer hung up in the top two strands of barbed wire. Wildlife was now free to move about the ranch.

I also proceeded to improve five hundred miles of boundary fence. Containment of bison within our boundaries was an early concern that proved less of a problem than trespass cattle from the outside. Bison raised on the ranch developed home ranges within wire boundaries and seldom tested fences unless pushed or frightened.

In 1995, the Nature Conservancy's Heritage Program led the first inventory of the ranch in search of unique and sensitive habitats and rare species. This survey would guide management decisions for bison, fencing and water developments. The consequences of some of these actions would surprise us. For example, overflow from solar-powered pumps became breeding habitat for the threatened Chiricahua leopard frogs that were especially vulnerable during times of drought.

We not only documented the existence of unique habitats, but we also became determined to manage them, emphasizing the conservation of imperiled species ranch-wide. In 1994, the Turner Endangered Species Fund (TESF) was formed to oversee threatened and endangered species on all Turner properties. The fund is dedicated to conserving biodiversity by ensuring the persistence of imperiled species and their habitats. The guiding mandate of Turner Enterprises Inc. (TEI) is to "manage and enhance Turner lands in an economically sustainable and ecologically sensitive manner while emphasizing the conservation of native species." Applying this philosophy and Ted's oversight, the Ladder Ranch became one of the most important private landholdings with respect to its contribution to biodiversity in the Southwest. Ted's vision has transformed the Ladder from a single-purpose cattle ranch to a multifaceted operation that not only produces bison meat for his restaurants but also cares for the environment.

During the early Turner years, the assignments and projects were daunting but doable. The speed at which things could be accomplished was vastly different than what I had been accustomed to with the government. The race to fulfill Ted's vision was highlighted by the immense satisfaction that I had in pleasing him and doing what I perceived was right for the land and the wildlife. Each day was a challenge and a thrill. Never was there an uninteresting or non-challenging moment. The early years focused on getting the ranch operational while developing the quail-hunting prospects.

We also developed habitat for mule deer; Coues whitetail; elk; pronghorn; javelina; black bear; mountain lions; bobcat; coyotes; gray foxes; kit foxes; ringtail; four species of skunks; wild turkey; and Gambel's, scaled and Mearn's (or Montezuma) quail. Coatis have recently been sighted on the ranch. In addition to quail and turkeys, 240 other bird species, including Mexican black hawks, zone-tailed hawks, yellow-billed cuckoos and burrowing owls, have been documented. Surveys of smaller native rodents have just begun. Restoration efforts are in place for black-tailed prairie dogs, bolson tortoises and Chiricahua leopard frogs. The ranch provides holding facilities for Mexican gray wolves in partnership with the U.S. Fish and Wildlife Service. Programs to support restoration of Rio Grande cutthroat trout and condors have been considered. We've also begun to study the history and origin of the Arizona sycamores.

I have no doubt that these efforts will be a lasting testament to Ted and all who work with him, making this a more complete ecosystem for future generations. The legacy will be carried forth by the Turner family. On August 7, 2012, Ted Turner was awarded the U.S. Fish and Wildlife Service Champion Award for his longtime efforts in promoting wildlife conservation. Fittingly, that presentation happened at the Ladder headquarters on Animas Creek.

On Animas Creek, we are the transients; wild species are the residents to be respected for their role in the ecosystem. This standpoint guides us but sometimes poses challenges for employees. Rattlesnakes, for instance, are not killed; they are merely transported away from residences if deemed dangerous to the occupants. All wildlife species are tolerated. They are not encouraged by supplemental feeding, except for a few farm plots where deer, elk, javelina, Canada geese and wild turkeys feed. Bears sometimes require relocation but are normally kept from being nuisances by ensuring that no garbage is available to them. Dogs are not allowed to run freely. Wildlife has the right of way. As a result, one can drive on the ranch and see a host of wildlife—unconcerned and willing to stand for a photo or two.

Following in the footsteps of managers like Tom Walton, Burton Roach and Art Evans was a formidable undertaking for me at first. While I did not have to prove myself as a cattleman, these men had not had to consider the needs of wildlife balanced with range use by bison. In particular, they did not have to keep unruly bison on the ranch or be concerned with needs of threatened or endangered species. Prior to Ted's ownership, the Ladder Ranch was known for its productive cow herds, tough cowboys and hard-handed bosses. All energy, time and money went to producing beef or wool. Predators, avian and mammalian, were relentlessly controlled. Rattlesnakes, prairie dogs, coyotes and cougars were dispatched on sight. But I believe that each generation of ranchmen loved the ranch because it was untamable and wild. I believe also that they admired in particular the peaceful and scenic landscapes of Animas Creek.

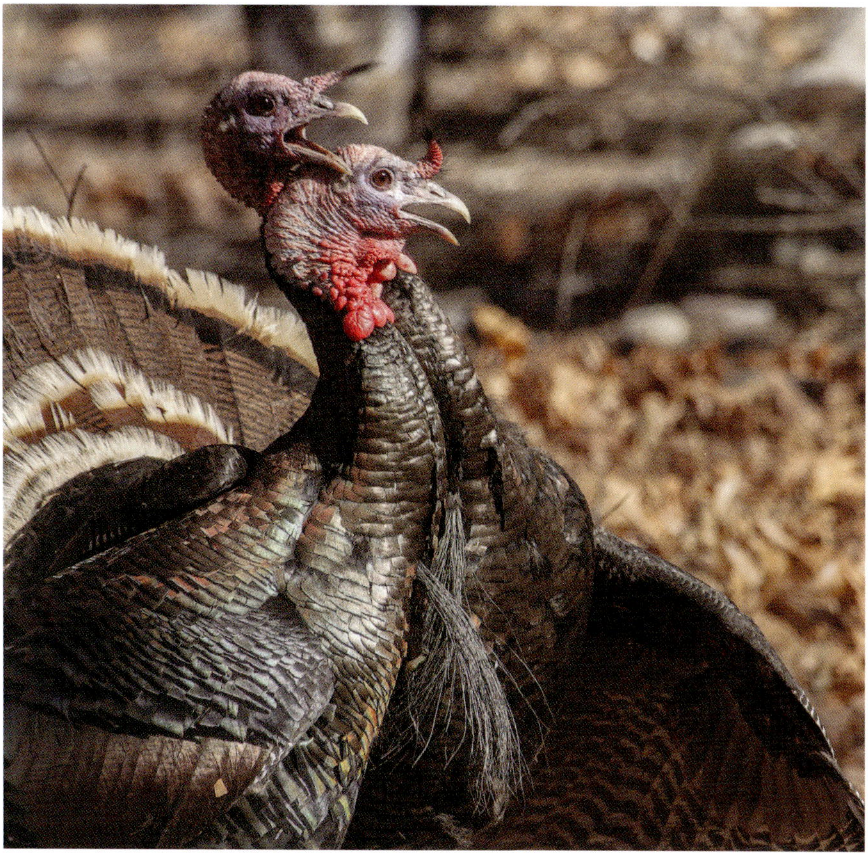

Turkey duet. *M. Gibson, photographer.*

Like the Mimbres people who inhabited the area from AD 1150 to 1500 or the later Apaches, Hispanics and Anglos, if, while on the creek, you close your eyes and listen, you will hear what the ancient ones, Apaches, Spaniards, U.S. Cavalry and homesteaders once heard. You might even hear their spirits crying in the wind.

I suspect I am not the first or last manager of the Ladder to venture horseback up this magical canyon on a fall afternoon to "check on water" amid the ghostly white trunks of the sycamores and colors and streamside fragrances of fallen leaves. Something about being on the creek soothes the mind. Local idiom describes the sound of the wind blowing through the trees in the canyon: "*En los Rios de Las Animas se oyen las almas llorando en la noche*" (On the Animas River one hears the souls crying at night). I propose this sense of spirit is why it was named. The name aptly represents all who have tasted its waters or lived and died along its banks. Once you have been there, you want to go back.

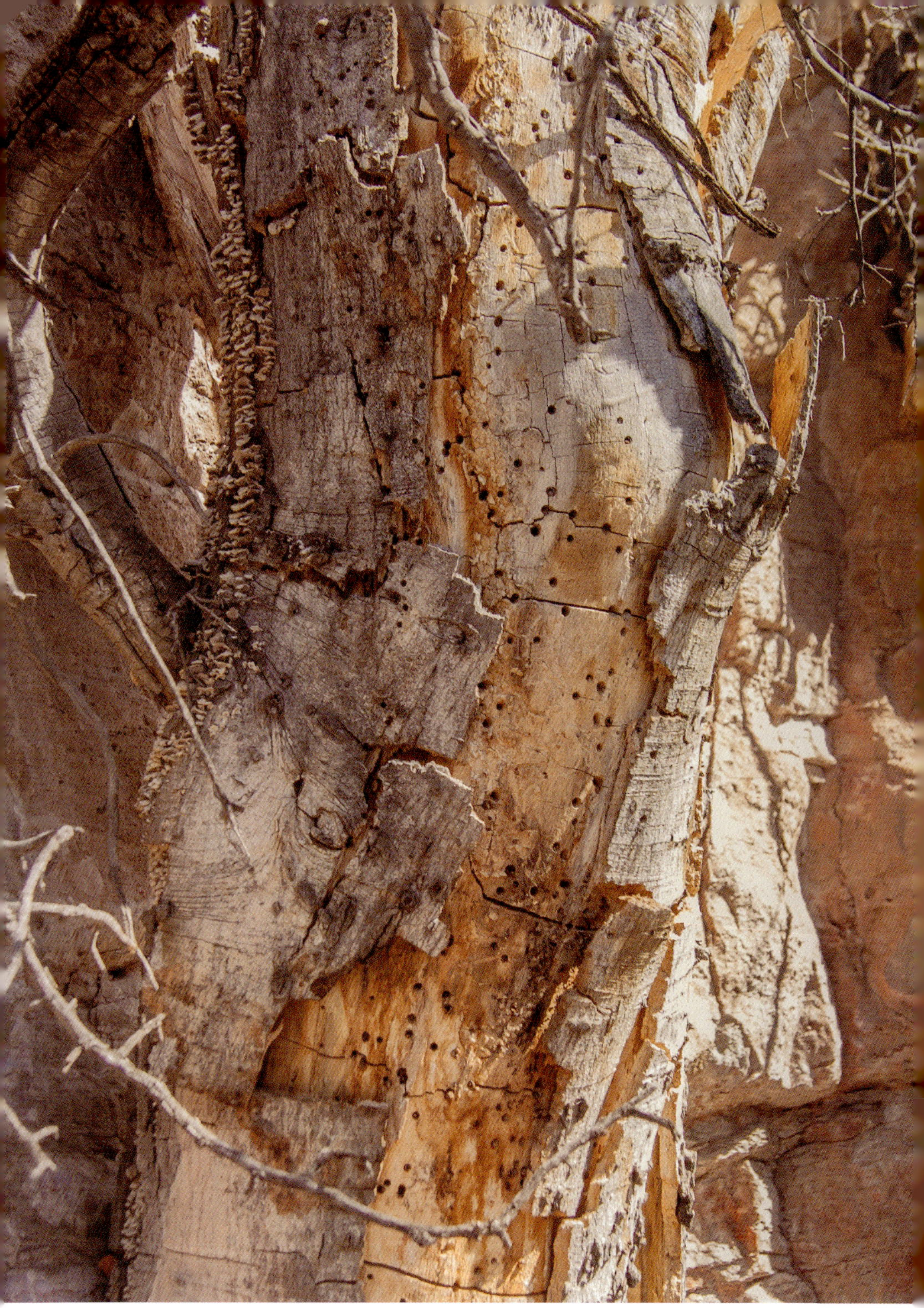

Golden decay. *M. Holzwarth, photographer.*

Chapter 10

WILDERNESS ADVENTURES

Harley Shaw

Stories of hunting, fishing or other forms of recreation in the Animas are sparse. I suspect this is because the tributaries of the Gila and Mimbres Rivers west of the Black Range are more easily accessible, had more dependable flow and hold a variety of game fish. As Hillsboro, Kingston, Hermosa, Chloride, Winston and Cuchillo grew, a few miners, ranchers, businessmen and visitors ventured into Animas Creek for adventure and recreation, but they left few records. Native cutthroat may have existed in the stream, although this is uncertain. The earliest record we've found of trout being brought to the upper Animas is in 1919. It is conceivable, even likely, that earlier stockings might have been tried.

The first mention of fishing in Animas appears in the diary of J.D. Whitham for September 1 to 3, 1883.[77] Whitham operated a toll road between Hillsboro and Kingston and speculated in mines. His brief entries about a horseback trip from Kingston into Animas read:

> *1st. Saturday. Left at 10 a.m. for Animas River. Camp on Garfield Creek, 4 p.m. Height 6700 feet.*
>
> *2nd. Sunday. White's Ranch, 11 a.m., 6000 ft. Heart of Mimbres Camp, 3 p.m. Hunted, fished & rested. Height 6700 feet.*
>
> *3rd. Monday. Left camp at 9 a.m. White's at 12, Garfield at 4 p.m., Percha City at 6:30 p.m., Kingston 11 p.m.*

No Garfield Creek appears on current maps, but based on riding time and the estimated elevation, Whitham's first camp must have been in the head of Cave Canyon, probably near the cave for which the canyon was named. On the second day, he entered Animas Creek. White's Ranch must have been near the site of present-day Apache Camp or the Kelsey site. Heart of Mimbres Camp was probably near the later Murphy cabin at the mouth of Holden Prong. Whitham's ride from the upper Animas all the way back into Kingston was a major undertaking, though certainly possible within the timeframe he presents. With a sound horse, a fourteen-hour ride would have put him back in Kingston.

Whitham's spurious ride into Las Animas fell between the time Victorio was killed and the uprisings of Geronimo and other Apaches. A solitary rider going into the Animas was taking considerable risk. The presence of White's Ranch in the Animas in 1883 suggests that the death of Victorio had provided some sense of security to settlers. Nearly all of these remote ranches were abandoned when Nana and Geronimo broke out. Whitham mentions fishing near the "Heart of the Mimbres" camp but doesn't say if he caught anything.

Hillsboro pioneer Edward Tittmann left an account of a 1909 hunting trip made into upper Animas. He came to New Mexico in 1908 from New York, where he had practiced law and served as assistant editor for the *New York Times* and *Wall Street Journal*. He attended school in Germany and received a law degree from George Washington Law School in Washington, D.C. He served as a Sierra County delegate to the New Mexico state constitutional convention in 1910. From 1913 to 1915, he served as district attorney of New Mexico's seventh judicial district and during 1917 and 1918 was an attorney for the Pueblo Indians in New Mexico. He was a member of the Civil Liberties Union and served on its national committee. He also served several years as a member of the Sierra County Board of Education. He fought successfully against an early attempt to move the Sierra County seat from Hillsboro to Cutter but lost a later fight against moving the county seat to Hot Springs (now Truth or Consequences). He died in 1957 at age eighty-four. His "Diary of the Hunt," published in the next chapter with permission from his grandson John Tittmann of Albuquerque, appears here in his own words.

Chapter 11

A 1909 PACK TRIP

EDWARD TITTMANN

Sunday, November 7th 1909. Although everything was supposed to be ready for our departure this morning we did not get off until after ten o'clock. Unable to secure a packhorse we had a burro and this restricted our pack in weight to about 100 pounds. The trail led over the Snake mine down to the Bonanza and from there past the cold springs and then the Warm Springs along the road to Hermosa to the top of the divide between Tank Canyon and Cave Creek. This was an uninteresting bit of journey along a valley desolate and bare of even oak brush, brown and yellow in tinge, and doubly wearying because the burro went so slow we had to walk our horses. Now and then the beast of burden created a little intermezzo in the ennui that enwrapped us by trying to throw his pack off his back, or running full tilt and with marvelous speed considering his ordinary travel for some other burro that he had discovered in the distance. Maybe our conversation was too intellectual to be understood by him though on the part of Stevens speech consisted mainly of cusswords flung at the long ears of the ass. [Stevens was undoubtedly Roscoe C. Stevens of Hillsboro. He was shown in the 1910 census as age thirty-three and employed as an electrician.] From the top of Cave Creek hill the trail into the canyon was steep, and about half way down the burro succeeded in throwing his pack so that it slid down on one side of him. We had to take off everything and repack. Thus we lost half an hour. The trail went up Cave Creek which soon became what the Germans call romantic, meaning wild, with steep cliffs ascending on either side several hundred feet. Finally the valley became so narrow that a wagon

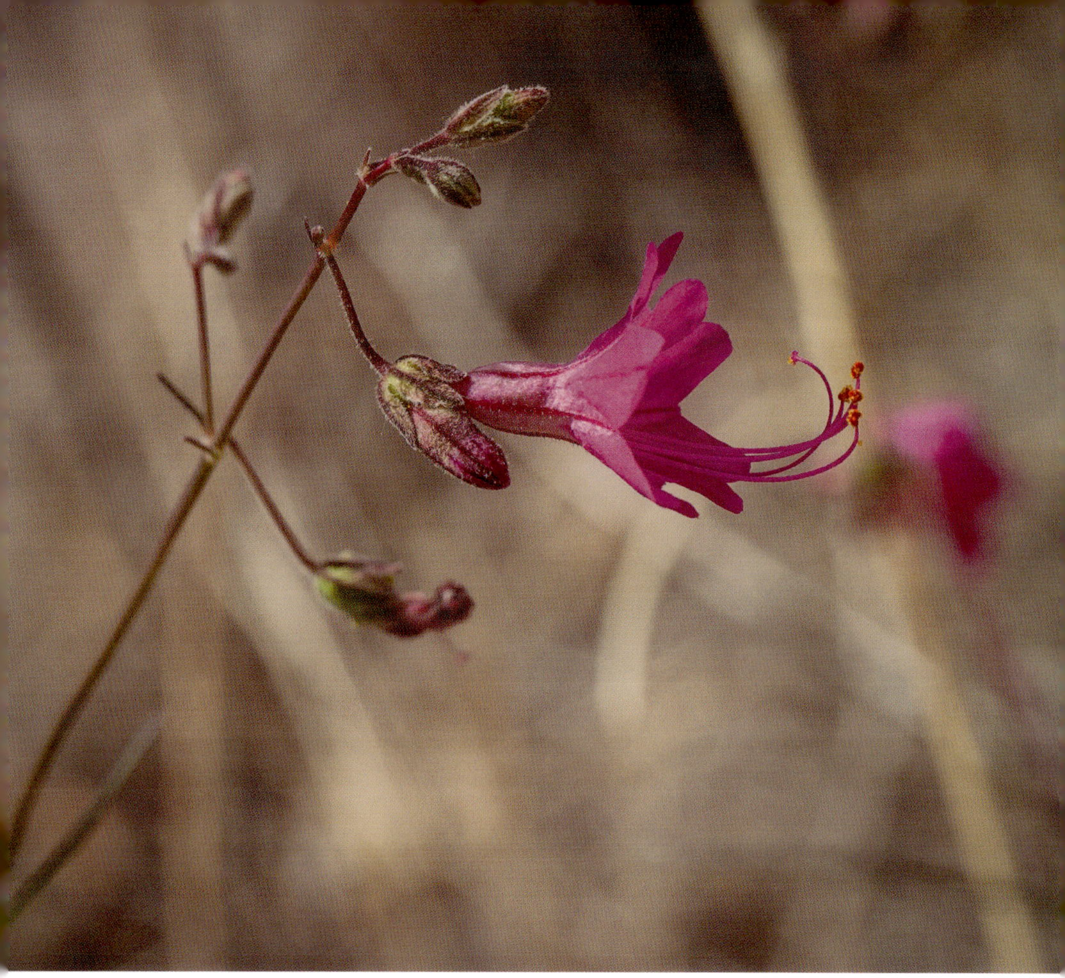

Delicate grace. *M. Holzwarth, photographer.*

could hardly have gone through it. The horses had to wade through deep pools of water, the burro being submerged almost to his body. The canyon widened again [as] we passed a goat ranch, where are now located the goats that used to bother us in the Ready Pay Gulch. We were getting into the pine country. Magnificent trees rose up everywhere some of them 70 feet high and five feet around. At four o'clock after we had travelled some 16 miles we made camp within sight of the goat ranch where Stevens' goats are located. We spread our bed under a spreading juniper tree. First we put down a large canvas. On this came three comforters, then each man's blankets, then two more comforters and then the end of the canvas or "tarp" was drawn up over the entire bed. We cooked supper, that is, Stevens cooked and I watched him. Bread made in a frying pan, much like a pancake, bacon and potatoes with a cup of weak coffee made up our meal. We had hobbled our horses and they had just finished eating some corn which we had taken along when an accident happened, which is difficult to relate in polite society. Brownie, Stevens' horse, mistook our towels for what I do not know but at any rate he seemed to think they were diapers and we had to wash them in the creek. As we finished supper the Mexican who has goats on shares came home with his wife and invited us into his cottage, made of upright logs with the spaces filled in with mud, a construction typical of Mexicans. Inside it was very nice and clean and he pointed out with pride what improvements he had made and what he still intended to do. He had a little girl who became very sleepy but the parents did not notice it till I called their attention to her whereupon they spread a comforter and some pillows on the floor and the little one was soon sound asleep. About half past nine we sought our beds and slept soundly until morning light broke over the hills. It was very cold. During the night winter had set in and the water had half an inch of ice on it. All the rest of the nights were cold or colder and every morning we had to thaw out the dishes and the bread made the night before while Stevens started to cook breakfast.

Monday morning I went after the live stock. I thought this would be easy but it proved otherwise as the horses, though hobbled, had wandered three miles down the creek so that before breakfast I had a six mile walk. About ten o'clock we pulled out of camp; up the creek we travelled only about five miles that day as I wanted to inspect the cave after which the creek is named and also desired to prospect a little as I saw plenty of mineral signs.

At Folgums Ranch about the head of the Cave Creek we made camp and then started out on a walk during which we saw lots of deer tracks, turkey tracks, tracks of wildcats and even of bear but the only game that fell before our prowess was a nice fat squirrel which had evidently been living luxuriously on Folgum's corn. I never saw a squirrel as fat. He made a nice supper.

We went to sleep under the stars without the shelter of a tree but as the moon was dark the starlight did not bother us. Lobo lay on the bed at my feet, our guns were at our sides and we slumbered peacefully and deeply. All at once—what was that?—I rose startled on one elbow. Again the cry weird and wailing sounded from the hilly side. This time it woke Stevens. It was some kind of a wild beast, most likely a coyote, calling to his mate. Then from the opposite hill came the answer or rather answers. It sounded as if there was a whole pack of them but there were only the two. Lobo barked loudly and started after them but I called him back for fear they might entice him away as the coyotes sometimes do. They kept their wailing up for a long time but finally they got tired and we went to sleep again. But just before morning when the stars first begin to pale we heard the beasts again. This time they were not alone but joined in a whole chorus of noises among which we distinguished the deeper notes of a real timber wolf. They were announcing the coming of morning. Then the cattle began to bellow and low and it was Tuesday.

Breakfast was the same as dinner except that the squirrel was all eaten up. After breakfast we started to climb up to the cave. This is a natural opening in the rocks resembling the shell in which orchestras play at the seashore and elsewhere. The cave was fully 30 feet high about 50 feet deep and about 75 feet wide. Within were all kinds of small holes to each of which led tracks easy and distinctly to read. I challenged the heads of the various families to come out and give me battle but no reply. Of course they knew I had a shotgun and they being unarmed with such weapons naturally hesitated. Above in the walls of the cave were multitudes of little nests but not of birds but rather of bats. One large nest belonged according to all the signs on the door to a Mr. Hawk who however happened to be out.

We descended and explored the surrounding country but found nothing great in the way of mineral. The country had been prospected once, twenty years ago, in part at the expense of the late Bob Ingersoll but though there are signs of mineral it will cost money to get it out.

We did not break camp that day, and when I went to bed it was in the hope that the musical coyote family might give us some more entertainment. But we were disappointed. We slept through without an adventure of any kind until Wednesday morning.

Again the bill of fare was the same and while Stevens was getting it ready I went after the horses. I found them all O.K. and brought them back into camp. For lack of a rope my horse had to remain untied a few moments and during those moments while I was getting his bridle Kid skipped out. He went to the waterhole in the creek and I went after him knowing: that as soon as he had drunk his fill he would let me fetch him but Stevens wanted to play cowboy and while Kid was still at the water hole Stevens rode up to him in spite of my warning and tried to rope him. Of course he missed and Kid indignantly galloped off and was seen no more as he was soon lost in the thick underbrush.

We learned afterwards that he must have gone straight home as he arrived there that very afternoon. I left my saddle etc at Folgums and went on afoot which I did not mind in the least as the trails were getting very steep and risky and a fall with the horse would have probably lamed the outfit at the bottom of the canyons. I climbed on afoot and Stevens led the burro. We went up at least 200 feet over the creek bed and then down again on the other side where flowed the beautiful Animas.

We went up the Animas about 4 miles and camped for the night near an abandoned goat ranch. Here lived some five years ago a goat rancher named Sanders who was killed by the Indians while out herding one day. Many people however think he was murdered by a worthless white man named Mills who was tried for the crime but could not be convicted for lack of evidence. It is a pretty place and adjoining it is another beautiful spot.[78] The Sanders ranch could be homesteaded and as the Indians have been removed to a reservation far away there would be no danger anymore. The place just above is known as the Kelsey place and can be bought for $10 an acre or $1600 for the 160 acres. Any man who controlled both these places would have a beautiful summer home as well as a remunerative farm as most of the land is bottom land tillable and rich. Everywhere are beautiful pines, spruce, juniper, cedar, cottonwood and other trees and the mountains are rugged and gorgeous, the views magnificent and the water never failing and good.

Branching beauty. *M. Holzwarth, photographer.*

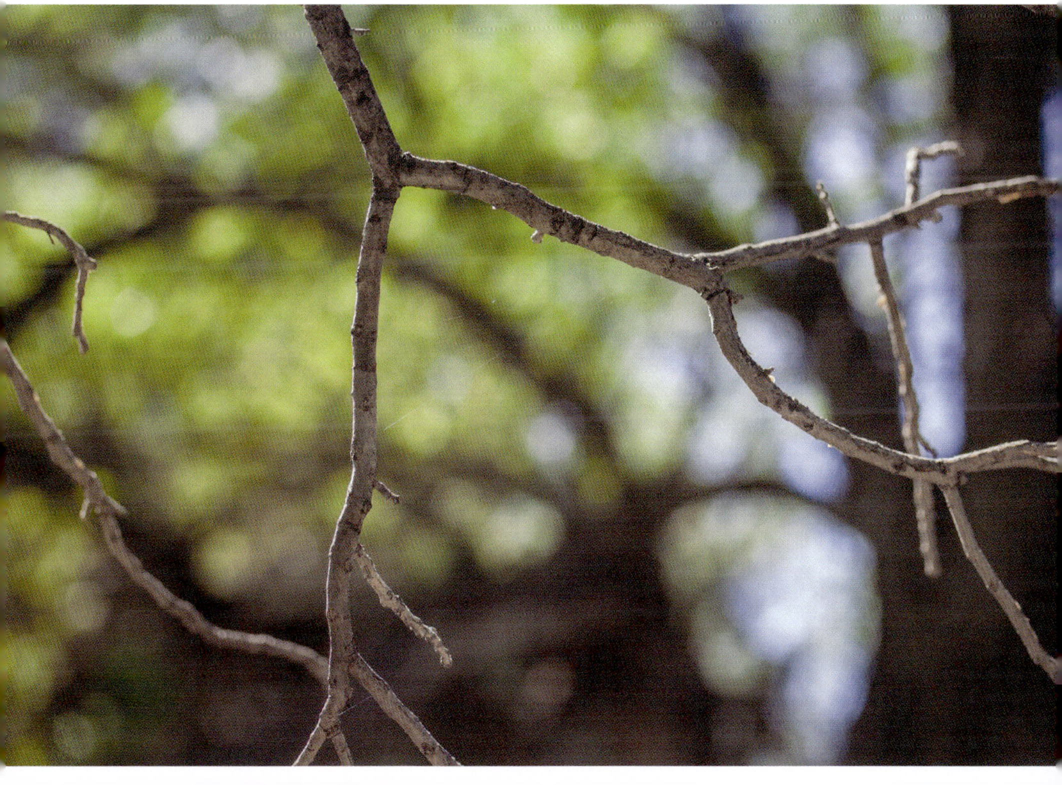

The place is easy of access and can be reached by wagon road from Hillsboro in about two hours.[79] There is plenty of timber and stone to build a nice home and outbuildings and by fencing the places in as you would have a right to do you would be secure from cattle or goats and could in fact have your own game preserve as it is impossible to descend from the tops of the hills into the valley at these points except at one or two places so steep are the canyons. The land around is forest reserve. If I had this place and a law office and newspaper in Hillsboro I would never have to fear for a living and a good one and I would be one of the leading citizens in every respect in this county. And I would rather be a leading citizen here than a nobody in New York, or even a little somebody there.

Thursday morn we broke camp early and still going up the Animas came at last to the place where the creek forks. We turned up what is known as the West Fork and camped in a lovely spot, where the brook murmured nearby while stately pines and balsam firs swayed in the wind. It was noon when we made camp and for the next two days I explored the beauties of this secluded nook. We shot several pine squirrels, which are the kind they make into fur coats and they made a very good stew a la chasseur. We found many bear tracks and one night Lobo barked at something that would not come into the range of the camp light but which by the tracks the next morning was a mountain lion.

Friday we devoted to hunting but got nothing. The deer were scarce and the wild animals were wary. However which way we turned the scenery was magnificent.

Saturday morning we started early and travelled back the road we came for a few miles and camped at the foot of what is known as the Monument, a natural stone column with a large flat stone on its top. This is where the trail to Vic's Park branched off where Vieg had said he had found such good mineral indications. A "park" in this country is flat place up in the mountains where there is plenty of timber and generally water. So there is Magnus (Magner) Park, Bear Springs Park etc. Vic's Park is named after Victorio, the Apache Chief, whose stronghold it was during the Indian troubles twenty five years ago. Here were several skirmishes between the troops and Victorio who held a practically unassailable position as we found out when we climbed up the steep hogbacks where a lone a man could get up without using a flying machine. Here the old chief was killed during a fight and Geronimo who only recently died took his place.[80] No one knew that old Vic was dead until the new chief took hold. Well we climbed and climbed and climbed and finally reached the sheltered plateau but saw nothing of mineral indications. Later we found out that Vieg had forgotten the place and that he had meant Bear Springs Park, several miles northwest. We returned to camp somewhat disappointed.[81]

Sunday morning we marched until half past three in the afternoon when we reached our old camping place at Folgums. On the way we secured five fat squirrels and had a fine meal of them. Monday morning we started for home as a fierce windstorm had blown up, which made it impossible to keep much of a campfire without setting the woods afire. This proved the only day I missed Kid as we had to go 20 miles and the last part of that through uninteresting territory. We got back about sundown and I sought an early bed as I had not walked that far since my student days in the Black Forest.

As a result I am convinced that there is not much to be found in the Black Range in the way of minerals. The rock is too uniformly granite.

Edward Tittmann's grandson John Tittmann of Albuquerque repeated his grandfather's trip in 2009. He took videos of the trip and plans to produce a movie.

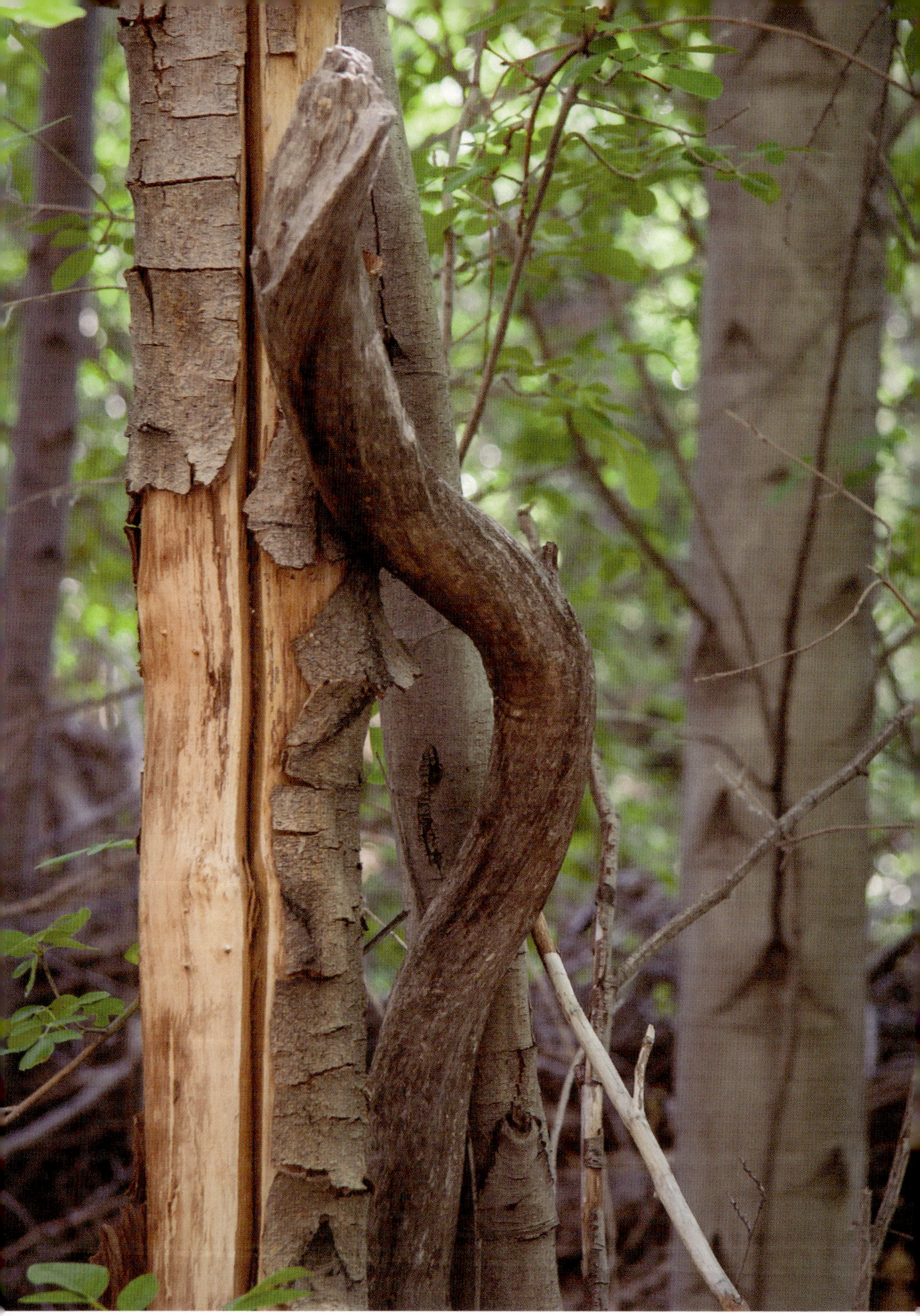

Animated river spirits. *M. Holzwarth, photographer.*

Chapter 12

FORESTRY BEGINS

HARLEY SHAW

As the western territories became populated and ultimately became states, the federal government retained ownership of large expanses of yet undeeded land. Early on, both the government and the public assumed that these lands would eventually be settled and placed under private ownership. Larger ranching, mining and logging conglomerates used them as public domain, capitalizing on their forage, ores and timber without assuming ownership. Poor, individual families homesteaded but couldn't make a living on the small plots of 640 acres or less.

At the same time, a broader American public began to see these western lands as unique and beautiful playgrounds, and resistance to their over-exploitation and privatization began to grow. A need for the government to manage its holdings was evident, and the forest reserves (later national forests) were created, with government-employed rangers present to protect the land from excessive use and establish long-term conservation practices. As noted in the chapter on goat ranching, Bob Reid was one of these early rangers. Another was Aldo Leopold, who used his experience in the Gila National Forest as a basis for writings and philosophies that led to being named the "Father of American Wildlife Management." Another young ranger, Fred Winn, arrived early in the Gila, worked the Black Range and carried out a long and successful career with the Forest Service in the Southwest. All three of these individuals spent time in the Animas, as did a relatively unknown youth named William Pinkney Lawson. We know little about Lawson because he disappeared from the public eye after writing a book about his summer working for the U.S. Forest Service and two unsuccessful western romance novels. His first book, titled *Log of a Timber Cruiser*, doesn't tell us what year he worked on the mountain, but the book was published in 1915.[82] Leopold started his career with the Forest Service carrying out a similar inventory in Arizona in 1909, and I suspect that Lawson was working on the Black Range about that same time. His chapters of the time spent in and about Las Animas (printed in the following chapter) characterize the canyon perhaps better than anything that has been written about it since.

Chapter 13

WORKING THE ANIMAS

THE FIRST TIMBER SURVEY

William Pinkney Lawson

The rainy season proper stopped on August 10, as abruptly as it had begun. Thereafter, we had an occasional storm, it is true, but the monotonous certainty of rain each day was gone.

We had just about completed our work on McKnight and were camped at the time near the head of that canyon, but still on the west side of the range. Just over the divide to the eastward stretched the Animas watershed. We had hesitated to cross while the rain lasted, but there was no reason now for delay in attacking that country, so preparations for the move were at once made.

I for one was glad of it. We had heard of the Animas country so often and with such a wealth of alarming detail, had discussed its possibilities so frequently, and were, in short, so obsessed with a nervous dread of this bugaboo that the suspense was becoming wearing.

We moved on Monday after a Sunday of rest. The atmosphere in camp that morning was similar, I imagine, to the tension of a squad going into battle. The smallest details of the day are printed ineffaceably upon my memory. I was awakened, I recall, by the sound of an axe. Peeping out from under the tarp, through the grey pall of dawn, I saw Bert vigorously splitting wood for the fire, which twinkled and smoked as if just kindled. It was a sight to make one shiver pleasantly and crawl deeper into the blankets. I lay still for a while, enjoying to the full the languorous mood that comes over one at such times.

But something was wrong. I became for some reason uncomfortable. A shadow in the background of my thoughts took shape and form. The Animas! There came that sinking at the pit of the stomach that one feels before a race, a football game, or a fight.

"Ye-ah-ah!"

Bert's "get up" scream cut the silence like a siren. No time now for nervous imaginations or forebodings! Breakfast was on the way.

Answering screeches lusty, feeble, sleepy, hoarse, or muffled, came from the tents around. One by one emerged half clad, tousled, yawning forms, making single-mindedly for the wash basins by the creek.

It was growing lighter now. We could see the sun on the high peaks, though the canyons were still in shade. The cook fire leapt and blazed. We stood in a half circle about it, soaking up the grateful warmth.

Suddenly Bert's voice shrilled once more:

"Breffo! Take her aw-a-ay!"

The summons called us to a steaming meal of bacon, beans, potatoes, coffee, hot biscuits and "lick." Our spirits, under this stimulus, rose rapidly to normal. Afterward everybody helped pack, and we were under way by nine o'clock.

It was nearly a mile from camp to the main divide, a gradual slope ending in an abrupt ascent by a zigzag trail. The nervy little burros, urged on by the yells of the entire outfit, made the climb cleverly.

The saddle crossed was narrow and steep. As we neared the top we saw the burros ahead worm slowly upward, stand out for an instant one by one against the skyline, then quickly disappear. And one by one the rest of us, following in single file, reached the summit and stopped.

I shall never forget that first sight of the Animas! We were on a bare and rocky ridge. No timber grew near to impede the vision. For weeks we had been picturing to ourselves this scene, but now, as we looked down over the maze of pinnacles, bluffs, rim-rock and boxes, the welter of formidable ridges and sharply cut canyons, we knew that nothing of our imagining approached this terrific fact in point of wildness or magnificence.

The whole great watershed lay open to our eyes. Timber grew thick and tall in the canyons, more sparsely on the ridges, but the entire rocky skeleton beneath was plainly visible in outline. We saw as on a map the network of waterways veins of the drainage system that carried the mountain rainfall and snowfall to the far plains of the Rio Grande.

For miles on either side, north and south, ridge upon rolling ridge shot out from the main range, constantly decreasing in height as they extended eastward. Between them were the canyons, which, beginning at the top in shallow draws, steep and boulder strewn, etched in by the overflow of snow and rain, merged ere long to make larger creeks. These in turn, further down, came together in ragged, rocky boxes, where sheer cliffs rose dizzily, and flowing on through canyons ever wider and deeper, formed the main rivers, for each of which its respective watershed was named.

The Animas proper was the chief of these final streams. The river bed itself was not visible from where we stood, but we could see the high walls of the canyon through which the stream flowed, and beyond the first confusion of mountains where the smaller tributaries came together, the two timber-covered ridges that outlined its course. Growing gradually lower and lower, these ridges flattened at length into open grassland, where the canyon seemed a mere dark gash in the soft green of the mesa. For many minutes we stood silent, rapt in the grandeur of the scene. No wonder the Spaniards picturesquely called the place Las Animas the Canyon of the Spirits. Its weird majesty seemed to fit the name; it looked a true abode for wandering souls or for disembodied beings.

Bert's matter of fact utterance at last broke the spell.

"Holy Mackinaw Moses," he ejaculated, in a tone of vast respect, "they's all the original fifty-seven varieties of country there, ain't they?"

"It shore looks like a piece of God's carelessness!" assented Bob Moak. No one could add to that comment.

Our intention was to camp on the main stream, some four miles from the top. There was but one trail down, and that none of the best. It had an alarming habit of vanishing at every particularly awkward place, as if its former users had been possessed of wings wherewith to fly over the more difficult stretches. At times we encountered obstacles that taxed even the ability of men on foot to surmount, but the packers by marvels of ingenuity and resource somehow got the burros through. About noon we found ourselves on the last ridge before the final drop to the bottom. This ridge separated the two main forks of the Animas. Where they came together it ended in a high, narrow, precipitous point, and here again the trail stopped abruptly. The descent seemed impossible but we had to get down somehow or go back to where we had started. So the packers, reconnoitering the edges, chose what seemed the least of many evils and drove the burros over.

Then our troubles began. The shrewd pack animals at once adopted a zigzag course of descent but even then, so steep was the slope, they could scarcely keep their feet. Luckily the surface rock was covered with a fairly deep humus which afforded a foothold. This was all, I verily believe, which kept the entire outfit from immediately sliding pell-mell down five hundred feet of mountain side to the bottom.

As it was we were not without excitement of a sort. Old Bed started things going. She carried the "office boxes," large wooden kyacks containing instruments, maps, drawing materials, and similar paraphernalia. They were bulky and clumsy enough on a level. And now Bed had not taken ten tentative, mincing, downward steps before one of the ill-fated affairs caught against the side of the hill and threw the burro off her balance. Over she went, sideways, and began to roll.

"Good-bye Bed, good-bye boxes!" sang out Frazer, dolefully. It seemed as if they were doomed. But as luck would have it, the falling animal, before she had gathered any great momentum, collided with a small tree, stopped abruptly in her spectacular flight, regained her feet and scrambled up again to where the others were. Nor did she again allow her protruding pack to interfere with an orderly, if slow, descent.

Methusalum was the next victim of the force of gravity. About half way down her breeching strap broke and the pack slipped over her head. She backed out of the harness with a skilful wriggle and standing unemotionally by watched the escaped burden go crashing down the hill. Later, as we neared the bottom and were beginning to breathe more freely, Whitey, who carried the dufflebags belonging to Conway and myself, slipped and went down hill end over end for a distance of some sixty yards, bringing up with a sheer drop of at least thirty feet. He landed on his back with a tremendous thump, the pack between himself and the creek bed, and lay there wedged between two rocks, waving his feet in the air and unable to turn over until we arrived at the bottom.

"There goes our snake bite cure," groaned Conway, as we witnessed Whitey's catastrophe. For each of us kept a flask in his bag against emergencies and it certainly seemed as if nothing breakable could have withstood the disintegrating force of that whirlwind descent. Strange to say, however, everything was found in good shape, including the whiskey and Whitey himself, who trotted off when released with no apparent injuries.

This ended our chapter of accidents and the worst leg of the move. The rest was comparatively easy. The canyon soon widened and we struck a very fair trail that led us about five o'clock to a first rate camping ground.

All of us except the baseline crew, Wallace, Conway and Wetherby, stayed in camp a few days on map work, while the baseline was brought over the top from Mcknight Canyon and extended down the canyon of the Animas to where we lay. Our few days' respite from physical effort was welcome. It gave us, in addition to the rest, an opportunity to examine our surroundings at leisure and to become accustomed to the sight of the awesome environment in which we found ourselves "growing a-climb-ated," as Conway called it, with a tragic effort at punning. We had time for exploring and sight-seeing in addition. For the country of the Animas was rich in localities connected by tradition with stirring events of Indian and outlaw fighting. We visited among other places "Vic's park," a pleasant, open glade on the very top of a high mountain. Here, in frontier days, the famous Apache War Chief Victorio was followed, it is said, by a regiment of U.S. regulars, whom he ambushed and practically annihilated.

One of the few survivors was a Negro horse wrangler. The story goes that this man afterward told a wonderful tale of how, while hunting horses on the morning of the massacre, he ran across a marvelously rich mass of gold bearing "float rock." He exhibited a piece of this as evidence of the truth of his story and announced an intention of returning before long to find the main vein. But he disappeared shortly after without leaving any more information than that. This is the local legend, and many have been the hopeful prospectors to toil away an arduous season in fruitless search for the fabulously rich "nigger diggins," as they were called. We contributed our mite of labor to this myth, but found no gold. Brown, however, did discover in Vic's park an old nearly decomposed army pack saddle, and nearby the bones of the animal which had, we supposed, carried it.

The park was also an excellent lookout point. The surrounding country could be seen in all its wild magnificence. And, as we gazed, something of its wildness seemed to disappear. The grandeur, the compelling solemnity of its spacious outlines, entered our souls. There was a strangely familiar effect apparent in the shapes of the vast, eroded rocks, in the slender pinnacles, the pillar like cliff formation, the whole grave spirit of the place. Frazer of all of us first hit it when he called the conception of the canyon "gothic." That was it, indubitably we were amid a multitude of temples. The true spirit of the gothic, apparent everywhere, sobered us like the distant chords of a great organ. One view in particular suggested, through the magic of the surroundings and the softening atmosphere, the famous cathedral of Milan. The rock walls rose mistily blue against the sky, delicate as the work of fairies. Buttresses gleamed in the sun, great arches shone as they shouldered the mass of intricate ornamentation, of pinnacles and points that topped the whole. Then as we looked the sun hid behind a cloud, the glistening, lacelike details were blotted out in a wave of darkness and the formless face of mystery, somberly impassive, stared us into insignificance and awe.

We were glad, strange as it may seem, when the day came for cruising. Several things accounted for this. In the first place we had rested thoroughly and were feeling the need of hard work once more. Then, too, conditions in camp were most uncomfortable. We had descended to an altitude of less than six thousand feet and for the first time during the summer began to suffer from the heat. All day the sun burned down wickedly. No rain came to cool the air. Even at night, which seemed strangely unjust to us, it was warm and sultry and we slept poorly.

To make matters worse all the flies and yellowjackets in the world seemed to have appointed our camp a rendezvous. Our sun baked sleeping tents looked now like hives, now like well filled fly traps. The cook tent was black and swarming with the little pests. They covered the food like a pall, they committed unpleasant suicide in the coffee or the soup, it was worth a sting or so to pass the sugar or jam, and eating soon became for us the most irksome task of the whole twenty-four hours. Our nerves and our dispositions suffered from these things. We were therefore distinctly relieved when the baseline came at last into camp and work was assigned for the following day.

The runs here were planned to extend north and south, up the high, steep ridges that shut in the stream and over into the cut up, rough country beyond where mountains and rocky spurs tossed like waves in a choppy sea.

When I reached my first station next morning and glanced upward at the prospect before me it seemed impossible that one could ever win to the top of the ridge. There was no hope in offsetting. On either side it was surely as bad, perhaps worse. One must simply make a beginning and trust to luck. So I started on the arduous ascent, working slowly up crevices in the bluffs, carefully crossing the broken surface of huge rock slides liable at a false move to go rumbling to the bottom bearing the unwary intruder haplessly upon the stony crest, and up steep, bare slopes so sharp that only by the timely aid of shrubs and stunted trees could one rise at all. It was hours before I even approached the top. Below, a thousand feet and more, ran the river I had left. Above remained some fifty feet of rimrock, almost perpendicular, but not difficult to negotiate provided one kept a cool head. Yet just here, with the long climb almost over, a thoughtless moment brought me as close, I think, to sudden death as I have ever knowingly been.

I was two-thirds up the rampart of rock, resting on a little ledge some eight inches wide and clasping with both arms a pillar of stone whose pointed top stretched two feet above my head. It seemed firm enough for my purpose, which was to pull myself up on this until I had gained a crevice, just above, that promised to make the rest easy. As a rule we always tested the stability of a support before trusting our entire weight to it, for in a great many instances the fault, a peculiarity of formation, splits a slab from the main body so that a touch or a pull will dislodge it. But this time, careless with the thought of imminent success, I quite

Winter still life. *M. Holzwarth, photographer.*

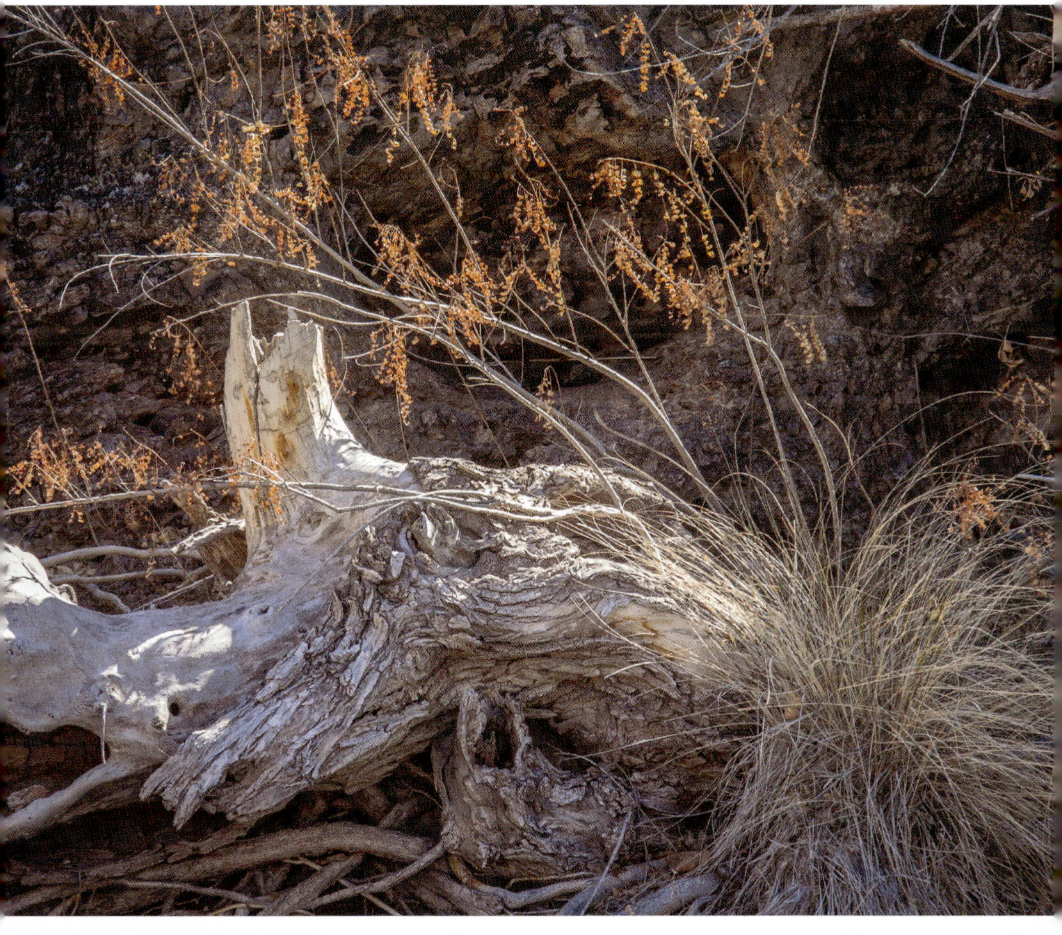

neglected such precautionary measures. I reached above, grasped the top of the oblong rock and with a sharp heave raised myself with my arms. As I did so the supposedly solid mass gave with my weight. For an empty moment I felt myself falling backward. There was no time to calculate. By a lucky instinct I glanced to the right, spied what seemed to be a narrow foothold a few feet away and leapt for it.

It held! And as I clung there, suspended above the abyss, I heard the great block I had dislodged a moment before go crashing down the dizzy slope followed by continually fainter and more prolonged reverberations. I felt my knees begin to weaken and realized, as clearly as if I were another person, that I was very much frightened. I dared not look below. Nor could I see much chance to ascend; but it was suicide to remain where I was. It seemed an age really it couldn't have been more than a few seconds before I moved. Every nerve was tightly strung, every faculty at highest tension, focused with straining single mindedness upon the one desire to scale the ten or twelve feet of stone that loomed between me and safety.

I don't know yet just how I reached the top of the ledge. So intent was I upon the task that I was unconscious of anything else. Slowly from cranny to cranny, from crevice to crumbly edge, I progressed till at length I felt the top with extended hands. One careful pull, one cautious last exertion and I fell forward with a gasp of relief and gave way to those wretched sensations that I had managed to ignore until safe.

It was a long time before I resumed my run. And it was days before I recovered from the effects of this adventure. As a matter of fact I don't believe I ever did quite overcome a tendency to nervousness that often caught me later at unexpected moments. Sometimes when clambering over cliffs that earlier in the season would have been mere child's play I would feel that sudden faintness, that suspicion of nausea, which preceded a fit of "the trembles," and would have to stop in my tracks, a prey to the most miserable sensations, until it was over. I used to force myself to climb the same place over and over in an effort to conquer this weakness, but it was not of much use. Even to-day when I stand in a high place and look down a wave of dizziness comes over me.

The rest of my run was as hard as any I had hitherto encountered. Up and down hill all day, one ridge after another, brush, dead and down stuff, locust and manzanita. I got back to camp at seven and found that I had not been alone in my discomfort. Each cruiser had tales to unfold of brush and heat and giant hills and impossible situations finally overcome.

Yet through the chorus there was a note of cheerfulness, of buoyancy even. We had at last come to grips with the bugbear of our season's task and won the first bout. Henceforth there might be hard work in plenty, but never again would we feel fear of our enemy, that haunting, superstitious dread that the Animas had inspired. Our imaginations were on our side now!

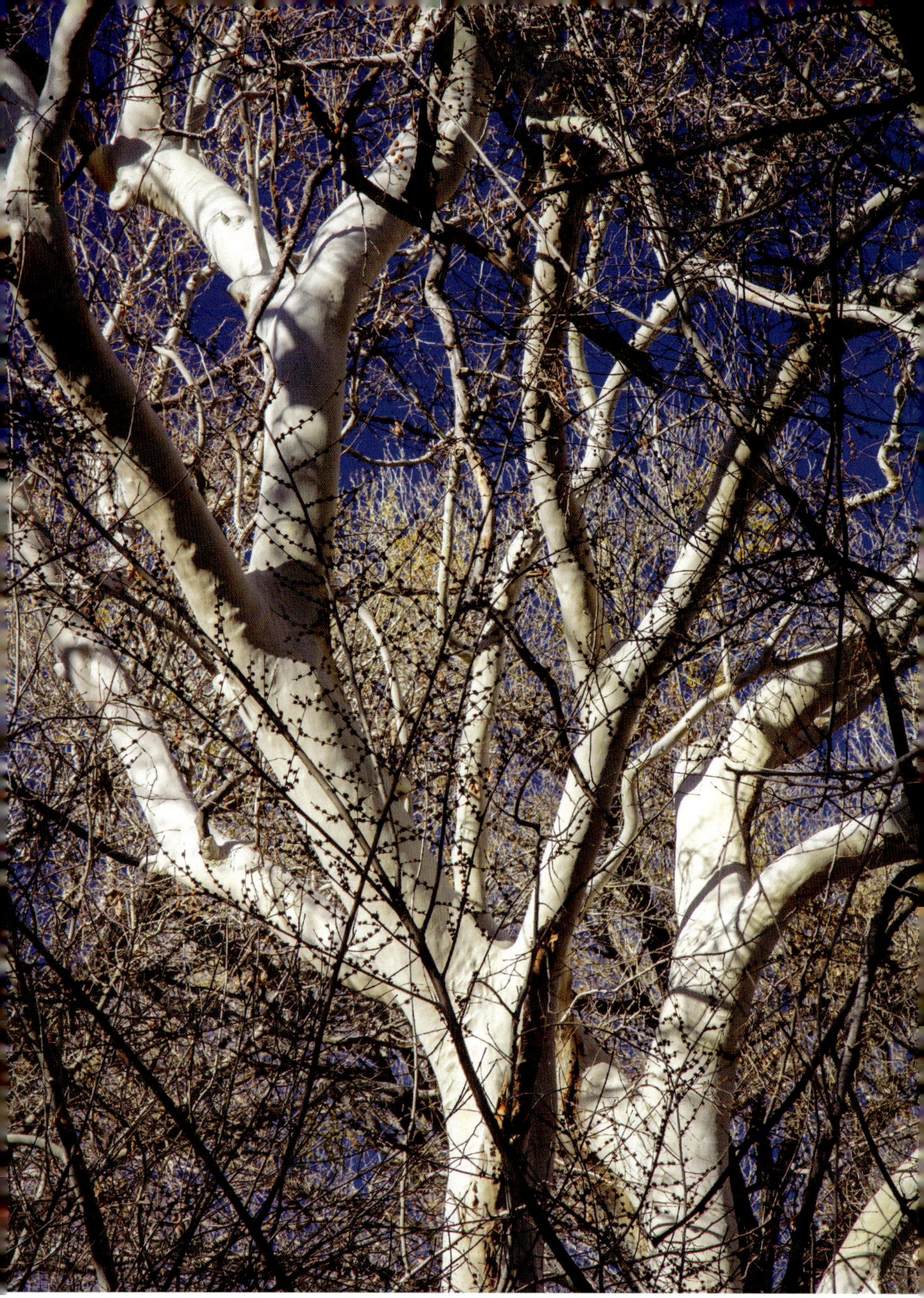

Sycamore grandeur. *M. Holzwarth, photographer.*

Chapter 14

FIGHTING FIRE WITH ALDO LEOPOLD

Compiled from 1922 field notes by Fred Winn and Aldo Leopold

Fred Winn was one of the earliest forest rangers in southwestern New Mexico. Brown notes:

> *Born in Wisconsin in 1880 into a well-to-do family, Fred's father was the personal physician to an important Chinese statesman and young Fred spent much of his youth in the Orient, living in or visiting China, Japan, the Philippines, India and Korea as well as South Africa. His education was Ivy League; he attended Princeton and was graduated with a B.S. degree from Rutgers in 1899. Upon graduation Winn went on to study art in New York, but finding the East without sufficient adventure, he headed west to New Mexico. Here he attempted to make his living as a prospector, cowboy artist, and a mailman on horseback. In May 1904 he took a summer job as Forest Guard watching for fires.*[83]

Winn viewed this first summer's work as a temporary position and had no particular plans to settle in the Southwest. However, in 1907, he took an assistant ranger position in the San Mateo National Forest, and his lifetime career began. By May 1922, Winn was the supervisor of the Gila National Forest and stationed in Silver City. On May 22, 1922, he was awaiting Aldo Leopold, planning to accompany him on an inspection of the Black Range portion of the Gila National Forest. From the following notes in his daily itinerary for this period, we can see that he had not lost his field skills as a result of becoming an administrator.[84] By the time Leopold arrived, a fire had broken out in Curtis Canyon, a tributary of Las Animas; both Winn and Leopold set aside their administrative assignments and entered fully into firefighting. Then as now, forest fires trumped any other activity in the national forests at that time.

On May 20, before Leopold's arrival, Winn was already at the site of the fire, noting that the area to the east was of low value and low hazard. In this, he referred to the south side of Las Animas Creek, approximately between Kelsey Cabin and the forest boundary. His greatest fear was that the fire would get into Holden Prong, where five hundred men would not hold it.

Up and out at 4:00 a.m. on May 21, Winn, District Ranger John Ray Painter and Robert Reid assessed the situation. The fire had been "corralled" by a hand-shoveled fireline, but it wasn't considered secure. Firefighters were exhausted, at least one was sick and supplies were running low. Winn left the camp at 8:30 a.m. and was in Kingston by 11:00 a.m., making the trip in two and a half hours. This speaks to the quality of their horses. He must have trotted and galloped all the way to make the trip, much of it in rough terrain, in this short time. By 1922, the Forest Service had phone connections to all the towers, and Winn immediately contacted Hillsboro Peak and McKnight Peak for reports of any fires in their areas. He also received notification that Leopold was en route.

Here we get a glimpse of the workings of the Forest Service, as well as the communities in 1922. Winn called the garage (undoubtedly the Slease Garage) and the Hillsboro store for a load of supplies, asking that it be delivered to the Reid Ranch the next morning. Most likely this was the ranch in North Percha. He also asked the clerk to find five more firefighters and send them out. Leopold arrived at 2:30 p.m. By 5:00 p.m., Winn had received reports of fires from Mogollon Baldy and from the Datil district. Thirty men remained on the East Curtis fire.

On May 22, Winn and Leopold headed back out to the East Curtis fire. The trip to Reid's ranch took two and a half hours, indicating that they were riding much slower than Winn had on the previous day. The time frame suggests that they had to be at the Reid Ranch in North Percha. At 11:00 a.m., the supplies and extra men arrived from Hillsboro, and by 11:15 a.m., they were en route to East Curtis, the new firefighters on foot. They spent two and a half hours in reaching the fire camp. Winn doesn't say if the men on foot also made the trip in this time, although it seems unlikely. Bob Reid was leading the fireline patrol; Leopold and Painter rode out to inspect the fire perimeter. Winn caught up time records and inspected supply needs in camp. Everyone turned in at 9:00 p.m.

On May 23, Winn, Leopold and Painter headed back to Kingston. Bob Reid took charge of the camp. They left the camp at 9:00 a.m. and were in Kingston by 1:45 p.m., taking four and three-quarter hours. Winn reported the East Curtis fire under control, with about 1,500 acres burned. The cost for fighting it was "about $1000." The East Curtis fire apparently was man-caused, and Winn shifted into an investigative role, planning to prosecute under state rather than federal law. Painter assumed the responsibility for investigation, with Winn noting that the justice of the peace, as well as "Aso Johnsen," would be interviewed. Aso Johnsen was apparently Asa Albert Johnson, a stock raiser. He was born in 1879. He and his wife, Bettie, ran a goat ranch in Animas Creek. He was apparently considered a witness regarding the cause of the Curtis Canyon fire.

Winn and Leopold left Kingston at 8:30 a.m. on May 24, headed for the McKnight fire cabin. They took a packhorse loaded with food for a fire crew at Hillsboro Peak. Winn notes that they took the "new trail," which probably went up Percha Creek and crossed to Ladrone Canyon near its head, ultimately hitting the crest trail south of Hillsboro Peak. At this point, they switched back into their administrative roles, inspecting the forest and assessing personnel, tools and general readiness of the district for emergencies. They were also looking at range condition and assessing timber. They spent the night at the Hillsboro Peak "dugout."

They rode on to McKnight Cabin on the twenty-fifth, staying on the "new" crest trail, which was still under construction. The ride from Hillsboro Peak to McKnight Cabin took them just under five hours. After lunch, they continued the inspection of the camp, tools and trail building. They retired at 9:00 p.m.

The next day, they worked with the trail crew, with Leopold demonstrating new guidelines for construction, which included water bars, "tread heel" and slope constraints. They spent the night at McKnight, contacting Kingston by phone and discussing the fire investigation. One of the Latham family was singled out for letting the fire go, and Painter was seeking action against him with the county attorney. The Lathams owned a ranch near Lake Valley. The diary entries dealing with Las Animas end here, although Ranger Painter notes on the twenty-eighth that he has taken out a warrant on Latham. Winn and Leopold continued on their inspection trip horseback and leading pack mules.

On June 4, Winn and Leopold rode to the West Fork of the Gila, where they managed to slip in three hours of fishing and chase a wayward mule. They then rode on to the TJ and XSX Ranches. On June 5, they left the XSX Ranch headed for Diamond Creek, stopping at the hunting lodge to bathe and wash clothes. They then rode ten miles up the East Fork to the Montoya Ranch and beyond it three miles before making camp. On June 6, they rode up Diamond Creek to the old Link Ranch and then along the North Star Road to the Tom Moore Place and on to the Diamond Bar Ranch. Through all this, Winn was taking advantage of phones to coordinate men all over the forest. On June 7, they rode back up Black Canyon en route to Diamond Creek, visiting the Reed Ranch. The owner of this ranch was not related to the Reids who ran goats near Kingston. Reed's Peak is named for him. On June 8, they inspected the Diamond Peak lookout and then headed for the Black Canyon Ranger Station to meet Rangers Painter and Putsch for a "conference." On the ninth, the four of them left the Black Canyon Ranger Station and rode to Reed's Peak, considering it for a place to build a lookout tower. They then rode thirty miles down the Mimbres to the Mimbres Ranger Station, stopping at the Cooney place en route.

They spent the tenth and eleventh at the Mimbres Ranger Station, interviewing several forest service personnel. Leopold apparently stayed at the Mimbres station on the twelfth, while Winn met local ranchers to view their range in the vicinity of Sheppard and East Canyon, swinging by the Mimbres store to buy grain before returning to the ranger station. On June 13, Winn and Leopold left the Mimbres Ranger Station. They rode to the GOS Ranch and then down to Sapello and old Gila Flat Road, where they separated. Leopold headed on to the XSX Ranch and ultimately to Mogollon; Winn headed for Silver City via Black Peak lookout. Winn stayed at the Goforth Ranch that night. On the fourteenth, he visited Black Peak and Redstone and then led the pack string on to Pinos Altos. At that point, he picked up his car and drove to Silver City, where he immediately took up coordination of firefighting all over the forest. His communications with Leopold continued through the seventeenth by phone. Leopold was apparently at Mogollon during this time.

Thus, Leopold and Winn carried out an incredible itinerary covering the Black Range District on an inspection tour, all the while helping with firefighting and coordinating fire crews elsewhere. The distances they were covering in rough terrain seem striking today to those of us who rarely have opportunities to ride the back trails—most of which are now too overgrown to ride anyway. In 1922, horse travel was still the main way to get around the forest, and the rangers were seasoned riders. Also, a high amount of cooperation existed between the Forest Service and ranchers, with rangers being welcome for stopovers on their routine tours. Fire was the enemy, and as noted regarding the Lathams, ignoring a fire was considered a criminal act.

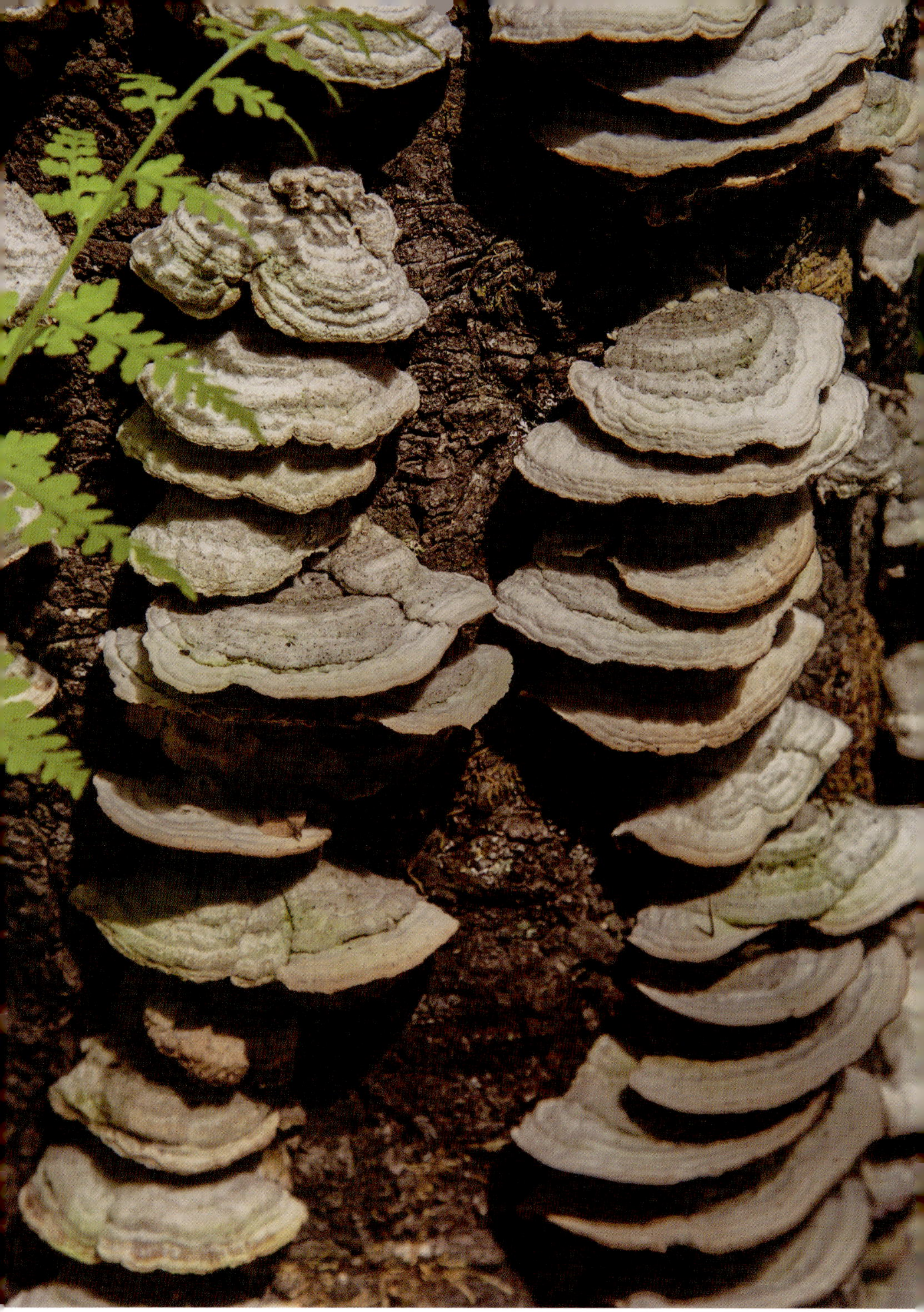

Abundant fungus. *M. Holzwarth, photographer.*

Chapter 15

SCIENCE AND CONSERVATION

HARLEY SHAW

On the whole, scientists were late coming to Las Animas Creek. Perhaps one of the earliest to penetrate the Black Range was J.W. Fewkes of the Smithsonian, who was surveying ruins in the San Mateos as well as the Black Range in the early 1900s. We've found no record of him reaching Las Animas, and he apparently spent most of his time in the upper Mimbres drainage. E.A. Goldman of the Biological Survey visited Kingston and Sawyer Peak in 1909 but did not venture into the Animas.

Amazingly, among the very earliest scientists to reach Las Animas after the decline of the Apaches were two unlikely and adventurous souls who were neither the usual general taxonomists seeking new mammals, birds or plants nor archaeologists digging ruins. In 1915, Henry A. Pilsbry and James H. Ferriss spent weeks packing through the Black Range, including Holden Prong, in search of mollusks and snails new to science. While most of their writings were rather drab and technical, Ferriss, who worked as an assistant to Pilsbry, took it upon himself to write of his Black Range adventures in a lighter frame of mind. In "A Shell Hunt in the Black Range," he describes a summer spent on the mountain with Pilsbry and "two ladies," presumably their wives, and later traveling by himself and his hired packer.[85] This party of collectors had planned to collect in the Mogollon Mountains, but during a brief visit in Deming with their friend Dr. Samuel D. Swope, they were persuaded by Swope to switch their attention to the Black Range. Samuel Swope would be worthy of additional study. He practiced medicine in Deming from about 1900 to the mid-1920s. He served as a physician with the Mexican Punitive Expedition under Pershing and also once treated victims of a shootout involving Butch Cassidy and the Wild Bunch. He was apparently well acquainted with the Black Range.

If the presence of Apaches kept early scientists away, the isolation and ruggedness of terrain have discouraged more recent naturalists. No study of the general natural history of Las Animas exists, and little early baseline data on the canyon are available. After the Ladder Ranch was purchased by Turner Enterprises, a variety of wildlife-related projects began. Some of these, though not focused on Las Animas, encompass it. Over time, elements of the creek have been recognized as unique. We try in the following chapters to discuss the research and science-based conservation programs occurring in Las Animas, the species that make it unique and the questions and issues surrounding the canyon.

Chapter 16

A SHELL HUNT IN THE BLACK RANGE, 1915

James H. Ferriss

Bypassing Cooke's Peak by way of the Mimbres River, the foursome traveled by wagon from Deming to Swartz, a settlement near present Faywood Hot Springs. At Swartz, they transferred their equipment to a pack string owned by Teodoro Solis, a Chihuahuan whom Ferriss described as "the best packer and camper alive." Their route led them to Mitchell Gray's mining camp on Silver Creek, on the west slope of Sawyer Peak, thence along the crest of the Black Range to Reed Ranch, where Pilsbry and the two ladies departed. Ferriss, still guided by Solis, describes the country and their adventures:

> *The work was continued for another month by way of Black Canyon, Diamond Creek (where we were detained briefly by enormous speckled trout), then over the range eastward, making our first camp at the ranch of Teodoro's brother near Chloride.*
>
> *This was the forest primeval. The trail ran about nine to ten thousand feet in elevation and the yellow pine, Douglas fir, spruces and quaking asps were large and thick. It was our highest and wildest range to date. The cattle, wild and keen of scent, are trapped for slaughter in corrals with swinging gates, something like monster turkey-traps. Black and silver-tipped bears and mountain lions were plentiful. A couple of untamed, off-the-reservation Apaches also were hiding in what seemed to be our best snail coves. We saw one a few seconds but did not catch him. Deer and turkey were fairly abundant, and the whole country is*

marked by interesting historical events. Near here Dr. Fewkes had dug some of his most valued specimens of prehistoric pottery. At one point a train of pack burros had rolled down into the Las Animas country. During our short stay two saddle horses also rolled down into that cavern of lost souls. In one of the gulches the bones of an unknown soldier had lain so long his clothing and a roll of money were destroyed by the weather. On the Kingston trail a bear dropped out of a tree upon a packer and killed him. Here Apache Kid had robbed and burned a miner's cabin, and at another point, lying in wait behind a rock, he shot a miner in the back; and when we dropped down into Chloride we met the men who followed this same Apache Kid into the San Mateo range and killed him—saw the mule that packed their dunnage, and located the men in Chicago who sent Kid's head to the Yale skull and bone fraternity. Also saw the carcass of a bull that killed a ranch-owner's saddle horse, and was killed and pried off the angry and pompous owner by an efficient cowboy.

I soon found myself in the whirl of Black Range society. Off upon an independent excursion of my own a mad cow obstructed the right of way. The law was upon my side but I knew the peculiarities of Spanish half-breed cattle well enough to get behind a tree, and did my best. Going around the tree rapidly, I kept behind it all but once and then in a fleeting second was fairly introduced. Grasping her heartily by the horns, I shook them; but the impulsive creature was really overwhelming in her attention, and upon her knees walked all over me. This spot is now marked, and it is quite a large one. Luckily the same cowboy with his 45 that killed the bull, came up the trail and with a bang released me from further embarrassment. Pride only received a jolt. My horsehide coat was cow-proof.

Again when alone, and my thoughts were far away, just at dusk, a robust mountaineer from the Great Smokies came into camp to show me the mummied right hand of the last man who climbed the trail to take him back to Tennessee. As a stranger, and a little timid, it was my part to show that I had no particular interest in the specimen; but those mountaineers possess keen insight into the minds of the tender-feet and I presume the camp site is marked also. However, the dwellers of the high and lonesome will never find the spot where I lay out the rest of the night watching to see if that uncanny naturalist was coming back with any more fragments of his specimen.

…I returned to Deming via Hermosa, Las Animas Canyon, Hillsboro, and Kingston.

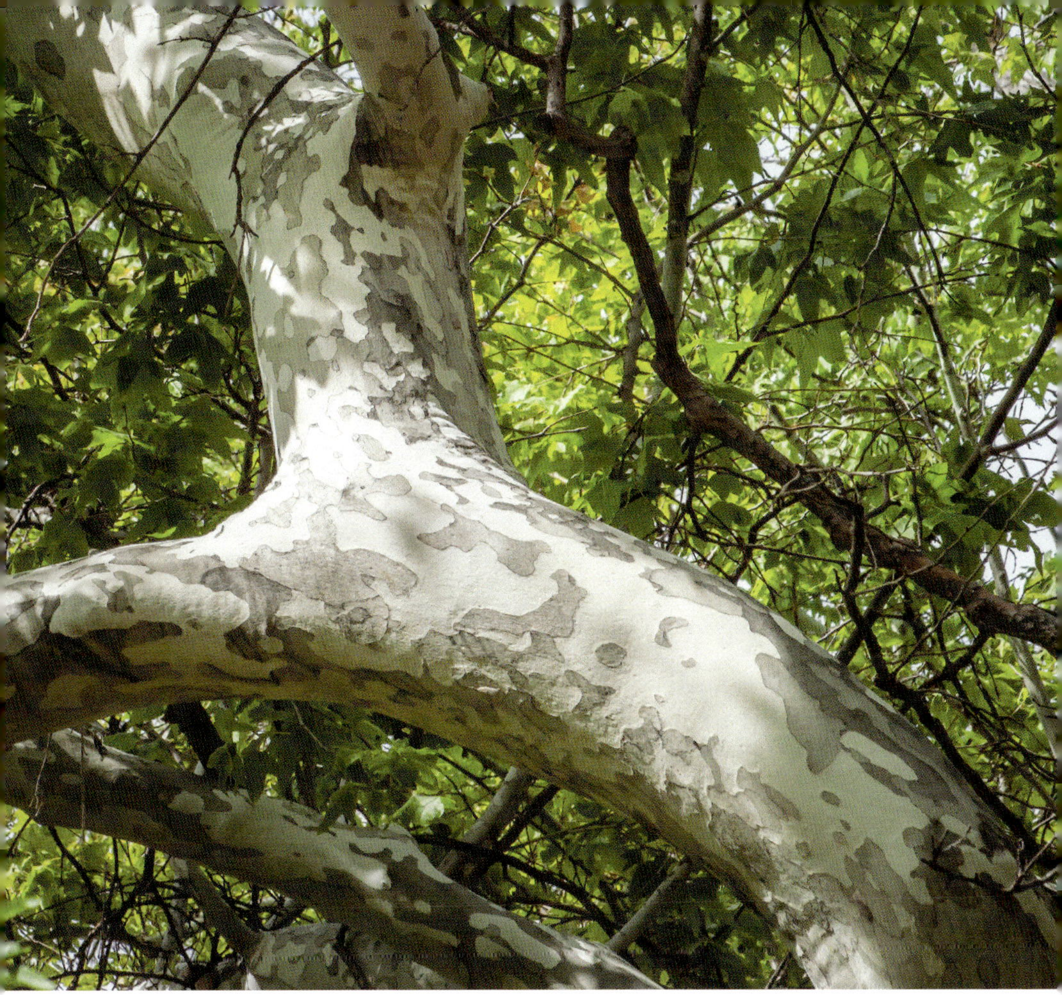

Patterns. *M. Holzwarth, photographer.*

Ferriss ended his article with descriptions and binomials of the shells he found on the expedition, but I have included here only those portions of his manuscript that provide a picture of the country and people in and around Las Animas in 1915.

Chapter 17

THE MYSTERIOUS SYCAMORE

Harley Shaw

The Arizona sycamore population along Las Animas Creek is one of its most striking features. These sycamores, growing along a twenty-five-mile reach, constitute the only known natural stand of this species within the Rio Grande watershed and functionally the only stand east of the continental divide. It lies at least thirty-five miles east of the nearest native stand along the Gila River. The Arizona sycamore was first described in botanical literature on the Santa Cruz River, Arizona, by botanist Charles Wright in 1851.[86] It occurs throughout riparian drainages between one thousand and six thousand feet from Southern California, through Arizona eastward to southwestern New Mexico and southward into Sonora and Chihuahua.[87]

Animas Creek lies within the northern Chihuahuan Desert ecoregion. Greatest precipitation normally falls in late summer. A lesser peak of precipitation falls during mid- to late winter. Las Animas is in a rain shadow on the eastern face of the Black Range and usually receives less rainfall than canyons on the west side of the mountain. This eastern slope is steep and brushy, descending from over 10,000 feet at Hillsboro Peak to about 3,500 feet at the Rio Grande in some sixty-five stream miles. Of this descent to 6,000 feet, 4,000 feet occur within the first sixteen stream miles from the summit. Sycamore grows below 5,800 feet, reaching its upper limit about one and a half miles downstream from the forest boundary, just below the Chacon Corral, and continuing nearly to the Rio Grande.

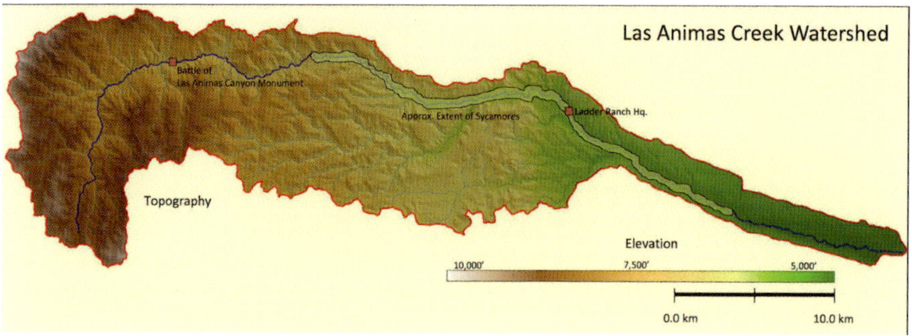

Sycamore distribution in Animas Creek Watershed.

We do not know when or how the Animas Creek sycamores were established. The genus *Platanus* is now less common in North America than it was during the Arcto-Tertiary period (sixty-three million years ago) and is restricted to wetlands of warm temperate to tropical climates. Sycamore fossils from the Arcto-Tertiary have been found as far north as Greenland.[88] The closest extant relative of Arizona sycamore is western sycamore in California, where some genetic gradations between the two species can be found. Holstein conjectured that the two varieties separated as the southwestern deserts expanded and left deciduous woodlands isolated along streams. If so, this would suggest that Arizona sycamore emerged as a separate taxon somewhere near the border between Arizona and California. Yun Feng and Manos, using DNA analyses, concluded that Arizona sycamore was a variety of western sycamore rather than a separate species.[89] These two western varieties are more closely related to *Platanus orientalis*, which is found in southeastern Europe and the Himalayas, than they are to sycamores in the eastern United States and northeastern Mexico.

We do not know if the oldest sycamores along Animas represent the first generation present or if earlier stands preceded it. Using a weighted average of all of Stromberg's regressions of age on diameter at breast height (dbh) for sycamores in Arizona (for trees growing from seed: age=2.7Xdbh-10.9; for trees sprouting from roots: age=dbhX2.7+0.1), the largest single-trunked trees measured near the eastern Ladder Ranch boundary are around 310 years old, hence could have been established about AD 1700.[90]

Estimated ages for the four trees we measured on private holdings east of the Ladder Ranch range from 328 to 456 years. Given room for variation, we might speculate that the biggest trees along lower Animas began growing between AD 1560 and 1612. If these oldest trees represent the first generation of sycamores in the canyon (which we don't know for sure), the trees were established well after the Mimbres had disappeared and not too long after the Athapascans came in. In fact, the dates seem close to Spanish arrival.

We measured one tree near the mouth of Cave Canyon that had a dbh of over nine feet and another over eight. Their growth form, however, was that of imbedded multiple trunks within an encased apparent larger trunk. The largest basal diameter exceeds ten feet. This multi-trunk form is characteristic of many large sycamores, and we are not sure exactly how such trees should be measured. We badly need age data for the larger sycamores.

Yun Feng and Manos considered long-distance dispersal to be a viable explanation for isolated populations of sycamores. Although the seeds are normally dispersed by wind, they might lodge in the feet and feathers of birds or fur of mammals and eventually be transported to remote areas. Thus, accidental dispersal by wildlife or humans or intentional transporting by humans could have created the Animas sycamore stand. A genetic comparison of twenty-five samples from the length of the Las Animas stand with a sample of twenty-five sycamore leaves collected near Gila Hot Springs on the Gila River did not disclose a clear separation between these populations. This comparison, however, involved a single gene, and more detailed genetic analysis is needed.[91]

So far, archaeological evidence has not confirmed the early presence of sycamores in Animas Creek at the time the eastern Mimbres culture was present (prior to 1400 or so). Nelson and Schollmeyer failed to find Arizona sycamore in structures or remnants of fuelwood in eastern Mimbres sites, including the Las Animas site on Ladder Ranch.[92] The Animas ruin represented the Black Mountain phase of Mimbres settlement and was populated from approximately 1200 to 1400 BC. None of ten samples of pollen collected at the Las Animas archaeological site contained sycamore remains.[93]

Within written history, Antonio de Espejo, traveling up the Rio Grande in the vicinity of the mouth of Las Animas early in 1583, noted, "Along the river banks there were many cottonwood groves and some patches of white poplars four leagues wide."[94]

The elevation here is much too low for aspen, and only one species of cottonwood is present. Espejo's "white poplars" might have been sycamores. If so, at that time they extended into the Rio Grande channel. This would suggest the presence of sycamores in the area for over four hundred years.

James Ohio Pattie, in 1825 and 1826, did not mention sycamores in Las Animas, the Mimbres or the Gila River drainages.[95] Lieutenant W.H. Emory, on October 15, 1846, crossed Las Animas but did not mention sycamores, but he noticed a "new sycamore" several days later when he arrived on the Gila River.[96] Philip St. George Cooke, on November 25, 1846, noted sycamores in a "Los Animos" Creek, but he was by this time southwest of Las Animas Creek and was undoubtedly referring to a different drainage in the New Mexico boot heel.[97]

E.L. Greene was the first to collect sycamore within the Las Animas drainage. Eugene Jercinovic notes, "Greene collected his [sycamore] specimen (#1111) on 13 July, 1904. The sheet is at the UNM Herbarium in Albuquerque. The only other specimen from the Animas Creek population that I know of was collected by Arthur LeRoy Hershey (#3022) of the New Mexico College of Agriculture and Mechanic Arts (now NMSU) in the summer of 1943. The specimen is at the NMSU Herbarium. The other early collectors who did major work in New Mexico, E.O. Wooton, Paul C. Standley, O.B. Metcalfe, and Edward Castetter, never visited the area."[98] Jercinovic suggests that the Animas stand could be a relic from more widespread paleo-distribution of the species.

We do not know why sycamores do not grow in the other drainages emanating from the east face of the Black Range. Their presence in Las Animas may tell us something of the unique nature of its watershed. Arizona sycamore forests have highest productivity and the greatest compositional diversity where groundwater averages less than two meters below the tree base during the growing season, less than one-half meter below the stream thalweg and fluctuates less than a meter annually. Where groundwater is deeper, trees grow slowly. Seedlings are largest and most abundant where groundwater is less than one-half meter below the flood plain surface, and productivity and diversity are highest in perennial streams or in ephemeral streams with high and stable groundwater tables.[99]

Sycamores reproduce by seed or by vegetative sprouting. Accurately distinguishing genets (trees originating as seedlings) from ramets (originating form root sprouts) requires genetic analysis, although sprouting can result in a clumped tree pattern while reproduction from seeds typically results in dispersed individual trees.[100] Sycamores appear to have more narrow environmental requirements for successful germination than other riparian tree species, and reproduction is sporadic.[101] Arizona sycamores reproduce sexually if their seeds and young seedlings are kept moist until the onset of summer rains, followed by a lengthy period when the seedlings and saplings are protected from flash floods.[102] Intervals of ten to forty years may elapse with no seedling establishment.[103] Summer floods do not help seedling establishment, but frequent winter floods and very wet springs stimulate regeneration, particularly along channels scoured and widened by floodwaters. Asexual regeneration from root sprouts is more common than seed regeneration.

The upper elevational limit of sycamores in Las Animas (5,800 feet) is similar to upper limits of Arizona sycamores in other parts of their range. Cold air drainage in canyons neutralizes the effects of the altitudinal temperature gradient, so groundwater depth, as affected by stream channel geology, is probably the main factor limiting their distribution. In the Animas, the uppermost trees grow within a narrow portion of the canyon where the stream leaves Tertiary extrusive formations and passes into Paleozoic sedimentary deposits and current stream bottom sediments. This is an area where a natural rock barrier undoubtedly forces groundwater upward to or near the surface. The presence of sycamore from this point downward suggests that groundwater remains fairly shallow for the remainder of the length of the creek.

To survive from seedling stage to old age, trees along Las Animas must withstand torrential flooding and the reshaping of the riverbed from the masses of mud, rocks and debris left by the surging waters. It also must withstand periodic droughts, when water is available only from the groundwater in an often cobbly substrate. Wetness is needed for roots to penetrate these rough-textured riparian soils. If the stream has downcut, trees that had germinated on sand or gravel bars in the old stream channel may be left high and dry on the resulting terraces.

Intensive surveys of wildlife within the Las Animas watershed are lacking. Bock and Bock assessed the importance of sycamores to riparian birds in southeastern Arizona, and their results may apply to Las Animas.[104] Canyons with sycamores held higher densities of birds. Twelve summer species were dependent on sycamore: white-winged dove, mourning dove, western wood-pewee, ash-throated flycatcher, Cassins and western kingbird, bridled titmouse, white-breasted nuthatch, American robin, Lucy's warbler, summer tanager, lark sparrow and

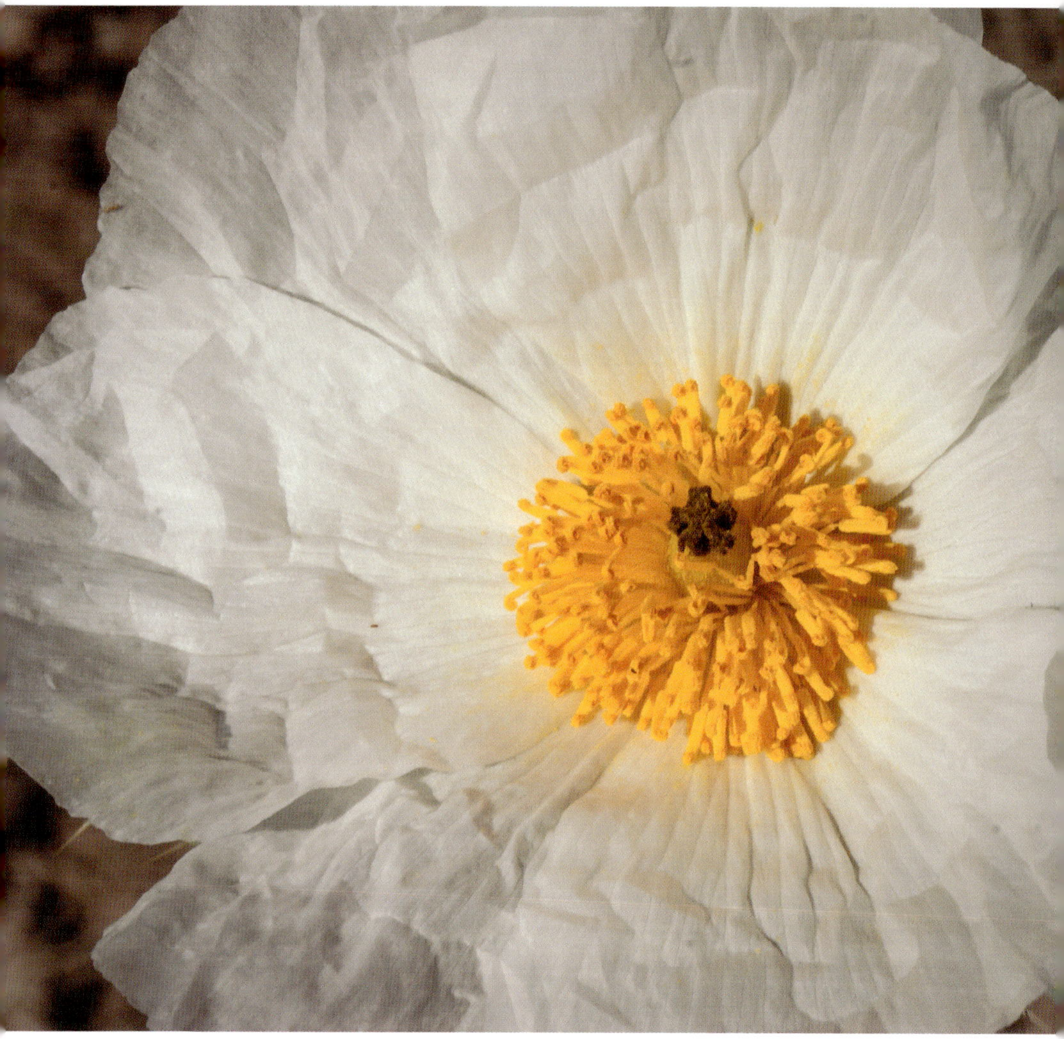

Cowboy fried egg. *M. Holzwarth, photographer.*

northern oriole. Winter birds showing dependence were ladder-backed woodpecker, northern flicker, bridled titmouse, white-breasted nuthatch, ruby-crowned kinglet, yellow-rumped warbler and American goldfinch. Only American goldfinches were seen feeding on sycamore seeds. Other species present were gleaning insects, such as the threatened yellow-billed cuckoo, or were using sycamores for nesting. Cavity nesters, especially, used the trees.

Bock and Bock also found that some species were more abundant in drainages without sycamores. These included brown towhees and rufous-crowned, Botteri's and Lincoln's sparrows—ground and shrub-nesting species that preferred areas without heavy overstory.

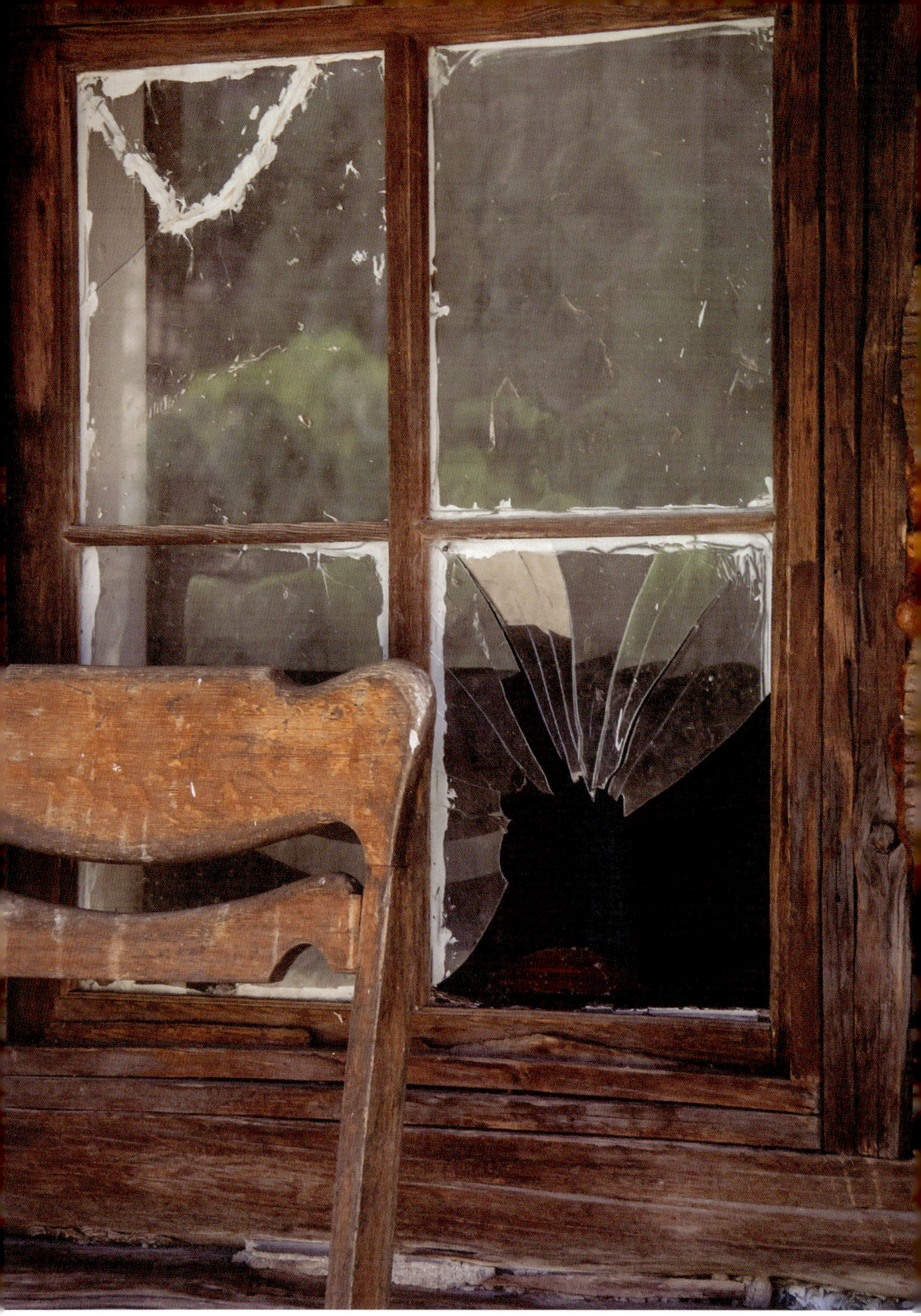

Last view. *M. Holzwarth, photographer.*

Chapter 18

MOUNTAIN LION STUDIES

Harley Shaw

The last recorded grizzly bear in New Mexico was killed in upper Animas Creek in 1932. With the disappearance of the "big bears," cougars became the top large carnivore in the Las Animas food chain. If early ranchers and hunters had succeeded in their eradication efforts, the cougar would have gone the way of the grizzly long ago. However, its secretive nature, wide dispersal and propensity to kill its own food made it less vulnerable to guns, traps or poison than wolves and grizzlies had been. Like the coyote, the cougar persisted through it all.

Initially, cougar research on the Ladder Ranch grew rather "like Topsy." It originated as an offshoot of a series of workshops designed to provide on-the-ground training in basic cougar biology and, most important, in identifying cougar sign. For decades, this author, as well as other western-state biologists with cougar experience, had received requests to evaluate reports of cougars in regions where the species had been extirpated. Mostly, these were the states and Canadian provinces east of the Great Plains. I had traveled east a couple times to work with biologists in what appeared to be cougar "hot spots" where people were sure, in spite of a lack of any hard evidence, that the species still existed. The results of these trips were less than satisfactory, ending with no good evidence of the cats being found and with the locals no less convinced that the "ghost cats" were present. I approached Steve Dobrott with the idea of holding training sessions for biologists who were having to respond to cougar reports without the benefit of any field experience with the animal. The idea fit well with the Turner vision of uses for Turner-owned lands.

The first workshop filled quickly and was generally a success. However, I and other instructors realized that attaining our teaching goals would be greatly improved with an educational aid in the form of a radio-collared cougar. The New Mexico Department of Game and Fish had provided support for the first workshop and quickly issued a permit to place a radio collar on a cat.

Orvel Fletcher, a longtime and mildly cantankerous houndsman from Albuquerque, had guided sport hunters for cougars on the Ladder Ranch, especially in Animas Creek, for years. He was a natural choice for helping to catch a cougar. On the opening morning of the second workshop, Orvel and his hounds treed a female cougar within three miles of our classroom and within fifty yards of a road. Everyone attending got to help handle the cat. Only after the workshop had ended did I, Furman University professor Travis Perry and Steve Dobrott realize that this radioed cat created an opportunity to develop cougar research on the ranch. Travis Perry quickly brought graduate student Megan Pitman into the picture, a study plan was designed and efforts were quickly afoot to capture several more cougars—something that isn't always easy in the rough landscapes of the Animas. The two stories that follow would stand alone as delightful tales of cougar research hardships. Associated with the study, they carry with them a moral as well: when you work with cougars in the wild, you do it on their terms and in their chosen terrain. The advantage is all theirs.

Chapter 19

A DAY (AND NIGHT) IN THE UPPER ANIMAS

Matthew McCollister

The summer after I finished my BS degree, 2005, I helped renovate Hermosa, a ghost town owned by Ladder Ranch, making it livable for a field semester class taught by Dr. Travis Perry. During that summer, I met Harley Shaw, a retired Arizona Game and Fish biologist who lived in Hillsboro, New Mexico. Harley had spent much of his career conducting some of the early long-term mountain lion field research in Arizona. One day, Dr. Perry and I went to Hillsboro and met Harley for lunch and inadvertently began our lion careers. Over the next six months, Harley and Travis would encourage me to attend graduate school at Clemson University. After completing course work at Clemson, I returned to New Mexico to work for Turner Endangered Species Fund on the Armendaris Ranch, monitoring desert bighorn sheep and trapping mountain lions. After six months, I returned to school and completed a master's thesis on North Carolina black bears. In 2008, with a couple years of experience trapping and studying cougars and black bears and with a fresh MS degree in wildlife biology from the University of Tennessee, I was seeking career-track employment. By this time, the cougar workshop at the Ladder Ranch—initially focused on introducing cougar ecology, study techniques and management to biologists—had expanded into a full-blown cougar study. Dr. Perry had asked me to attempt to snare and radio collar a cougar during the week of the workshop. In particular, he was eager to recapture an adult male lion (LM1) that had a malfunctioning collar. I took off for New Mexico, excited to snare lions again. I was feeling pretty good about catching one and started planning where to run a snare line. Before I could set snares, however, ranch manager Steve Dobrott said that lion hunter Orvel Fletcher was coming to the Ladder with his hounds and that my snare line couldn't happen while Orvel was there. I would, instead, help Orvel. While Orvel was more than capable of catching a lion, it would be up to me to drug and collar it.

Orvel showed up the next day with a dozen hounds and two mules. He asked about my experience with mules, and I admitted that it was next to none.

We started the next few mornings well before dawn, checking roads and arroyos for fresh lion tracks. Throughout these days, I would listen with radio telemetry from high points, hoping to hear the VHF signal from LM1, but never did. Over these first days, Orvel got increasingly frustrated. He wanted to set his hounds on a track and didn't particularly want to focus on a specific animal. Dr. Perry was anxious to re-collar LM1 and arranged with a pilot out of Truth or Consequences to fly with a telemetry receiver. On the morning the pilot flew, we were waiting for a call on the radio. We were finally informed early that afternoon that the lion was high in the Black Range near the headwaters of Animas Creek. Orvel immediately started to prepare to leave, despite warnings from Steve Dobrott and Harley Shaw regarding roughness of that country and forecasts of a storm. Fortunately, a younger houndsman named Billy Jack had arrived to work with Orvel. Billy Jack was familiar with that country, and he, too, cautioned that we were about to put ourselves in peril. Orvel reluctantly agreed to postpone our hunt until the next day.

Carrying the capture gear aboard a mule would be up to me, along with a cumbersome directional antenna and receiver. My pack had to be bare bones. I packed a pint of water and an apple for sustenance.

The next morning at 3:00 a.m., we loaded mules and dogs and drove thirty miles to our jump-off point. Orvel stopped on the frozen road at 4:00 a.m. and asked if I could see tracks. I couldn't, and Orvel concluded that we were ahead of Billy Jack. We waited. Then, at about 4:20 a.m., Orvel decided Billy Jack must be ahead of us. At the end of the road, we found Billy Jack's rig parked with dog boxes and his horse trailer empty.

Orvel started saddling his mule and yelled for me to do the same. I was still trying to saddle my mule, something I had never done, when Orvel turned out the dogs and took off up the trail. I managed to get the saddle on, but it was loose and the stirrups were much too long. I grabbed my gear, mounted and tried to keep up. After a while at a jarring trot, we caught Billy Jack. I was already aware that this was going to be a painful day. The mule I was riding had been injured when she spooked at a bear. Long story short, I was riding her for her first day back at work, and she was seeing a bear behind every bush.

Orvel and Billy Jack started up the slope through a mix of mountain mahogany, cat claw acacia and ponderosa pine. I was barely able to see the others well enough to know which way to go. My mule was trying to scrape me off on brush and low limbs, my saddle was slipping and the overly long stirrups left all of my weight on my butt, pounding hard against the saddle. I jumped off and pulled the cinch tight but couldn't get to the stirrups before I could hear Orvel yelling at me to catch up. When I found them, I was already disheveled enough that Billy Jack offered to carry the antenna, giving me both hands free for riding. By the time we got close to LM1's expected location, twenty-four hours had passed since the pilot had located the cat's signal. My butt and back were bruised, and the acacia had shredded my shirt and scratched my arms. Somewhere around here, the hound packs separated, with most of Billy Jack's dogs heading one way on a track and most of Orvel's seemingly following a different track.

Orvel and I continued up slope, and Billy Jack followed his dogs, leaving me once again carrying the antenna. As Orvel pushed up the mountain, my mule began to stumble. Orvel yelled at me to get off and lead her. I wasn't in any better shape than she was. In no time I was giving out, and Orvel was worried that we'd lose the pack. Fortunately, he couldn't leave me, because at eighty-three, his hearing was bad, and he needed my ears to hear the hounds. It was late morning and getting hot. I was already worn out, and my mule didn't seem much better. Most of the dogs began milling around, trying to line out the track, but one young gyp was missing. I took this opportunity to shorten my stirrups and finally was able to hold some weight on my feet. I also ate my apple and drank all of my water. We eventually decided that we could hear a single dog barking toward the Animas. Orvel was convinced she was barking treed, so we headed straight toward her. The steep slope had several small, sheer rock faces that blocked the mules. We went on afoot. Before long, we were using all fours to climb and eventually hit a bluff that stopped the dogs. Orvel climbed down to the next bench, and I stayed above and used a rope to lower one hound at a time. In a few more minutes we were at another drop-off and realized that we were blocked. We climbed back to the top, pulling hounds up by rope as they fought and squirmed. Both of us, as well as the dogs, were worn out and feeling the by now midday heat. To make things worse, the missing gyp wasn't barking anymore, and we were a long ways from the truck. I filled my water bottle with snow. Orvel chose a new route down the ridge to the Animas, which seemed to be the best way if we wanted to get off the steep slope by dark.

Before long, my mule started to sulk. Orvel told me to pound on her to keep her going, but all that did was wear me out. I eventually tied my mule's lead rope to Orvel's saddle, and his mule dragged mine down the slope. This turned into a mess, as Orvel's mule would kick mine in the chest and mine would plant her feet and refuse to move. However, the soil was loose, so she'd end up sliding, pushing rocks and dirt down slope. Through all this, Orvel was leading and I was bringing up the rear, trying to keep clear of hooves and debris. The saddle on my mule slid up onto its neck, and for a moment it looked like she was about to explode, but Orvel stopped, and we pulled the saddle off before we ended up in a real mess. I felt like I was dehydrated and wondered about Orvel. I hadn't seen him drink any water all day. I hoped we could soon find a spring. We would soon run out of daylight, so Orvel kept pushing on as fast as he could. We ended up in a small draw with a stagnant pool, and both mules drank a long time. The water wasn't anything Orvel or I were going to try.

A little way farther, the draw turned into a dry boulder-strewn stream bed. We found another stagnant pool. Orvel was walking alongside his mule, and my mule dropped its head to drink. Orvel's mule kept plodding along, and as the rope between the mules tightened, it flipped Orvel across the wash, slamming him down into the rocks. He hit hard and went limp. I was afraid he had cracked his head. He wasn't responsive at first, but he eventually groaned, so I knew he wasn't dead. I found some potable water seeping from a crack and filled the bottle several times while we drank and rested. I couldn't see any blood from his head and concluded he had taken most of the impact in his back. It was a long time before he got up, but he didn't complain, although it slowed him down a good bit when we finally moved on.

After a while, we reached flatter ground, and he was able to climb in the saddle. I did the same, hoping my mule had recovered enough to carry me. We tried to raise Billy Jack on the radio. Surprisingly, he answered. We told him that we were heading downstream and asked if he could radio the Ladder Ranch office to have someone meet us at the national forest boundary in Animas Creek. Orvel was feeling better and picked it up to a trot. I hadn't shortened my stirrups enough, and the trotting mule was pretty hard on my sore butt. We followed the creek for several miles, passing the buffalo soldiers' graves at dusk and reaching Apache Camp just before dark.

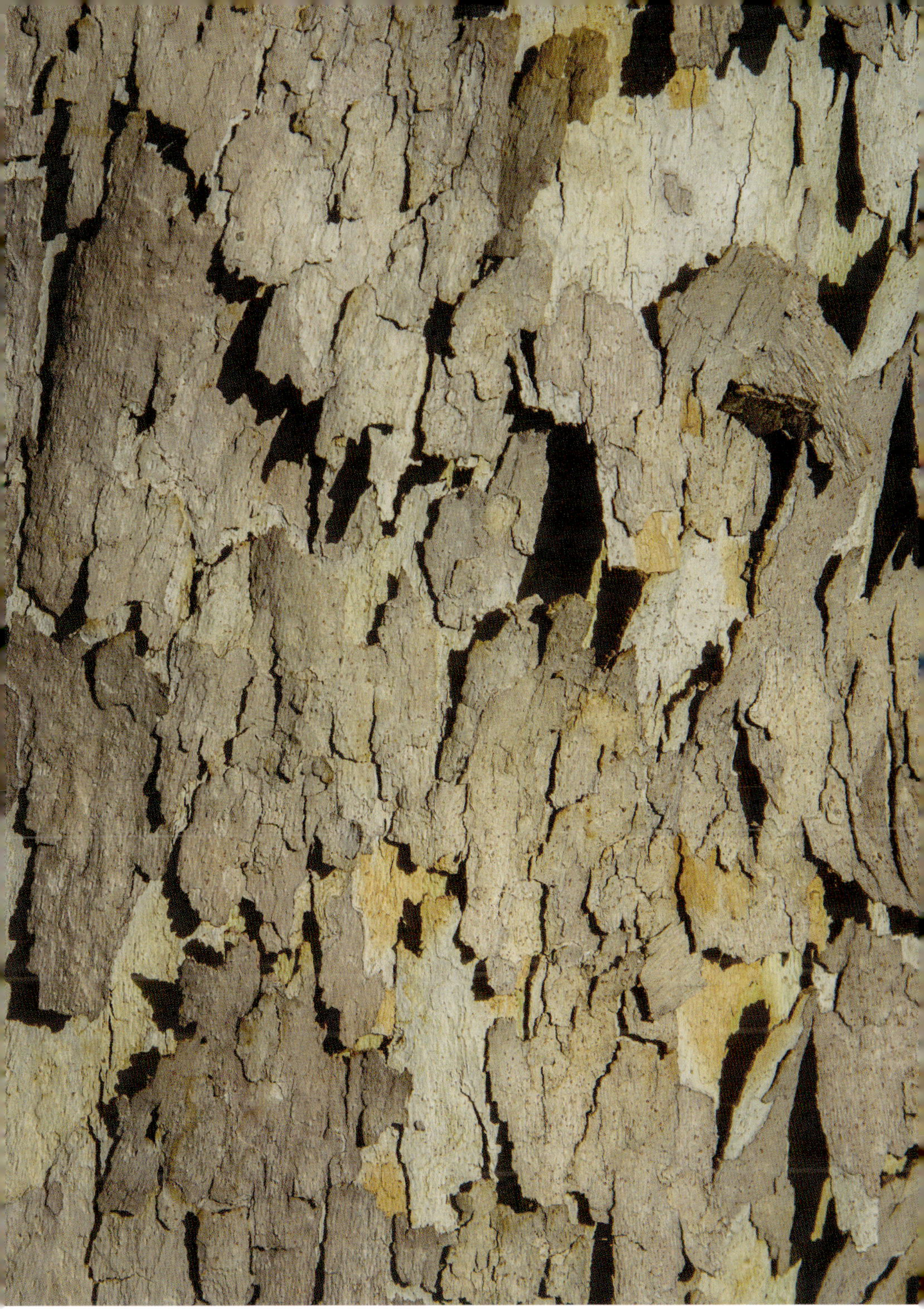

Bark palette. *M. Holzwarth, photographer.*

As we neared the ranch boundary, rain was falling. We were relieved to see Dr. Perry's Ford pickup. Graduate student Megan Pitman had come to our rescue but had stopped when a tire blew.

We helped her change the tire, stripped the mules, loaded the tack and dogs and started the long drive to the ranch office around 10:00 p.m. We left the mules to find their way back to the ranch. We finally crawled into our beds about 1:00 a.m. I knew it had been a rough day when even Orvel didn't get up the next morning until long after sunrise. I was sore everywhere. My shirt was in rags, and my arms were scratched all over. During the day, we got an earful from the rest of the workshop and Steve. Apparently, they had heard all the radio talk from the day before but weren't able to communicate with us. Billy Jack had spent the night stranded in a snowstorm and sat out the night by a fire, high on the mountain. By the morning, he had gathered the rest of his dogs plus one or two of Orvel's. Our mules wandered into headquarters two days later. We'd had an adventure, but we never got close to making it a success.

The workshop ended the following day, and I drove back to Louisiana for a bear project. Two months later, I was leaving that project to work in Colorado on bighorn sheep. I stopped in at the Ladder Ranch for a week to try, once again, to snare cougars for Travis. The first afternoon, I set two snares on the Animas. The next morning, I checked the sets, and I had caught LM1.

Chapter 20

ANIMAS MOUNTAIN LION PURSUIT

Travis Perry

In 2005, when I was making plans to begin a mountain lion research program, I was fortunate enough to have connections with the Ladder Ranch through previous biodiversity surveys. The Animas watershed and surrounding country would make an ideal study area for the big cats.

The Animas Creek watershed is a gem of biodiversity in the Southwest. Latitude, variable topography, the elevation gradient, relative isolation and water are the major reasons. At around thirty-three degrees north, the Animas is far enough south to receive abundant solar energy, a common factor in diverse systems. It is also far enough south to pick up some neotropical species such as the zone-tailed hawk and white-nosed coati. The various slopes and canyons of the watershed begin at near 10,000 feet and descend to around 4,200 feet where the Animas meets the Rio Grande. Variable topography over variable elevation produces a wide array of abiotic conditions and resulting habitat types, from creosote-dominated Chihuahuan desert scrub to mixed coniferous forest. The Animas has its headwaters on the eastern slope of the Black Range in the Aldo Leopold Wilderness, which is but a hop, skip and a jump from the Gila Wilderness. These large wilderness areas provide a reservoir of species to colonize and recolonize the Animas drainage. They also provide a buffer from human activity that might otherwise diminish the wildlife here. An additional buffer is provided by the conservation-minded management of the Ladder Ranch, through which the Animas flows. And then, there is the holy grail of the Southwest: water. Although the Animas doesn't flow its entire length all year, it does much of the year, and there are nearly always pools of surface water along its length.

In 2008, we began our mountain lion research on the ranch. The project had several objectives, including development of a cost-effective technique to estimate mountain lion populations. Another objective was to create an educational resource for the public, students and wildlife professionals. This field workshop was a venue of lectures, field practicals and idea exchange for wildlife professionals from the East and Midwest who were beginning to deal with what appears to be a slow eastward spread of mountain lions. In February 2008, during our Mountain Lion Field Workshop, LF1(Ladder female no. 1) was bayed by Orvel Fletcher's hounds in a colossal cottonwood on the Animas flood plain near the Ladder office. Our workshop participants got front-row seats to mountain lion research.

Another of LF1's milestones was reached during a different educational outing. While I was giving a tour of our program to the public for the New Mexico Museum of Natural History, one of my colleagues discovered that LF1 had produced a litter of cubs in a boulder pile on the south side of Dollar Mesa, eight and a half miles upstream from the giant cottonwood in which she was captured. For the touring "students," although a mile or more away, being able to actually see the rock outcrop where a female mountain lion lay with her new cubs was a learning experience to which no classroom setting could compare.

By the fall of 2008, LF1's radio collar had only a few weeks of battery life remaining. With a litter of cubs in tow, her value as a research animal had skyrocketed. Fitting her with a new collar was imperative. Her collar e-mailed us her cumulative locations every three days—usually. My graduate student Megan Pitman and I, both based in South Carolina, had decided to take a week off of classes in late October and attempt to recapture LF1. We hoped the radio collar would send us LF1's locations, allowing us to stalk the cat close enough to shoot her with a tranquilizer dart, thereby eliminating the need for a prolonged ground search in rough and rugged country. It didn't.

On our first morning, beneath the vast blue expanse of a cloudless sky, I scanned the slope in front of me with binoculars for sign of the mountain lion among the oak, yucca and mountain mahogany. I could still feel my pulse throbbing in my ears from the steep climb from a side canyon of the Animas. I stood atop the west end of Dollar Mesa, sweeping my radio antenna across a vista of wild, rough country. Staccato beeps from the receiver told us that LF1 was in a dauntingly steep canyon about a mile east of Apache Peak.

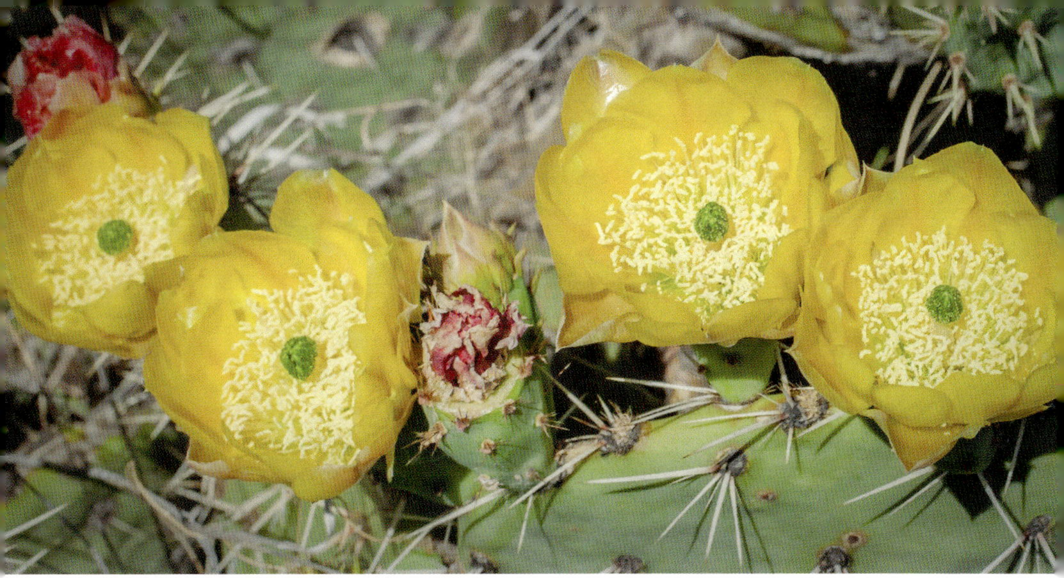

Cactus blooms. *M. Holzwarth, photographer.*

Loaded with equipment, we ventured into the Animas Creek drainage. Neither the cat nor the terrain was making this easy.

This wilderness of deep canyons, precipitous brushy slopes and fantastic rock outcrops was where Apache leader Victorio had lured Navajo scouts and buffalo soldiers of the Ninth U.S. Cavalry to a smashing military defeat. Victorio's men led the cavalry into a side canyon of the Animas, where the men and their horses were trapped by difficult terrain and blazing gunfire. Over several hours, soldiers and mounts were killed and wounded by Apache bullets until the cover of darkness allowed survivors to slip away. The place was afterward named Massacre Canyon. And in that direction we were headed.

The plan was to either find her on a kill and set foot snares on her prey cache (ideal) or locate her day bed and place foot snares along the path she was most likely to travel the next night (risky). My pack weighed 65 pounds and Megan's 45 pounds. We were moving 110 pounds of gear to effect a safe and sure capture. Over the next few days, we'd become keenly aware of every ounce of that weight.

From the top, we could see lumps and spires of yellow-gold, olive-gray and dark green along the sinewy path of the creek lying in the canyon bottom. As we hiked down, the splashes of color became identifiable as box elder, cottonwood, Arizona sycamore, New Mexico alder and the occasional ponderosa pine. Once at the bottom, we got our feet wet for the first of many times in the cold, flowing water of the Animas. We walked slowly up the canyon, scanning the sandbars and occasional mud banks for mountain lion tracks and stopping periodically to turn on our radio receiver to listen for LF1's signal. We hiked into the afternoon, looking at the signatures of black bear, coyote, gray fox, deer (either whitetail or mule), elk, skunk (spotted, hooded, striped and hog-nosed all occur on the Animas), raccoon and even a white-nosed coati as the October sun heated us and the sweat ran down our backs beneath the heavy insulation of our packs. We found bobcat tracks and mountain lion tracks, including those of a big tom, but none that we could be sure belonged to LF1 and her cubs.

The last locations we'd received showed her to be on the southern edge of Chacon Park. When we reached this meadow, we thankfully dropped our packs and waded through the waist-high brown and crackling grama grass, sunflowers, four o' clocks and asters to the bottom of the slopes that formed the southern boundary of the park. Beneath an alligator juniper, we found handfuls of deer hair and, nearby, a small, fresh mountain lion scat. Given the volume of long white hair, I suspected it was a Coues deer, a subspecies of whitetail, characterized by small body and antlers. We found no bones, no entrails, nothing—a situation typical of a kill of a small deer made by a female with cubs. Many mouths, growing bodies and the energy demands of lactation mean that mother and cubs can't afford to waste even a mouthful. Males, on the other hand, are more concerned about what female may be over the next ridge or in the next canyon. Traveling is their priority, and they often don't stay in place long enough to consume an entire adult deer.

We made camp that first night within view of Chacon Corral, where I imagined many a cowboy had thrown down his bedroll after a hard day of driving cattle out of the many side canyons. We lay out our sleeping bags on a bench close enough to the Animas to hear the murmuring water flowing over stones and heard a western screech owl in a nearby juniper. It had been a long day, and we were starving. Given the exceedingly dry conditions of this country in October combined with the abundance of tinder in the form of dead forbs and grasses, we had decided we wouldn't make a fire during this expedition. We opened some prepackaged Indian food we'd bought in Albuquerque and dug in with enthusiasm. The food was eye-watering, air-gaspingly hot. Having drunk all of our water just to get the Indian food down, we made a short hike back to the stream to refill our canteens. We hiked back to our camp late with still-smoldering mouths and sore feet beneath a black velvet sky and vivid Milky Way, the night's waning half moon not yet risen.

We woke to frost on the second day. By the time the temperature had climbed to the forties, we'd eaten our granola bars shivering, loaded our packs in grateful anticipation of the hot sunshine to come and were back in pursuit. We hiked to higher ground south of Chacon Park and then climbed west to a seven-thousand-foot peak just north of Cottonwood Canyon. On the rocky side of this peak, after a hardy (or should I say "hardly") meal of more granola bars and some dried apples, I heard that siren song that has lured many a field biologist to hardship and occasional satisfaction: a faint beeping on the radio receiver. The signal was coming from slightly north of Apache Peak, now about two miles to our west. Given our elevation, the signal could have been coming from a couple of ridges or canyons between us and the peak. We decided to hike next to a ridge below us that had a two-track along its crest. This ridge was to our west and rose at a high angle from the Animas. We hefted the leaden packs to our already sore shoulders and walked and slipped five hundred feet to the bottom of a small canyon. We then climbed to the top of the two-track ridge. And here, on this steeply ascending ridge, breathless from the uphill scramble, I turned on the receiver and heard the signal booming in my ear.

After thirty-six hours, we'd located our mountain lion. Time now to really get to work. We wanted to set the snares on her kill, if she had one. Later collar data confirmed that she had a kill on this hillside at this time. Without GPS data to show us the location of a kill site, we had two problems. First, she wouldn't be on her kill during the day; she'd most likely be one hundred yards or more away from it. Second, we didn't want to go bumbling around a steep hillside covered with dense brush playing hide-and-go-seek with a female mountain lion with cubs. And there was another problem. If we were too intrusive with our search, we might bump her out of this canyon and into even rougher and more remote country. At this point, the bane of all field expeditions presented itself: logistics. We'd been hiking since early morning, and it was now mid-afternoon. We were out of water. Rather than move down the ridge we were on and potentially bump our cat, we returned to the narrow canyon from which we'd just come and made our way to the sweet, cool waters of the Animas to slake our thirst.

With the little daylight we had remaining, we moved quietly into the canyon bottom just below the hillside where our mountain lion lay with her cubs. As quickly and quietly as possible, we constructed two snare sets along a game trail. A mountain lion scrape with mountain lion scat along the trail told us this was indeed a highway for the big cats. We located a solid anchor tree and removed any branches the cat could get hung up on. We wrapped the anchor chain, attached to the three-sixteenth-inch cable snare, around the anchor tree and secured it with a quick link. Then I dug an eight-inch-diameter hole in the trail and inserted a third of a two-pound coffee can, opened at both ends, to prevent the sides of the hole from caving in. Next I positioned the snare spring arm such that the treadle fit through a slot in the coffee can and lay perpendicular to the trail. I placed six lengths of metal measuring tape to span across the top of the coffee can and beneath and perpendicular to the treadle. When our mountain lion stepped on the treadle, the brittle measuring tapes would ensure that she committed her full weight to this foot before the treadle dropped with a snap, thereby releasing the spring and tightening the cable loop well above her paw. I next covered the can, tapes and treadle with a square of canvas and pinned it down with four lengths of welding rod. I sifted soil over the canvas and blended it with the substrate of the trail. Then, I threaded the snare cable through the end of the spring arm and positioned the cable on the welding rods about three-quarters of an inch above the sifted soil covering the treadle. Finally, we placed a stick horizontally above the snare loop at a height of about twenty-eight inches. The stick, referred to as a "jump stick," was secured to the anchor tree and woody vegetation on the opposite side of the trail. Deer, elk and all but the smallest bears would encounter this stick barrier and either jump or climb over it. In 90 percent of cases, however, mountain lions would choose to go under the stick—a simple and effective filter to prevent capture of non-target species. We repeated this setup fifty yards up the trail as the sun was setting. When we'd finished, the receiver told us the cat was still on the hillside far up the canyon.

As the light faded and the temperature dropped, we found a weedy flat adjacent to the Animas, dropped our packs and prepared for a night of eager anticipation. We laid out our sleeping bags in the open, beneath another brilliantly starlit New Mexico night, and ate a cold supper of salami, cheddar and M&Ms. Despite the cold and the excitement over what we might find in the morning, sleep came quickly.

Frost was thick on the sleeping bags as the sky began to brighten around six o'clock the next morning. I pulled on some clean socks and shoved my feet into frozen hiking boots. (They'd gotten wet during the last water refill from the Animas the night before.) The receiver told an encouraging story: our mountain lion was still up the canyon. That meant one of two things: either she was caught and would soon be wearing a new collar or she was on a kill, greatly increasing our chances for a capture and producing some good prey data as a bonus. We hurriedly repacked our gear, now two snares lighter. We didn't want to blunder up the game trail where we'd set the snares, in case the lion was only out for an early morning stroll. Remote cameras' data had told us that mountain lions were regularly active as late as 8:00 a.m. but rarely after that time. It wasn't yet 7:00 a.m.; we could expect her to still be active. We climbed the ridge as quickly as gravity would allow, and I began taking bearings on her about every two hundred yards in an attempt to triangulate her position. Bearings converged high on the slope, close to her location the day before. She wasn't caught. We hiked on, climbing the ridge until we reached a relatively level spot where we stopped to eat from our dwindling supply of food and plan our next move.

We decided to first locate her position with the receiver as precisely as possible to avoid any surprise encounters. Once we felt confident about her position, we would carefully search the hillside for her kill. If we failed to find the kill, we would place two cubby sets in the bottom of the canyon.

We spent the first part of the day attempting to pinpoint her location. We hiked to the highest point on the ridge and then descended, taking regular bearings. The terrain produced signal bounce, confusing our efforts. By noon, after hiking up and down the ridge and trudging up yet again, taking repeated readings, we had only succeeded in narrowing her location to several hundred square yards. Our plan now was to scour the hillside with hope of finding her kill and also hoping that our radio telemetry had been accurate enough to prevent us from bumping into the mountain lion and her cubs. But before we could begin that delicate task, we had to return to the Animas. We were out of water.

This time, we left our packs near the top of the ridge and carried only a lunch and our empty water bottles. On this hike, without the static and beeps of the receiver buzzing in our ears, we were able to take a more thoughtful look at this landscape. It was ideal mountain lion habitat—and by that, I mean it was ideal mountain lion *prey* habitat. The floodplain was perhaps eighty yards wide and filled with riparian gallery forest through which flowed a perennial stream—a fantastic rarity in southwestern New Mexico. Flanking the wide flood plain, the canyon sides slope gently and then steeply up to mesas and peaks, and everywhere these canyon sides are incised by smaller canyons and shallow drainages. The Animas flows eastward out of the Black Range, and thus one canyon side faces almost due south while the other faces north.

In a land of harsh sun and little rain, the aspect of a slope determines which and how many plants grow on it. The south-facing slope is relatively warmer and dryer than its north-facing counterpart in all seasons. The species that can grow, or grow well, on the cooler, wetter north slope dominate there, and the same is true for the south-facing slope. On the south slope of Animas

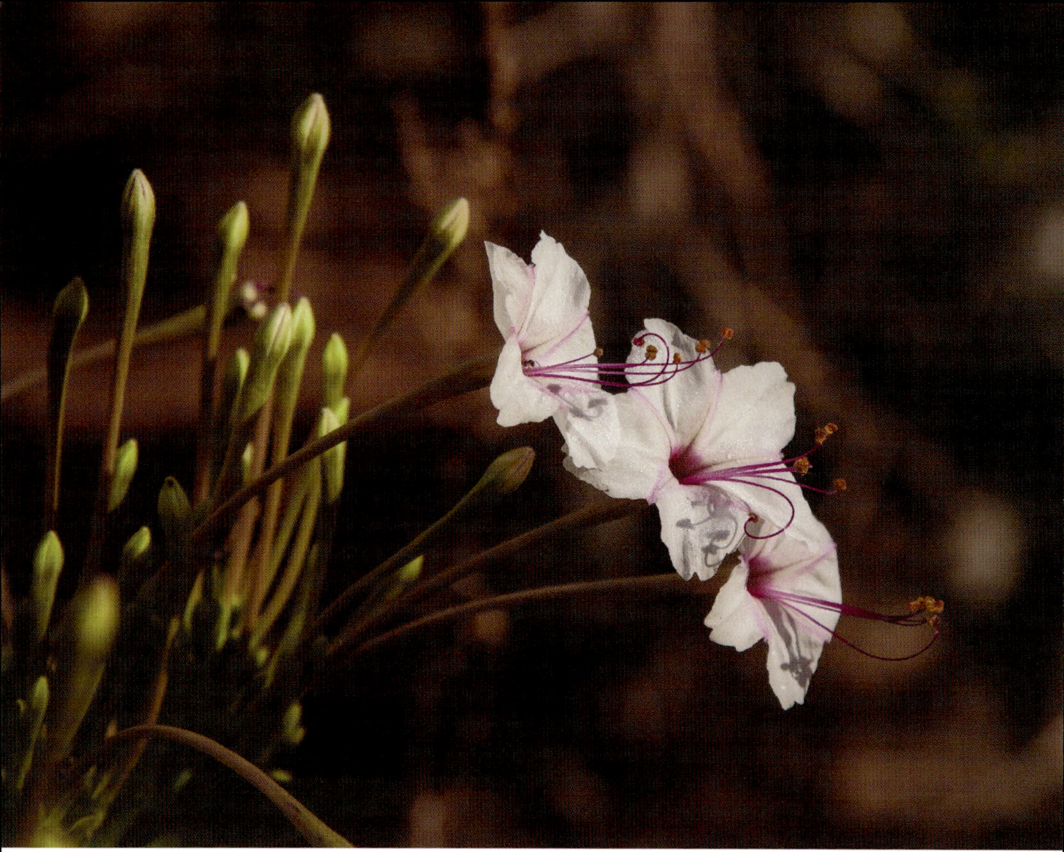

Sweet four o'clock (*Mirabilis longiflora*). *M. Holzwarth, photographer.*

canyon, the grass is thinner; bare rock, prickly pear, sotol and cholla cactus are common; and gray oaks and one-seeded juniper are widely spread. By comparison, the north-facing slope is a jungle. Vegetation is ten times denser on that slope. Juniper, both one-seeded and alligator bark; gray oak; mountain mahogany, a favorite deer browse species; and Datil yucca cover these slopes. Ponderosa pine grows tall in some of the shallowest north face drainages. Add the riparian forest of Animas Creek, and the result is a haven for deer and elk, with the essentials: food, water and cover for all seasons. In other words, it was an ideal place for mountain lions.

In the shade of the alders, we sat on rocks and let the cool stream flow around the soles of our boots. We drank our water bottles to the bottom and then repeated twice while we ate our lunch of summer sausage, peanuts, chocolate and cheddar cheese. I saw a little fellow in a rock crevice on the bank behind me and had a closer look. Peering from the shadow was a canyon tree frog, one of only two tree frog species found in New Mexico. The scientific name (*Hyla arenicolor*) refers to Hylas, one of the argonauts who sailed with Jason, who bent down to drink from a spring and was taken to reside there forever by a water nymph, and arenicolor, meaning the color of sand. As scientific names go, it's a good one—a sandy-colored fellow that can't stray far from water. The fact that our amphibian companion was here at all was testament to the permanence of water in this canyon, shaping animal and plant communities for centuries.

We trudged slowly back up the hill where our packs lay to begin the rather tense search for LF1's kill among the rocks and thick brush while she watched us from her hiding place. On the walk up, we startled a Coues buck browsing among the mountain mahogany. Only a hundred yards farther on, we flushed a group of five mule deer does—mountain lion country to be sure. After reaching our packs, we crossed the now very narrow side canyon to begin searching her hillside for the hidden kill. For the next few hours, we scoured the steep slope as quietly as we could. It seemed there were always the thick, pointy-sharp leaves of a yucca or the spines of a cholla below us as we slipped along the slope. We found nothing. With visibility in most places less than ten yards, I was not surprised. We returned to our packs to collect our gear and dropped back into the little canyon we'd just crossed to construct two cubby snare sets with predator calls.

The cubby set is the preferred set when you can use a bait or some other attractant. We were going to use an electronic predator call, set to mimic the cry of a gray fox, as our attractant. The cubby set differs from the trail set in that it is a one-way route. Brush is piled in a circle about eight feet in diameter with a narrow opening on one side, like a donut with one bite taken out of it. A series of foot placements lead through the opening. At the opposite side of the circle from the opening is a tree used to anchor the snare cable. As in the trail set, the snare loop and the trigger for the spring that will tighten the loop are positioned in one of the foot placements leading into the circle. The attractant, in this case our predator call, is placed at the opposite side of the circle from the entrance opening, usually by the anchor tree. A mountain lion coming to investigate can only enter this brushy corral (this is the "cubby") from one direction, forcing it to step on the spring trigger. Having used up most of our day searching for her and her kill, we worked as quickly as we could to cut and pile brush, dig an emplacement for spring and snare and arrange foot placements before the sun sank too low and our cat began to move. For the second night in a row, as the sun was setting we put the finishing touches on our snares and slipped away to camp.

We decided to keep the high ground this night and had to search for a spot on our narrow ridge to lie where we wouldn't roll or slide. For supper, we ate the last of our food, the bits and pieces that had survived the last three days. We hoped for a morning capture, as that would mean a one-way trip back to the food in the car on Dollar Mesa after the triumphant re-collaring. No morning capture meant a long round trip to the car to resupply.

It was a long, cold night, almost too cold for sleeping. When the cold on my face woke me up, I threw a dirty shirt over my head. The insulation of the shirt worked for a while, but as the temperature continued to drop, the cold crept in again. I was up before the sun just to be able to move around and generate some heat. Thick ice in my water bottle assured me that I wasn't exaggerating the cold. The temperature had hovered around eighteen degrees Fahrenheit that night. As soon as my frigid, stiff boots were on my frozen toes, I turned on the radio receiver and pointed the antenna at the large area where we'd located our cat the day before. To our surprise and disappointment, she was still there. Mountain lions rarely stay in the same spot for more than a couple of days, and this is nearly always when they are on a kill. We've only seen mountain lions spend several days in one spot under two circumstances; one is when they are having cubs and the second is when they've killed a large prey animal and the weather is cold. I could certainly attest to the cold weather, and we already knew she had cubs. She must have a nice fat deer on that hillside. We took one more shot at finding that carcass on the slope, without success.

The plan for the rest of this day was already determined by circumstance: hoof it to the truck on Dollar Mesa to resupply and then hoof it back to this side canyon. Needing to be prepared for any contingency or delay, we packed up all our gear yet again. Although we were now four snares (including sixteen feet of chain) lighter, the prospect of topping out on Dollar Mesa and returning to this spot before dark was not welcome. Before we could begin the long walk to Fritos, we had to lock down our snare sets. We didn't want to take a chance on catching an animal during the day while we were away. Although the nights and mornings were below freezing, the sun was still warm on your skin and downright hot under exertion. Afternoon temperatures were reaching the upper seventies or low eighties. We couldn't take a chance on an animal becoming overheated. We hiked down into the canyon and then on to the Animas, locking down first our cubby sets and then our trail sets

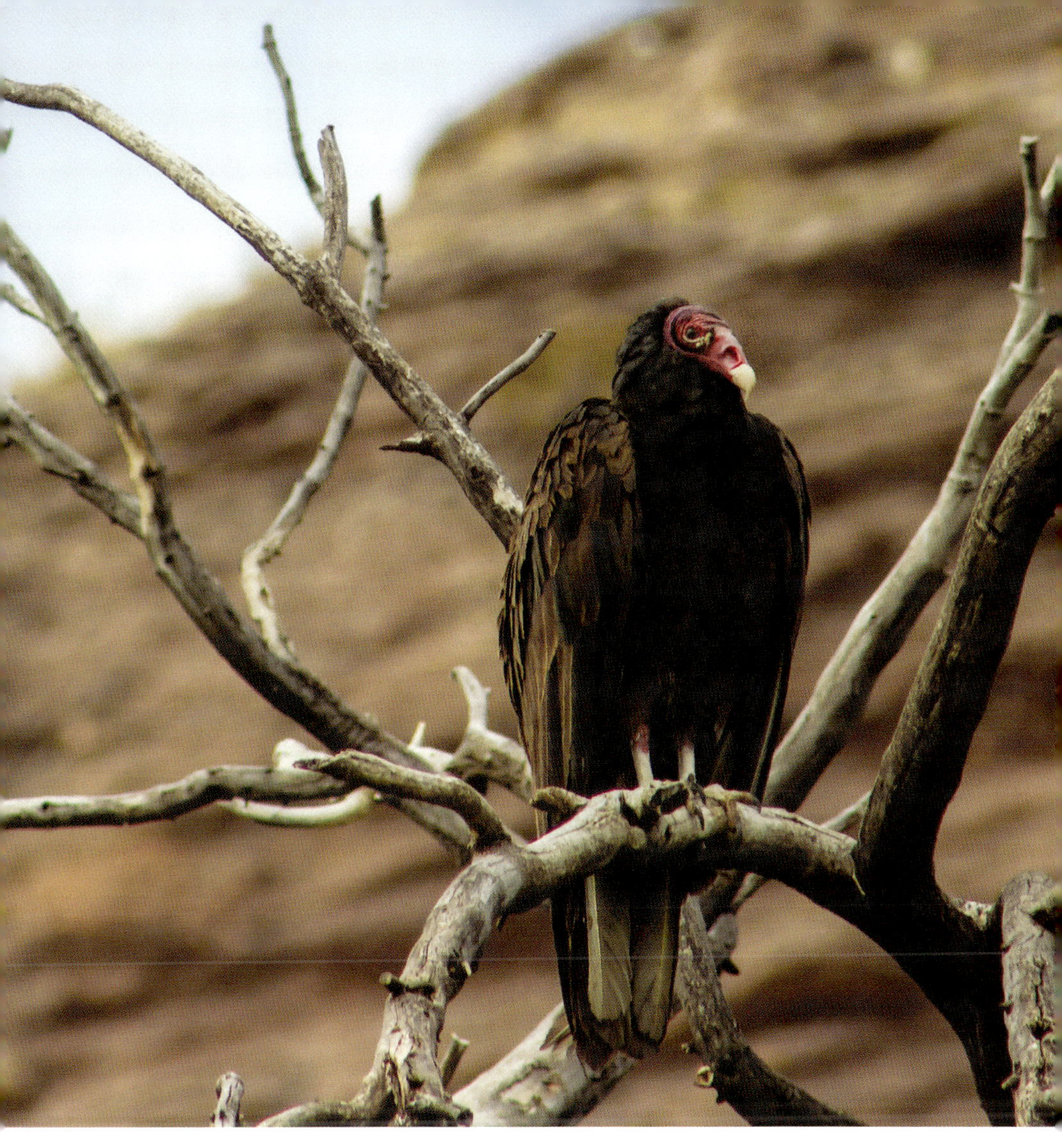

Waiting. *M. Holzwarth, photographer.*

along the way. With the snares locked down, we now had a deadline to meet. We had to get back to this canyon, unlock our snares, turn on our predator calls and get out of the way before LF1 decided to leave her lair. We walked as fast as we could through the morning, along the forested sides of the Animas, through the open expanse and waist-high plants of Chacon Park, past the weather-beaten corral and again over the tracks of many animals like lumbering bears, fleeting deer and stealthy bobcats. After about three hours of fast walking with limited water breaks, we reached the bottom of the CC road. We fortified ourselves for the final push out of the canyon with some cold Animas water and began the long climb. Just after one o'clock, we reached the top of Dollar Mesa and the truck. The sweat running down my back and dripping off my nose seemed unreal after the night I'd spent freezing in a sleeping bag. In the shade of the cab with the doors opened wide to allow a cooling breeze, we ate too much and stayed too long, savoring the minutes of relaxation before the long trek back. While we ate, we watched a herd of elk grazing on the mesa.

On the windshield, we found a note left by Steve Dobrott. The note told us what we already knew. A pilot we'd hired to locate LF1 had found her on the hillside where we'd been listening to her signal for three days now. Ahhhh, timing.

Sleepily, with overfull stomachs, we loaded cookies, M&Ms, apples, another dastardly packet of Indian food, suspicious-looking cheese and summer sausage into our packs. Because the CC road was not as bad as we'd feared it would be and because we were dreading climbing it again, we drove the truck back down as far as the end of the CC road and parked beside the Animas. Then we double-timed it back up the big canyon with the sun beginning its slide down the western sky to meet the Black Range.

The receiver indicated that LF1 had not moved all day, and we were not surprised. It's a rare thing for an undisturbed mountain lion to move during the day, especially one with a belly full of venison. Arriving back to our sets around 5:15 p.m., we just had time to reset our snares and sneak away before dusk. Sunset was due at 6:20 p.m., and we didn't want to be in the way when the mountain lions and long shadows started to creep. Snares were set and predator calls activated as the light faded.

Ten steps at a time between rests, we staggered back up the steep ridge to camp. We were deep bone tired with new blisters in our hot boots; our eyelids, crusted with the paste made from dust and sweat, were sticky when we blinked or squinted; our backs and leg muscles complained about the packs filled with heavy old gear and new food; and our feet felt like blocks of stone. Packs thumped to the ground at our small, level sleeping area. I rolled out my sleeping bag and stretched out on my back. I think I ate lying down for a while before mustering the energy to sit up. We'd hiked a total of 14.25 miles that day after a sleepless night shivering on the ground. In total, we'd climbed 2,400 feet in elevation since wriggling out of our cold sleeping bags before sunrise. I wondered if those buffalo soldiers felt a little like this back in 1879. At least I didn't have anyone shooting at me. And I would have rather been here, in this wild, beautiful place, attempting do my small bit to understand this enigmatic cat, than anywhere else. Layered with every article of clothing I had, sore, exhausted, crusty, dusty and cold, I fell asleep planning the individual steps of a safe capture for each snare site, contented.

Shivering and stamping my feet the next morning, I turned on the receiver and swept the antenna over the hillside and small canyon bottom. I was transfixed. The signal had moved to the vicinity of one of our snare sets. We had her!

Adrenaline and elation in equal parts were pumping through my brain. Immediately, I began the quick but methodical recheck of all of our capture gear—dart gun, extra CO_2 cartridges, darts, extra darts, dart prep supplies, immobilization drugs, reversal drug, eye gel, topical antibiotic, injectable antibiotic, insulated foam pad, emergency heat blanket, eye cover, hand warmer packets, isopropyl alcohol, tape measure, calipers, thermometer, spring scale, block and tackle to lift scale, weighing harness, camera, cable cutters, ear tags, ear tag marker, ear tag punch, 5cc syringes, 10cc syringes, 50cc syringe to pressurize dart, sterile gauze, medical tape, quarter-inch nut drivers to remove old collar and to fasten new collar, data sheets, clipboard, pens, new GPS collar. Everything was in order, hands and eyes had been on everything as it was repacked. Now for the prep talk. Although Megan and I had captured several puma by this time, we approached each capture as if it were our first (we still do). In our program, there is only one person in charge at a capture. That person talks the entire group of participants through a step-by-step narrative of everything that will happen at the capture, emphasizes safety rules (for cats and people), assigns specific tasks to specific individuals, sets priorities and attempts to prepare everyone for the unexpected. This narrative is given whether there are two people or ten people involved in the capture. I don't allow captures with fewer than two people and only allow more than five participants for exceptional reasons.

Using this approach in almost every instance, we've never had an injured or compromised person or mountain lion in over eight years of fieldwork and sixty captures. In any wild animal capture, there is a particle of risk. We've been lucky; but I have to believe that we've helped create some of this "luck" with careful planning, methodical procedures, erring on the side of caution and heeding the advice of many excellent veterinarians and wildlife professionals.

Finally, we were ready to catch this cat. With the radio receiver in hand, we began our slow walk down to the snare set. As we got closer, the signal got louder; it was booming. I turned down the gain as we pushed through the brush. The signal then got weaker. I turned up the gain. The signal continued to get weaker. The damnable thing was moving! It was good that we were alone. At the moment I realized she was slipping away, words unfit for children, sensitive folk and print burst forth in hisses between clenched teeth. She moved down the canyon floor below and slightly ahead of us, away from any hope of capturing her today.

What followed was one of the most astonishing feats of animal behavior I have ever seen, or rather, not seen. She glided out of the canyon bottom and onto our side of the steep ridge. She continued down the ridge toward the Animas at the pace of a leisurely walk. I knew this because of the radio signal, not because I saw her. I didn't. Now that she was off the steep, high, rocky hillside and in front of me, the resolution of the directional antenna was much better. Fortunately, I was able to follow her movements with some precision; otherwise, I wouldn't have believed what was happening. I turned the gain down to almost nothing to improve our ability to follow her. We were at most one hundred yards from her and often within fifty or less. At one point, I disconnected the antenna from the receiver, and still the steady beeping could be heard. Unlike the hillside where she'd been lying with her kill for the last three days, this hillside had relatively few trees and bushes. It was mostly covered with grasses, knee high and shorter, and widely scattered shrubs and juniper. We moved around one of the few juniper and saw a group of four mule deer does foraging on our hillside about one hundred yards ahead of us. The mountain lion's signal was coming from a point in a straight line between us and the browsing deer. Our cat was moving right toward them. We held our breath in anticipation for perhaps thirty seconds and then the deer exploded in leaps and bounds like fireworks in every direction, except toward us. Undoubtedly, our girl had gone undetected by them until she was under their very noses. Again we pursued her signal.

We had perhaps covered one-quarter of a mile at this point, always within tens of yards of this signal, and we saw nothing. We watched these deer foraging in plain sight. We could see them down to their knees and below. We saw dust and rocks fly as they rocketed away in terror from her presence. Of her, we saw nothing. We followed close on her heels all the way down to the creek. We watched her tracks and the tracks of her cubs filling with water on the banks of the Animas. We followed her up a nearly barren section of south-facing canyon side. In this near moonscape of mostly bare rock, there was a shallow drainage with a few cacti, yucca and scattered bunches of grass and shrubs. The antenna even told us where to look as she climbed the side of the canyon, and still we saw nothing. The incongruity between what the radio receiver told me and what I was *not* seeing caused me to doubt the equipment and my ability to use it. The truth the radio signal told was soon confirmed as we traveled the drainage behind her and saw her tracks.

The signal climbed ahead of us and stopped at a large rock outcrop. We circled the outcrop wide to assess the situation. On the side facing the creek, there was an overhang, perhaps three feet high and we couldn't tell how deep. By circling and listening closely to the strength of the signal, we could tell that she was beneath this overhang, in what amounted to a very shallow cave with a wide opening of perhaps thirty feet. We hiked around to the back side of the outcrop and then climbed up on top of it. Here we were now sitting about twenty feet above her. By removing the antenna and turning down the gain to almost nothing, we again had concrete verification that we'd followed a mountain lion and her cubs for over half a mile, at times as close as fifty yards, in mostly open habitat and even up a barren canyon side, without ever seeing so much as a patch of tawny hide, the flick of an ear or the twitch of a tail—a ghost cat indeed. It was an experience that bordered on the supernatural; it defied the senses. The stealth, the silence, for all practical purposes the invisibility of that mountain lion I would not have believed if I had not seen it for myself.

I had turned off the radio receiver. Up to this point, we had the benefit of a reasonable plan to guide our work. What now? We quietly took out our water bottles and lunch and ate while we tried to formulate a new capture plan. I stared down to the opening of the overhang in grateful amazement. I saw a ghost. A mountain lion cub about the size of a beagle rolled out from the overhang and lay on its side, swatting its oversized paw at a sibling that was out of sight. The little cat's spotted coat made it nearly imperceptible in the dappled sunlight. If not for the movement, the switching tail, the batting paws and the roll out from under the overhang, I'm sure I never would have seen this miniature ghost.

There are many reasons people choose careers in field biology. Common to almost all of them is a profound wonder at the natural world. Starlit skies, the yellow-gold of cottonwood leaves fluttering in an autumn breeze, the effortless bounding away of a mule deer, a tree

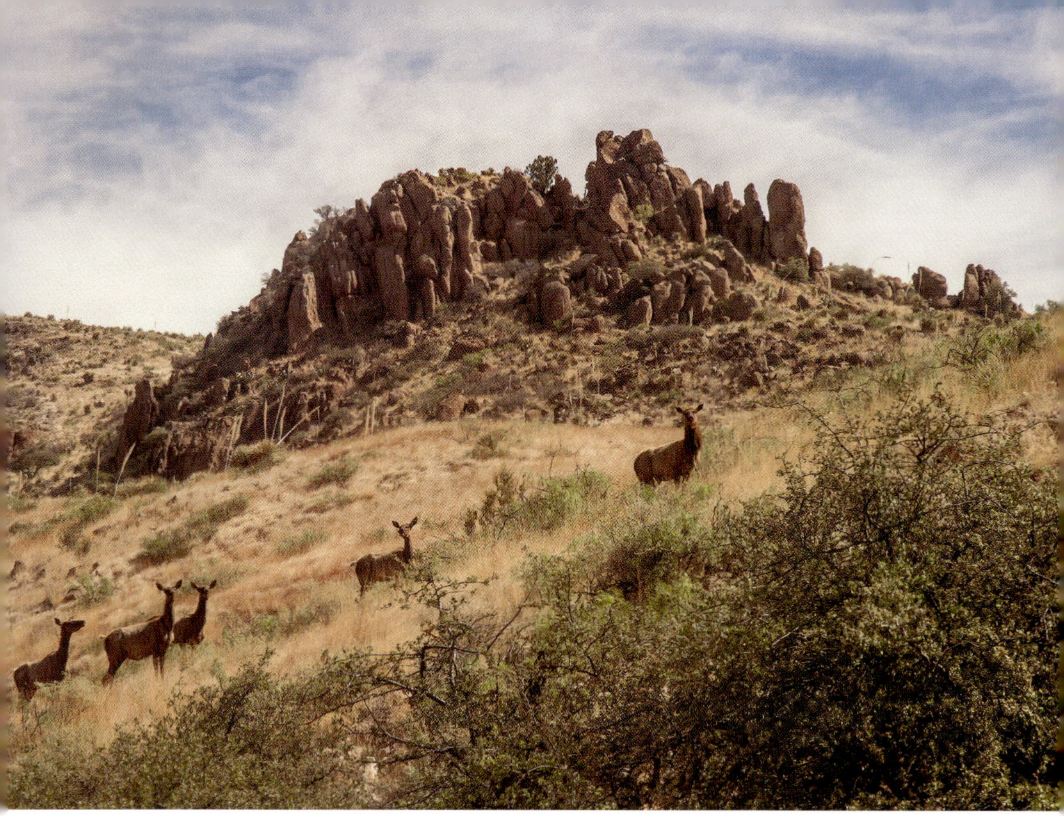

Single file. *M. Holzwarth, photographer.*

frog in a canyon oasis—all these things stimulate the soul and inspire joy, appreciation, contemplation and curiosity. And for all the magnificence of nature taken as a whole, there are, for every individual biologist, some special set of species that epitomize the awesome mystery, that are pinnacles of nature's grandeur, spellbinding to behold. For me, of course, the mountain lion is one of these. I sat and sweated in the noonday sun, dirty, smelly, blistered, sore, scraped, bruised, exhausted and foiled in a capture attempt that had cost me so much in time, money, energy and effort. And I was satisfied. I was grateful for my station. I was privileged. I was sitting on the edge of a vast wilderness, high above a stream of life in an arid land, watching a wild mountain lion cub playing in the October sun.

LF1 and her cubs drifted away like smoke on a misty day. We did not see them leave. Eventually, the radio told us they had moved on. There was a small opening at the back of this overhang that she led her cubs through. She headed for Maverick Spring on the back side of our point, but the distance was too far and we were out of time and supplies. We spent a final frigid night on the ground, rose early and packed all of our gear. With pack weights back up at forty-five and sixty-five pounds, we walked the seven miles of Animas Creek for the fourth time to our truck. In the end, we hiked a little over forty miles and climbed nine thousand feet in elevation to witness firsthand a family of mountain lions move invisibly through this landscape and to share a moment of their lives on an autumn afternoon. I feel it was more than worth it.

Since 2008, we've captured and collared twelve mountain lions—eight females and four males—on the Ladder. Of these, three males and three females were captured on the Animas. All but two of these cats spent most of their time in the Animas watershed.

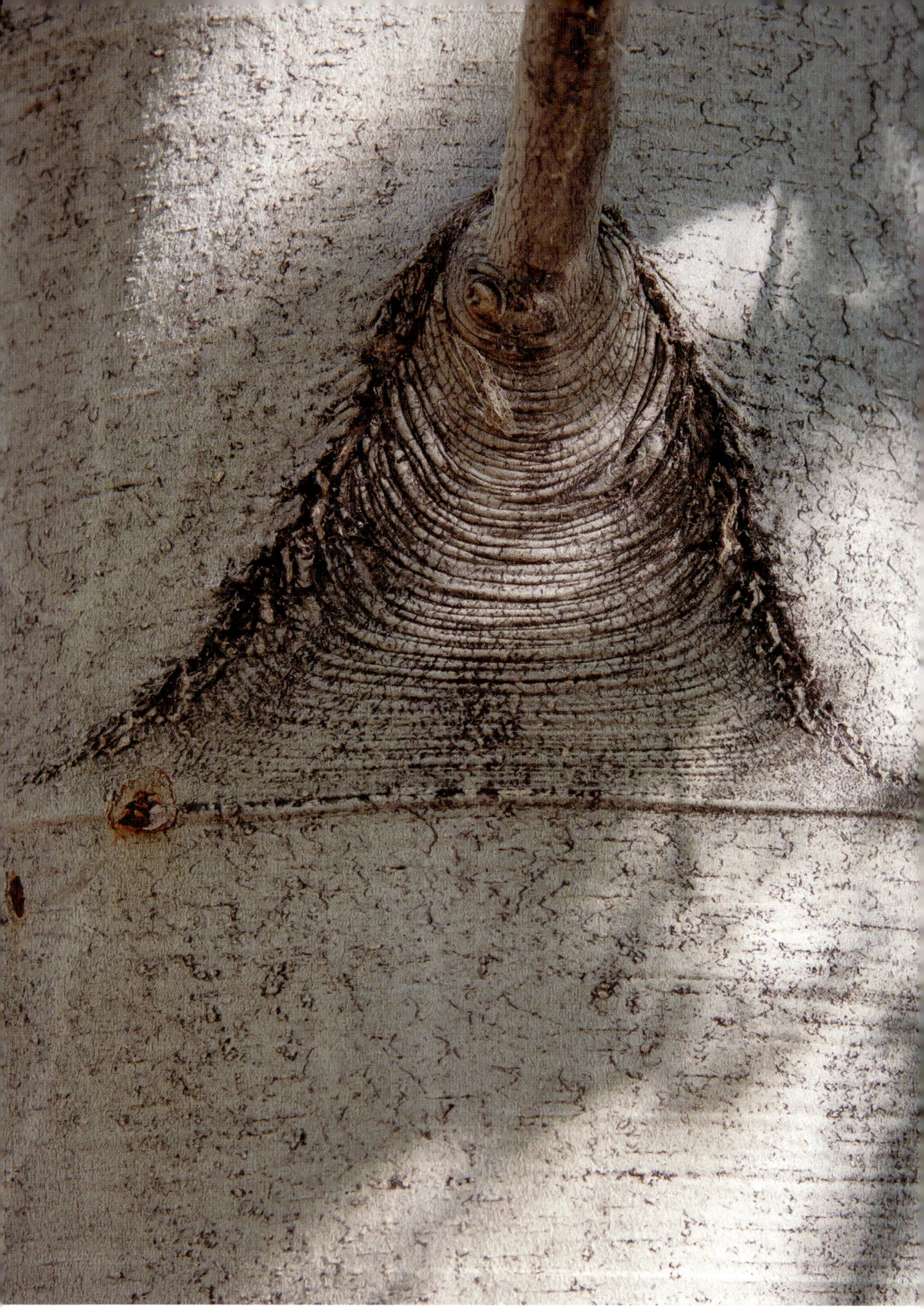

Wrinkles. *M. Holzwarth, photographer.*

Chapter 21

RESTORING THE PIECES

STEVE DOBROTT

BISON

One of Ted Turner's primary objectives for his ranches has been to provide well-managed herds of American bison. Since bison are primarily grazers, they do not impact woody riparian plants as do cattle. This has resulted in the regeneration of several plant species along Las Animas that had suffered from cattle grazing. Even though a wandering herd of bison sometimes visits Animas Creek, they do not spend much time there, preferring the more open grassland mesas, where the breezes keep the horn flies at bay. The ranch discourages grazing by bison in Animas Creek, and any trespass cattle from surrounding ranches are removed as soon as possible. Livestock grazing in riparian areas stopped when the last cow left the ranch in 1992, allowing regeneration of cottonwood, sycamore, alder and ash. The growing number of elk in the Black Range may eventually have a deleterious effect on the riparian vegetation, but as yet not to the extent of the domestic bovine.

RIO GRANDE CUTTHROAT TROUT

One of Turner's first projects in Las Animas Creek was clearing the brush from trout pools to facilitate fly-fishing. This was soon acknowledged by Ted as a "dumb idea"; angling for the diminutive Rio Grande cutthroat was hardly worth the effort. Nonetheless, he recognized the importance of conserving native trout. It became apparent fairly soon, via DNA analysis, that the supposed Rio Grande cutthroat in Animas Creek were actually hybrids, genetically compromised by historic stockings of rainbows and Yellowstone trout. The fish showed varying degrees of genetic introgression all the way to the head of Holden Prong.

In 2000, Turner biologists, New Mexico Game and Fish Department and the U.S. Forest Service developed plans to establish a pure strain of the Rio Grande trout subspecies in Animas Creek. By this time, the stream had at least an eighty-year history of stockings that included brook, rainbow, brown and cutthroat trout originating from a variety of sources. Turner's endangered species biologists and biologists from the two agencies recommended eliminating the existing trout population and starting over with pure Rio Grande cutthroats from New Mexico Game and Fish Department hatcheries.

Such a venture seemed worthy, but the program quickly ran into opposition. This was not, as might be expected, from budget-wary politicians but instead a combined front of local scientists, fishermen and environmentalists. Only a few fishermen were hardy and dedicated enough to hike or pack into the upper reaches of Animas to catch trout that rarely exceeded twelve inches in length, but some of these worthies questioned the wisdom of eliminating fish, hybrids or not, that were adapted to the austere conditions of the Animas. At least one environmentalist joined the fight by challenging the chemical, antimyocin, that had been chosen to kill the genetically tainted fish population. The program was complicated by the fact that at least one endangered species—the Chiricahua leopard frog—resided in the drainage that would be vulnerable to the piscicide. In addition to the frog, sensitive fish species, the Rio Grande chub and Rio Grande sucker, were also present, and the potential effects of the chemical on invertebrates was considered a problem.

Preparations for renovation included getting clear title to all reaches of the creek on the ranch. Ladder Ranch negotiated a trade of its North Palomas Allotment for the Animas Creek Allotment and pursued a partnership with the Forest Service relative to trout and other unique resources within the entire watershed. A newly built fish barrier on middle Animas just above ranch headquarters ensured that nonnative fish could not reinvade the upper reaches after treatment. However, due to the local opposition, the plan to renovate Animas Creek was tabled by the New Mexico Game and Fish Commission in 2001. The fact that some of the former range of the Rio Grande cutthroat farther north in the state had been compromised by the wildfires of 2011 and the realization that the Animas also held the native chubs and suckers (compromised by the introduction of the nonnative long fin dace) created a broader and more urgent need. If the above species were classified as threatened or endangered, the department might be forced into designation of critical habitat throughout the Rio Grande watershed. This would have implications on management of other wildlife species in addition to the native fish.

The project was nominally conceived as a restoration effort—putting the Rio Grande trout back into its southernmost historic habitat. However, efforts to document the presettlement presence of the subspecies have so far produced no record of trout of any kind in the creek prior to about 1920, when stocking by New Mexico Department of Game and Fish began.[105]

As noted earlier, J.D. Witham mentioned fishing in Animas Creek near the Murphy place in 1883. Edward Tittmann camped at the Kelsey Ranch and near the juncture of Animas and Water Canyons on his 1909 pack trip. Although this was a recreational outing of sportsmen—people who might notice trout—Tittmann does not mention fishing or presence of trout. Lawson, working on a timber survey for the U.S. Forest Service about 1910, camped for over a week in upper Animas Creek and did not mention trout. Once on the west side in the Diamond Creek watershed, Lawson noted that two of the survey party members were fishing enthusiasts and frequently walked two miles after a hard day of work to fish for trout. It seems likely that these worthies would also have taken advantage of trout in the Animas, had fish been present. Hatch found no records of scientific specimens from the creek before 1961.[106] According to Patten:

> *Stocking records indicate seven stocking events in the Rio Las Animas from 1920 to 1963 by New Mexico Department of Game and Fish Department. Species stocked include brook trout, native black spotted trout, rainbow trout, and New Mexico cutthroat trout. "New Mexico cutthroat" were stocked in 1958, 1961, and 1963 after the 1951 McKnight Fire allegedly killed all trout in the Rio las Animas (NMDGF files). The New Mexico cutthroat were probably hybrids between Rio Grande cutthroat trout and Yellowstone cutthroat trout. Undocumented stocking events may also have occurred on private lands, i.e. the Ladder Ranch. Considering the prevalence of rainbow trout alleles in the lower watershed, at least some of these plantings included rainbow trout. The increase of rainbow trout alleles over time in Holden Prong, including the extreme headwaters, indicates upstream hybridization and population connectivity throughout the watershed. Hitt et al.*[107] *observed a similar*

upstream pattern of hybridization between west slope cutthroat trout and rainbow trout. If true, the degree of rainbow trout hybridization in the extreme headwaters of Holden Prong is expected to increase over time.[108]

Patten provided a summary of New Mexico Department of Game and Fish stocking records for Animas Creek:

1920 Brook Trout 10,000
1935 Native Black Spotted Trout 35,560 (Black-spotted is another name for cutthroats. These were probably Rio Grandes.)
1940 Rainbow Trout 48,000
1947 Rainbow Trout 114,780
1958 New Mexico Cutthroat 100,000
1961 New Mexico Cutthroat 100,000
1963 New Mexico Cutthroat 40,000[109]

These plantings included hatchery stock that had grown from northern New Mexico trout, hence the presence of Rio Grande cutthroat genes.

New Mexico Department of Game and Fish information branch chief Marty Frentzal provided an authoritative history of fish management in Las Animas Creek. He, too, attempted to ascertain if a historic population of trout had existed in Las Animas prior to settlement. According to Frentzel:

The release of exotic trout in the state had grave implications for the state's native fish fauna. Both the Rio Grande cutthroat and the Gila trout have experienced competition with brook trout and brown trout.…Those fish hybridize with natives as well as compete for food. They therefore can dilute native gene pools and even swamp the natives out of existence.…Although the…rainbow trout is recognized as the most common species capable of hybridization with cutthroats, several other species of Oncorhynchus *were introduced to the state, including 166,005,750 Black Spotted Trout. These fish arrived by rail and were stocked throughout New Mexico waters. The source for those fish in 1920, and possibly much earlier is believed to be Yellowstone National Park.*

Rainbow trout came to the Black Range in 1904 with the delivery by rail of 1,000 fish to Nutt, destined for the North Percha "River." Black-spotted trout were sent to the Gila River in 1907, that first load being 50,000 fry. In 1920, shipments of brook trout were sent to Hatch for planting in Las Animas Creek.[110]

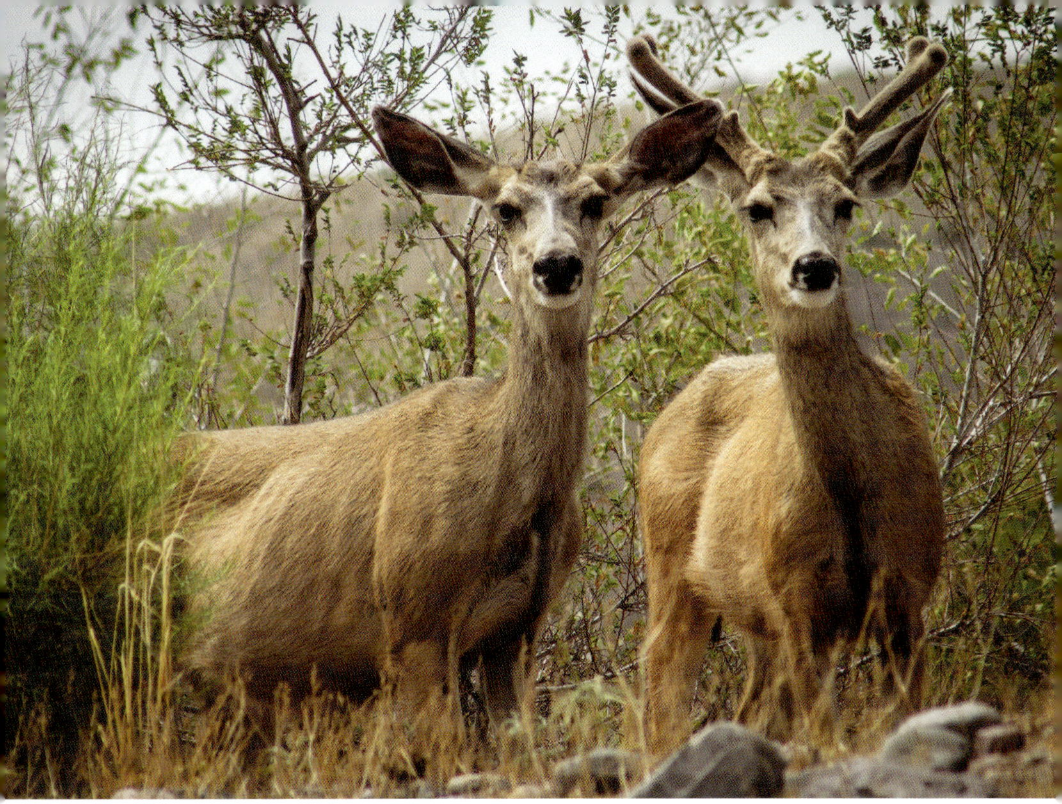

Mule deer pair. *M. Holzwarth, photographer.*

The Black Range was recognized as a destination fishing area by the U.S. Forest Service as early as 1907, but historic presence of trout in Las Animas cannot be confirmed. The only historic "literature" suggesting presence of trout in the stream is one large petroglyph about halfway up Animas that shows a fish with an adipose fin—a trait limited to salmonids and catfish.

The restoration project, with modifications, was approved by the commission and scheduled for 2013, but nature interceded. An extended drought leading up to 2013 resulted in reduced flows in Animas Creek and restriction of trout entirely to Holden Prong. Even in this upper drainage, pools became low and flow sluggish. During the summer of 2013, the lightning-started Silver Fire consumed 140,000 acres of timber on the Black Range. Early assessments of the effects of this fire suggest that ash flows and habitat modification were even more devastating than the ash flows of 1951. The trout and all other fish species were destroyed, and post-fire flooding and debris flows destroyed the road up Las Animas.

Once the road up Las Animas is restored, U.S. Forest Service, New Mexico Department of Game and Fish and Turner Endangered Species biologists will evaluate the status of the creek. If nothing else, the effects of the fire have made the conflict regarding stream renovation moot. With all fish populations gone, the question now is only when conditions will be right to stock the Rio Grande cutthroats.

Chiricahua Leopard Frogs

In 1994, Steve Dobrott identified native leopard frogs in North Seco and Animas Creeks. At the time, this species was not considered uncommon in the Southwest. It wasn't until 1995, when the Nature Conservancy Heritage Program was invited to the Ladder Ranch to conduct surveys of biologically sensitive habitats, that the Chiricahua leopard frog was recognized as unique to the area. Many years later, when this species began to disappear from 85 percent of its range, it became of concern to conservationists. The decline of the species was likely due to disease, loss of habitat, introduction of invasive species and range-wide persistent drought. In 2002, the frog was listed as threatened under the Endangered Species Act. In 2001, the Turner Endangered Species Fund began working with the U.S. Fish and Wildlife Service and the New Mexico Game and Fish Department to conserve this species. In 2012, TESF implemented an ambitious program to assist the service with a frog breeding program to enhance wild populations. A "ranarium" was built on the Ladder Ranch for the purpose of propagating the rare frogs. A full-time biologist was employed to run the facility and assist in the recovery program. Since that time, thousands of tadpoles derived from dwindling Arizona and New Mexico populations have been produced from this one-of-a-kind facility. The development of ranch frog refuges contributed greatly to the program. The importance of this work was realized after a rash of wildfires scorched thousands of acres, resulting in the loss of at least two populations of this species primarily by persistent ash runoff that decimated fish and frogs in places like Beaver Creek and Las Animas. Fortunately, breeding stock had been collected from these areas and was being held at the Ladder Ranch ranarium, affording the opportunity to restore these populations. Today, the Ladder Ranch reportedly has the most robust populations of Chiricahua leopard frogs within their New Mexico range. In 2013, Ted Turner was presented the U.S. Fish and Wildlife Service Endangered Species Recovery Champion Award for his team's important work on behalf of this species.

Mexican Wolves

In early conversations, Turner mentioned his desire to restore wolves, prairie dogs and condors to his properties, where appropriate. No one knows when the last wolf was killed in the Black Range, but they were effectively gone by the 1930s. In 1994, the U.S. Fish and Wildlife Service approached Turner for assistance with the Mexican gray wolf reintroduction program. While the Ladder Ranch was not within the legally defined wolf release area, a "transitioning" facility was needed to re-wild wolves on their way from captive bred populations to the wilds of Arizona and New Mexico. The result is five one-third-acre pens, built using five thousand hours of volunteer labor. The pens overlook middle Animas Creek and are managed in partnership with the U.S. Fish and Wildlife Service and Turner staff. Since receiving the first wolves in 1994, dozens of wolves have come and gone from this facility. Although the wolves are confined within chain-link pens, one can once again hear their howls echoing down the Animas canyon on a windless, full-moon night.

Prairie Dogs

In 1996, Steve Dobrott was queried by a graduate student regarding past existence of black-tailed prairie dogs on the ranch. An old Bureau of Biological (Animal Damage Control) Survey map indicated that, indeed, prairie dogs were poisoned, eliminating them from the grassland south of Animas Creek. Depressions along an upland swale revealed what was left of a collapsing burrow system. The rediscovery of the site prompted an effort to restore prairie dogs to the ranch. Under senior biologist Joe Truett of the Turner Endangered Species Fund, five colonies were reestablished, and for a while, the Ladder had the only black-tailed prairie dogs west of the Rio Grande. Since that time, the ranch has become a source for prairie dogs and has been instrumental in restoring colonies at the Bosque Del Apache National Wildlife Refuge and the first reintroductions of this species back into the grasslands of southern Arizona by the Arizona Game and Fish Department.

CONDORS

In 2001, the Turner Endangered Species Fund attempted to assist the California condor restoration program, hoping to provide a remote location on the Ladder for a captive condor breeding facility. Breeding pairs would be housed and used in an experimental program resulting in the release of parent-reared condors into the Gila National Forest and Aldo Leopold Wilderness. Unfortunately, funding took a downturn in 2003, and the project was terminated. Visions of vultures with nine-foot wingspans on the Animas were dashed in favor of less expensive projects. The prospect of poisoning from long use of lead-based ammunition by hunters in the area was another consideration that gave pause to biologists who voiced skepticism of success.

QUAIL

"How many coveys of desert quail can we find in an hour?"

Ted Turner asked this question just after he bought the Ladder Ranch.

"Well, sir, here in the Southwest, it's not how many coveys you hunt per hour, it's how many hours you hunt the covey."

One of the limiting factors in quail distribution is water. Large coveys of Gamble's quail were congregated around leaky livestock drinkers at the wells. After consulting a map, the ranch decided to install quail drinkers every half mile in between the wells. Today, there are approximately 150 sources of water and at least one covey of Gambel's, scaled or Mearn's quail at each site. While some quail managers believed that southwestern quail didn't need standing water, quail distribution and numbers on the Ladder was enhanced by increasing water sources. In a desert environment, water is the key to ensuring that all three quail species survive and reproduce in an otherwise marginal habitat.

OTHER BIRDS

Ornithologists have recorded 252 species of birds on the ranch; 80 percent of these species are associated with the creek's cottonwood and sycamore forests. Summer-breeding neotropicals, winter migrants and year-round residents all benefit from the riparian forest and water. With the increase in prey came raptors—Cooper's hawks, prairie falcons and peregrines.

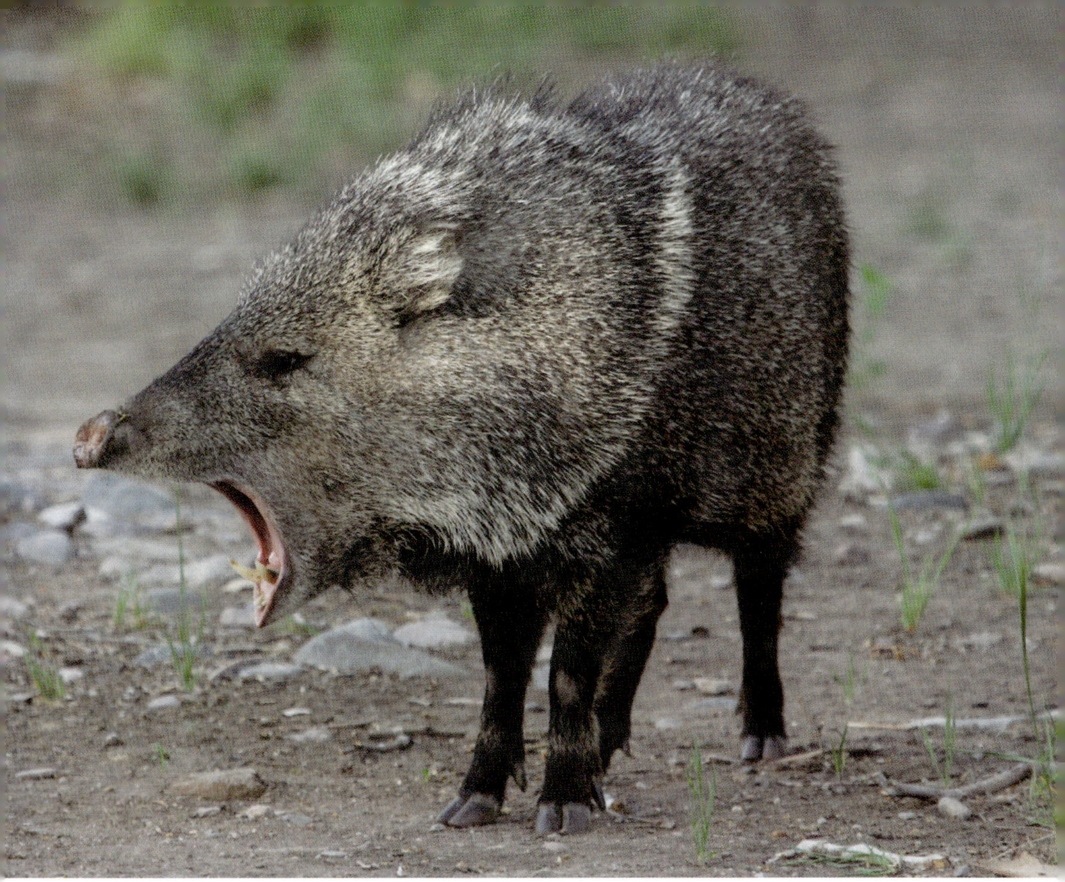

Javelina. *M. Gibson, photographer.*

Riparian obligates like the Mexican black hawk and zone-tailed hawk nest along the creek.

Las Animas Creek is a major corridor for migrating and breeding birdlife. A high percentage of the bird species utilize the riparian stream vegetation for travel and nesting. The Animas drainage affords opportunities for neotropical species like tanager, orioles and cuckoos to find refuge among the cottonwood and sycamore forests along its forty-mile length from the Black Range to the Rio Grande. The Audubon Society has nominated the Animas as one of its Important Bird Areas.

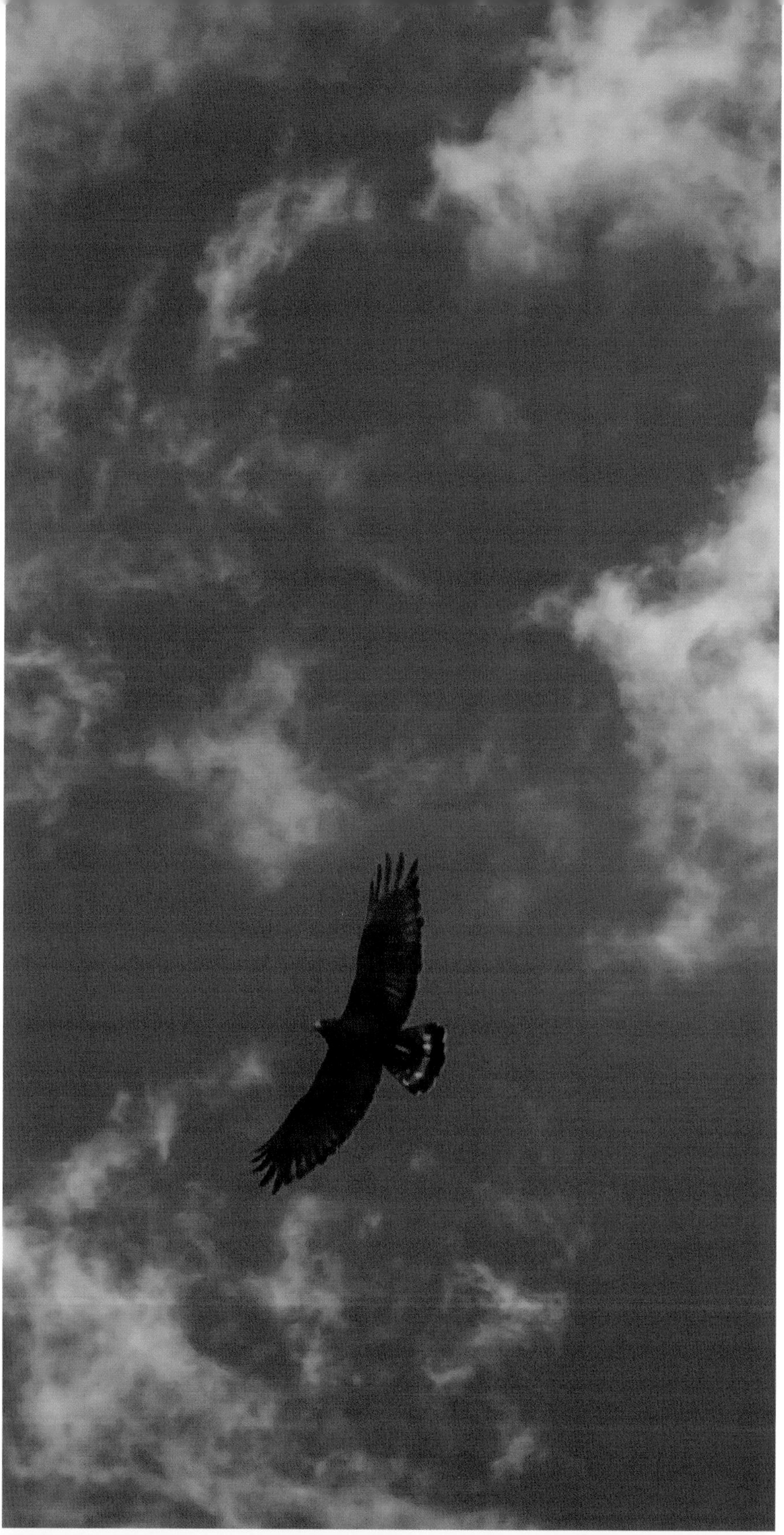

Epilogue

LAS ANIMAS FUTURE

HARLEY SHAW

Perhaps our most significant discovery in this synthesis of Las Animas literature is how little we really know about the canyon. Beginning with geology, our authors have been able to provide an overview of the mechanisms of formation of the Emory Caldera, hence Black Range, and the subsequent development of the canyon down its eastern slope. But we have no detailed description of either the canyon's lithology or hydrology. Such information is not easily acquired and may be long in coming for Las Animas if, indeed, such studies are ever accomplished. Geologist and Hillsboro resident Gretchen Kerr notes, "This type of geology is...so hashed and trashed and then geochemically-altered with the follow-on hydrothermal events, that it usually takes about a dozen PhD dissertations to get any conclusive structure nailed down." So there is work to be done and discoveries to be made, but the very remoteness of Las Animas, its complexity and its limited history of commercially valuable minerals may discourage any but the most curious and dedicated of geologists from any exploration.

Moving forward in time, virtually no paleontological studies have been carried out in the canyon. Insofar as our synthesis has explored, not a hint exists of what species occupied it during Pleistocene or earlier times. As we move forward from the Pleistocene, knowledge accrues incrementally and more uncertainties exist. Did elk range into the canyon prior to their

Opposite: Soaring. *M. Holzwarth, photographer.*

extirpation from the state in the 1880s? What have been the changes in vegetation through the various stages of human settlement? How did the Mimbres cultures use the canyon? Where, actually, was Victorio's camp? Was it at Victorio Park? If so, how and how frequently was it used? Was it a summering place in peacetime? A launching base for raiding? Or was it a bastion used only when raiding parties were pursued by Spanish and, later, U.S. troops? Are artifacts still present that could tell a more detailed story? Does the single peel tree found in Massacre Canyon signify occupation during hard times? Do other such trees exist in the area?

And what of the rock art scattered along the drainage? Which cultures chipped out the murals of fish and turtles? What art hasn't been found? What stories do the drawings tell? Is the large fish on the canyon wall evidence of native trout in the stream? If so, what does the drawing itself tell us about the astuteness of the early humans ranging up and down the creek? How were the other Mimbres culture villages located on points along the canyon related to the Las Animas Village near the Ladder headquarters? What could excavation of these upper sites tell us of early wildlife, early vegetation? How did these early occupants use the higher reaches of the canyon?

And then there were the Anglo and Hispanic families who settled along the canyon. Some obviously moved into the area as the Apaches were being subdued. But who were the Frazers, Kelseys, Dunns and Murphies? Why did they seek such isolated sites? Were they hiding from some past or merely seeking property on which to survive? How successful were they? What drove them out? Who first settled Apache Camp? These people left their names on places but left no knowledge of themselves. Is anyone left alive who can tell their stories? Did any of them write, leave photos? We have only scratched the surface and truly as yet do not know where to look for answers to these questions.

Unfortunately, after the Silver Fire of 2013, answering many of these questions may become more difficult or impossible. This mountain-wide and very hot forest fire eliminated the remains of all of the cabins except Apache Camp. Post-fire flooding scoured much of the channel of the creek from the top of the mountain to its mouth at the Rio Grande. Damage to prehistoric and historic archaeological sites has yet to be assessed, but many artifacts were undoubtedly destroyed. Fortunately, the fire did not extend outside the national forest boundary, so much of the canyon downstream and above the flood channel is intact. Most of the sycamores survived.

While some of the natural history and human history may now be beyond discovery, other aspects of the canyon are already being explored. Graduate students from the University of New Mexico are assessing the small mammal populations. The array of cameras maintained for the Furman University cougar studies have also accumulated masses of records of mid- and large-sized mammals. With the Turner philosophy of supporting science on the land, our knowledge of the River of Spirits can only increase—and with knowledge comes deeper appreciation. Thanks, Ted.

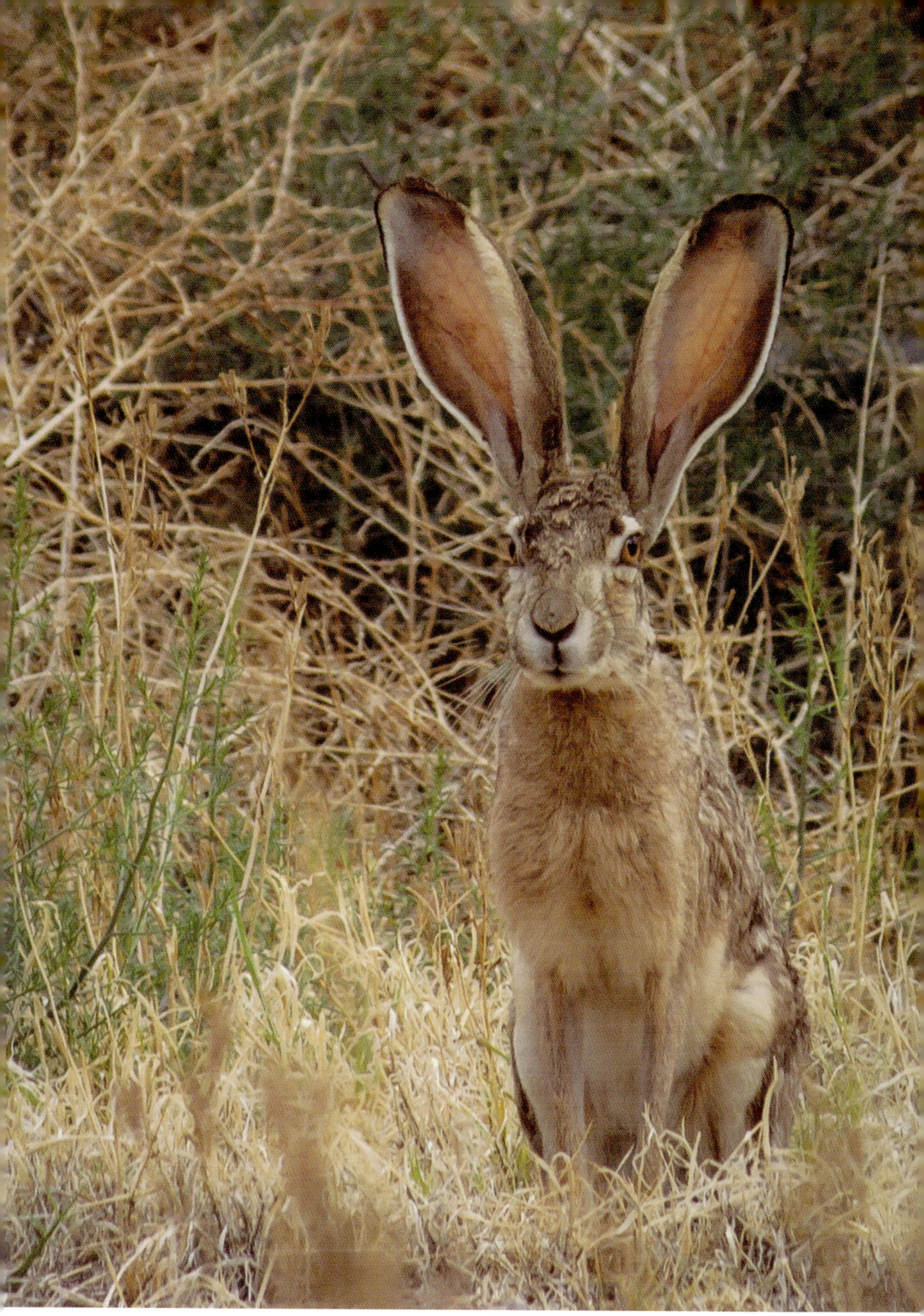

All ears! *M. Holzwarth, photographer.*

NOTES

Introduction

1. Zamora, recorded oral history.

Chapter 1

2. Harley, "Geology and Ore Deposits."
3. Davie and Spiegel, "Las Animas Creek Hydrographic Survey Report."

Chapter 2

4. This chapter represents the only portion of the book that Joe started before he died. In it, Joe summarizes a lot of historic and prehistoric information, but in many cases, he had not yet cited his sources. Where possible, I have provided references that make sense considering the information Joe presented. For some of his more general statements, I have no way of determining his source. Knowing Joe, I can only say that I'm sure his thoughts and interpretations are based on solid scholarship. Ed.
5. Hegmon and Nelson, "Archaeological Research on the Ladder Ranch."
6. Nelson and Hegmon, "Abandonment Is Not as It Seems," 213–35.
7. Nelson and Hegmon, *Mimbres Lives*.
8. Cannon, "Large Mammal Relative Abundance," 317–47.

9. Hallenbeck, *Alvar Nunez Cabeza de Vaca.*
10. Oviedo y Valdez, *Historia General y Natural de las Indias.*
11. Pattie, *Personal Narrative of James O. Pattie.*

Chapter 3

12. Forbes, *Apache, Navajo, and Spaniard*, xvi.
13. Hodge, Hammond and Rey, *Frey Alonso de Benavides*, 24–28.
14. Thomas, *Foregotten Frontiers.*
15. Wilson, "Between the River and the Mountains."

Chapter 4

16. Day Medal of Honor report.
17. According to Gibson, *Life and Death of Colonel Albert Jennings Fountain*, on June 4, 1885, Albert Fountain claimed to have led a column of New Mexico militia into Las Animas Canyon and drove Geronimo's band out of Victorio Park. This story is repeated by Owen, *Two Alberts*, quoting Gibson. None of the other historians researching Apache warfare mentions this incident. All other sources say that Geronimo was in Mexico at this time.

Chapter 5

18. Wilson, "Between the River and the Mountains."
19. Bolton, *Spanish Explorations in the Southwest.*
20. Crouch, *Jornada del Muerto.*
21. Feather, "Colonel Don Fernando," 285–304.
22. Pike, *Exploratory Travels.*
23. Pattie, *Personal Narrative of James O. Pattie.*
24. Emory, *Notes of a Military Reconnoissance*; Clarke, *Original Journals of Henry Smith Turner.*
25. Larson, *Annals of the Mormon Battalion.*
26. Lieutenant C.C. Morrison, Sixth Cavalry, USA, acting engineer officer.
27. Alberts, *Rebels on the Rio Grande.*
28. Connor, *Joseph Reddeford Walker.*

29. Bell, *New Tracks in North America.*
30. Wheeler, *Geographical Surveys.*
31. Wilson, "Between the River and the Mountains."

Chapter 6

32. Harden, "Cowboys and Cattle Rustlers."
33. Harwood, *History of New Mexico Spanish and English Missions*, 242.
34. Stanley, *Hillsboro, New Mexico Story*, 2.
35. Federal patent information in this chapter is from a land status search (LSR) of the Bureau of Land Management General Land Office Records. Retrieved from www.glorecords.blm.gov/search/default.aspx.
36. Hutchinson, Foreword, in *Best Novels and Stories of Eugene Manlove Rhodes.*
37. Stanley, *Grafton, New Mexico Story.*
38. Johnson, "Half Breed Tract."
39. Candelaria, "Gregorio Chavez," 122.
40. Harwood, *History of New Mexico Spanish and English Missions*, 242.
41. Bean, "Settlement and Stages of Frontier Systems"; 1880 U.S. Census.
42. Merlan, *Historic Homesteads*, viii–ix.
43. *Albuquerque Daily Citizen*, "Weekly Crop Bulletin."
44. Montoya, "Edward Carbajal," 92.
45. Torres, "Frances R. Torres," 92.
46. Ebeling, "Elizabeth Ebeling," 122.
47. White, *History of Sierra County Post Offices.*
48. Chatfield, Chatfield and Chatfield, "Chatfield Family," 95.
49. Gordon, "John N. Gordon," 144.
50. White, *History of Sierra County Post Offices.*
51. "Emmett L. Nations," 206.
52. Munger, "Descendents of Santiago Majalca."
53. Chatfield, interview, February 18, 2014.
54. Wilson, "Monroe M. Faulkner," 129.
55. Wilson, interview, March 6, 2013.
56. Chavez, interview, February 25, 2013.
57. Wilson, interview, March 6, 2013.
58. Chatfield, "Chatfield Heritage."
59. Chatfield, interview, February 18, 2014.
60. Chatfield, "Chatfield Heritage."
61. Chatfield, interview, February 18, 2014.

62. Chavez, interview, February 25, 2013.
63. Chatfield, interview, February 18, 2014.
64. Chavez, interview, February 25, 2013.
65. Wilson, interview, March 6, 2013.
66. Chavez, interview, February 25, 2013.
67. Chatfield, personal communication, February 22, 2014.
68. Wilson, interview, March 6, 2013.
69. Chavez, interview, February 25, 2013.
70. Chatfield, interview, February 14, 2014.

Chapter 7

71. Reid, "Book on Angora Goat."

Chapter 8

72. Incorporating smaller homesteads into what was to become the Ladder Ranch ultimately benefited the Las Animas drainage by reducing the number of people scattered along it.
73. Hopewell's efforts on behalf of the railroad included arranging for employees of the railroad and the Pennsylvania Development Company to buy land, which was then turned over to Hopewell. In the resulting scandal, President Roosevelt asked for the resignation of the territorial governor. In Congress, opponents used this scandal to delay statehood.
74. Wigmore was implicated in scurrilous dealings with senatorial candidate Myron T. Herrick. Herrick had been ambassador to France, and Wigmore's involvement with munitions occurred at the same time Herrick returned to the United States, apparently carrying inside information. According to the Lima, Ohio *Times Democrat* of Tuesday, September 26, 1916, Wigmore (undoubtedly partnering with Herrick) parlayed an initial $1,000 investment to $5 million within a single year, selling munitions through French connections. This scandal came to naught because Wigmore's holdings grew and his company, the National Munitions Corporation, received the Army-Navy "E" award for excellence in 1942.
75. Patterson, *Hardhat and Stetson*, 99.
76. Wilkinson, *Last Stand.*

Chapter 10

77. Whitham, unpublished diary.

Chapter 11

78. Sanders's death figured in the later killing of an Apache whom many thought was the so-called Apache Kid. A posse from Chloride trailed this Indian to a wikiup near the top of the San Mateo Mountains and shot him. Sanders's watch was found among the Indian's possessions, thereby clearing Mills of the murder. Sanders may have been Walter Sanders, who was married and had two children in 1900. His occupation was shown as miner.
79. This is an unrealistic estimate of the time traveling from Hillsboro. A stage route connecting Hillsboro and Hermosa crossed Animas Creek several miles downstream from Kelsey, but I doubt that the trip could have been made in less than a day.
80. Tittmann is mistaken here. As noted earlier, the Battle of Massacre Canyon occurred near here, but Victorio was killed later in Mexico.
81. I found no record for anyone named Vieg in Sierra County at this time.

Chapter 12

82. Lawson, *Log of a Timber Cruiser*.

Chapter 14

83. Brown, "Frederic Winn."
84. Winn, "U.S. Forest Service Notes."

Chapter 15

85. Ferriss, "Shell Hunt in the Black Range," 99–103.

Chapter 17

86. Little, "Checklist of United States Trees."
87. Benson and Darrow, *Manual of Southwestern Desert Trees.*
88. Holstein, "California Riparian Forests."
89. Yun Feng and Manos, "Phylogeny and Historical Biogeography of the Genus Platanus," 786–99.
90. Stromberg, "Flood Flows and Population Dynamics," 170–87.
91. Nativig, personal communication, February 7, 2015.
92. Nelson, *Mimbres during the Twelfth Century*; Schollmeyer, "Prehispanic Environmental Impact," 375–98.
93. Popova, "Initial Pollen Analysis."
94. Hammond and Rey, *Rediscovery of New Mexico*, 219.
95. Pattie, *Personal Narrative of James O. Pattie.*
96. Emory, *Notes of a Military Reconnoissance.*
97. Cooke, *Conquest of New Mexico.*
98. Jercinovic, personal communication, December 12, 2011.
99. Stromberg, "Influence of Stream Flow Regime," 227–39.
100. Kamman Hydrology & Engineering, Inc., "Phase 2 Technical Report."
101. Siegel and Bock, "Germination Requirements," 3–8.
102. Bock and Bock, "Patterns of Reproduction."
103. Stromberg, "Flood Flows and Population Dynamics," 170–87.
104. Bock and Bock, "Importance of Sycamores," 97–105.

Chapter 21

105. Frenzal, "Trout of Animas Creek."
106. Hatch, "Native Fish Fauna."
107. Hitt, Frissell, Muhlfield and Allendorf, "Spread of Hybridization," 1440–51.
108. Patten, "Genetic Status of the Trout Population."
109. Ibid.
110. Frenzal, "Trout of Animas Creek."

BIBLIOGRAPHY

Alberts, D.E. *Rebels on the Rio Grande: The Civil War Journal of A.B. Peticolas.* Albuquerque, NM: Merit Press, 1993.

Albuquerque Daily Citizen. "Stock Notes." May 24, 1902, 14. chroniclingamerica.loc.gov.

———. "Weekly Crop Bulletin." April 28, 1898. chroniclingamerica.loc.gov.

Arizona Historical Society MS: 0875, Winn Papers. Box 5. Cover Page, Fred Winn. Forest Service. Silver City, NM. April 17, 1922, to June 30, 1922.

Bean, K.M. "Settlement and Stages of Frontier Systems: The Historic America Settlement of New Mexico's Black Range Region." Unpublished doctoral dissertation. State University of New York–Buffalo, 1996.

Bell, W.A. *New Tracks in North America.* New York: Scribner, Welford, and Company, 1870.

Benson, L., and R.A. Darrow. *A Manual of Southwestern Desert Trees and Shrubs.* Tucson: University of Arizona, 1945, 411.

BLM. Land Status Search, United States Bureau of Land Management General Land Office Records, 2014. www.glorecords.blm.gov/search/default.aspx.

Bock, C.E., and J.H. Bock. "Importance of Sycamores to Riparian Birds in Southeastern Arizona." *Journal of Field Ornithology* 55 (1984): 97–105.

Bock, J.H., and C.E. Bock. 1985. "Patterns of Reproduction in Wright's Sycamore." In *Riparian Ecosystems and Their Management: Reconciling Conflicting Uses*, R.R. Johnson, C.D. Ziebell, D.R. Patton, P.F. Folliott and R.H. Hamre, 523. First North American Riparian Conf. USDA Forest Service, Rocky Mountain Forest and Range Experiment Station.

Bolton, Herbert E. *Spanish Explorations in the Southwest, 1542–1706*. New York: Charles Scribner and Sons, 1916.

Brown, D.E. "Frederic Winn (1880–1945): A Forester's Forester." Unpublished manuscript, 2010.

Candelaria, A. "Gregorio Chavez." In *History of Sierra County, New Mexico*, 122. Truth or Consequences, NM: Sierra County Historical Society, 1979.

Cannon, M.D. "Large Mammal Relative Abundance in Pithouse and Pueblo Period Archaeofaunas from Southwestern New Mexico: Resource Depression among the Mimbres Mogollon?" *Journal of Anthropological Archaeology* 19 (2000): 317–47.

Chatfield, H. "Chatfield Heritage." Unpublished paper.

———. Interview by Margie Ann Gibson. February 14, 2014. Animas Creek, NM.

———. Personal communication with Margie Ann Gibson. February 22, 2014. Animas Creek, NM.

Chatfield, H., J. Chatfield and E. Chatfield. "Chatfield Family." In *History of Sierra County, New Mexico*, 95. Truth or Consequences, NM: Sierra County Historical Society, 1979.

Chatfield, Leoma. Interview by Margie Ann Gibson. February 18, 2014. Animas Creek, NM.

Chavez, Lorraine "Dogie." Interview by Margie Ann Gibson. February 25, 2013. Animas Creek, NM.

Clarke, Dwight L. *The Original Journals of Henry Smith Turner with Stephen Watts Kearney to New Mexico and California, 1846–1847*. Norman: University of Oklahoma Press, 1966.

Connor, D.E. *Joseph Reddeford Walker and the Arizona Adventure*. Norman: University of Oklahoma Press, 1966.

Cooke, P.S.G. *The Conquest of New Mexico and California in 1846–1848*. From 1964 reproduction of book. Chicago: Rio Grande Press, Inc., 1878.

Crouch, B. *Jornada del Muerto: A Pageant of the Desert*. Spokane, WA: Arthur H. Clark Company, 1989.

Davie, W., Jr., and Z. Spiegel. "Las Animas Creek Hydrographic Survey Report: Geology and Water Resources of Las Animas Creek and Vicinity." Santa Fe: New Mexico State Engineer Office, 1967.

Dils, Lenore. *Horny Toad Man*. El Paso, TX: Boots and Saddle Press, 1966.

Downs, Winfield S., comp. *Encyclopedia of American Biography*. Vol. 8. New York: American Historical Society, 1938, 361–63.

Ebeling, E. "Elizabeth Ebeling." In *History of Sierra County, New Mexico*, 122. Truth or Consequences, NM: Sierra County Historical Society, 1979.

Elston, W.E., W.R. Seager and R.E. Clemons. "Emory Cauldron, Black Range, New Mexico, Source of the Kneeling Nun Tuff." *N.M. Geol. Soc. Guidebook*, 1975, 283–92. 26th Field Conf.

"Emmett L. Nations." In *History of Sierra County, New Mexico*, 206. Truth or Consequences, NM: Sierra County Historical Society, 1979.

Emory, W.H. *Notes of a Military Reconnoissance from Fort Leavenworth, in Missouri, to San Diego, in California Including Parts of the Arkansas, Del Norte, and Gila Rivers*. New York: H. Long and Brother, 1848.

Evans, Art. Personal recollections. Geronimo Springs Museum. Truth or Consequences and Ladder Ranch Files, n.d.

Feather, A. "Colonel Don Fernando de la Concha Diary, 1788." *New Mexico Historical Review* (1959): 285–304.

Ferriss, J.H. "A Shell Hunt in the Black Range with Description of a New Oreohelix." *Nautilus* 30, no. 9 (1917): 99–103.

Forbes, Jack D. *Apache, Navajo, and Spaniard*. Second ed. Norman: University of Oklahoma Press, 1994, xvi.

French, W. *Some Recollections of a Western Ranchman: New Mexico, 1883–1899*. N.p.: Argosy Antiquarian Ltd., 1965.

Frenzal, M. "The Trout of Animas Creek: Native Stock or Hatchery Product?" Unpublished manuscript, New Mexico Department of Game and Fish.

Gibson, A.M. *The Life and Death of Colonel Albert Jennings Fountain*. Norman: University of Oklahoma Press, 1965, 134–36.

GLO 2014. Moutre, Josette, Sierra, New Mexico. Homestead patent no. 567 D. CRI search, digital image, United States General Land Office Records. www.glorecords.blm.gov/search/default.aspx.

Gordon, V. "John N. Gordon." In *History of Sierra County, New Mexico*, 144. Truth or Consequences, NM: Sierra County Historical Society, 1979.

Hallenbeck, C. *Alvar Nunez Cabeza de Vaca: The Journey and Route of the first European to Cross the Continent of North America, 1534–1536*. Glendale, CA: Arthur C. Clarke, 1940.

Hammond, G.P., and A. Rey. *The Rediscovery of New Mexico, 1580–1594*. Albuquerque: University of New Mexico Press, 1966, 219.

Harden, P. "Cowboys and Cattle Rustlers." El Defensor Chieftain, September 1, 2012. www.dchieftain.com.

Harley, G.T. "The Geology and Ore Deposits of Sierra County, New Mexico." *New Mexico State Bureau of Mines and Mineral Resources* 10 (1934).

Harwood, T. *History of New Mexico Spanish and English Missions of the Methodist Episcopal Church from 1850 to 1910*. Albuquerque, NM: El Abogado Press, 1910, 242.

Hatch, M.D. "The Native Fish Fauna of Major Drainages East of the Continental Divide in New Mexico." Master's thesis, Eastern New Mexico University, 1985.

Hegmon, M.M., and M.C. Nelson. "Archaeological Research on the Ladder Ranch, 1994." Unpublished report by Department of Anthropology, Arizona State University, Tempe, 1995.

Hitt, N.P., C.A. Frissell, C.C. Muhlfield and F.W. Allendorf. "Spread of Hybridization between Native Westslope Cutthroat Trout, Oncorhynchus clarki lewisi, and Non-native Rainbow Trout, Oncorhynchus mykiss." *Canadian Journal of Fisheries and Aquatic Sciences* 60 (2003): 1440–51.

Hodge, F.W., G.P. Hammond and A. Rey, eds. *Frey Alonso de Benavides' Revised Memorial of 1634*. Albuquerque: University of New Mexico Press, 1945, 24–28.

Holstein, G. "California Riparian Forests: Deciduous Islands in an Evergreen Sea." In *California Riparian Systems: Ecology, Conservation and Productive Management*, edited by R.E. Warner and K.M. Hendrix. Berkeley: University of California Press, 1984.

Hutchinson, W.H. Foreword. In *The Best Novels and Stories of Eugene Manlove Rhodes*, edited by F.V. Dearing. Lincoln: University of Nebraska Press, 1987.

Jercinovic, Eugene. Personal communication. December 12, 2011. Deming, New Mexico.

Johnson, F.L. "The 'Half Breed Tract' and Scrip." MNOpedia. 2014. www.mnopedia.org/event/half-breed-tract-and-scrip.

Kamman Hydrology & Engineering, Inc. "Phase 2 Technical Report." Sycamore Grove recovery program, 2009. Sycamore Grove Park, Livermore, CA.

Kelley, V.C. "Tectonics of the Rio Grande Depression of Central New Mexico." In *New Mexico Geo. Soc. Guidebook*, 93–105. 3rd Ann. Field Conf. Rio Grande Country, Central New Mexico, 1952.

Larson, C.V. *The Annals of the Mormon Battalion, 1846–1848: An Eyewitness Account*. Spanish Fork, UT: 1700 East Electronic Media, 2000.

Lawson, William Pinkney. *The Log of a Timber Cruiser*. New York: Duffield and Company, 1915.

Little, E.L., Jr. "Checklist of United States Trees (Native and Naturalized)." *Agriculture Handbook* 541 (1979): 375. Forest Service, USDA.

Merlan, T. *Historic Homesteads and Ranches in New Mexico: A Historic Context*. Santa Fe, NM: Historic Preservation Division, Office of Cultural Affairs, 2008, viii–ix.

Montoya, L.C. "Edward Carbajal." In *History of Sierra County, New Mexico*, 92. Truth or Consequences, NM: Sierra County Historical Society, 1979.

Munger, D. "Descendents of Santiago Majalca." Unpublished manuscript. Sierra County Genealogical Society.

Nativig, Donald, University of New Mexico. Personal communication, February 7, 2015.

Nelson, M.C. *Mimbres during the Twelfth Century: Abandonment, Continuity, and Reorganization*. Tucson: University of Arizona Press, 1999.

Nelson, M.C., and M. Hegmon. "Abandonment Is Not as It Seems: An Approach to the Relationship between Site and Regional Abandonment." *American Antiquity* 66 (2001): 213–35.

———. *Mimbres Lives and Landscapes*. Santa Fe, NM: SAR Press, 2010.

Oviedo y Valdez, G.F. *Historia General y Natural de las Indias*. 4 vols. Madrid: Academia de la historia, 1851.

Owen, G.R. *Two Alberts—Fountain and Fall*. Las Cruces, NM: Yucca Tree Press, 1996.

Patten, K. "Genetic Status of the Trout Population in Upper Holden Prong of Animas Creek, Sierra County, New Mexico." New Mexico Department of Game and Fish Special Report, 2008.

Patterson, P.E. *Hardhat and Stetson: Robert O. Anderson, Oilman and Cattleman*. Santa Fe, NM: Sunstone Press, 1999, 99.

Pattie, J.O. *The Personal Narrative of James O. Pattie: The 1831 Edition Unabridged and with an Introduction by William H. Goetzmann*. New York: J.P. Lippincott Company, 1962.

Pike, Z. *Exploratory Travels through the Western Territories of North America: Comprising a Voyage from Saint Louis, on the Mississippi River, to the Source of that River, and a Journey through the Interior of Louisiana, and the North-eastern Provinces of New Spain*. Denver: W.H. Lawrence and Company, 1889.

Popova, L. "Initial Pollen Analysis of Samples from LA 3949, New Mexico." Special report. Barrett Honors College, Arizona State University, Tempe, 2014.

Reid, J. "Book on Angora Goat and Mohair Industry." Unpublished manuscript, 1928. Armer-Reid Papers, Rio Grande Collection, Branson Library, New Mexico State University.

Rhamy, R. "H.A. Ringer." In *History of Sierra County, New Mexico*, 237. Truth or Consequences, NM: Sierra County Historical Society, 1979.

Schollmeyer, K.G. "Prehispanic Environmental Impact in the Mimbres Region, Southwestern New Mexico." *KIVA: The Journal of Southwestern Archaeology and History* 70, no. 4 (Summer 2005): 375–98.

Sherman, J.E., and Barbara H. Sherman. *Ghost Towns and Mining Camps of New Mexico*. Norman: University of Oklahoma Press, 1974, 110–11.

Siegel, R.S., and J.H. Bock. "Germination Requirements of Key Southwestern Woody Riparian Species." *Desert Plants* 10 (1990): 3–8.

Sierra County Clerk's Office. Miscellaneous record book A, 327–29.

Sierra County Tax Assessor. 1887. Microfilm. New Mexico Records Center and Archives, Santa Fe.

Socorro County Clerk's Office, New Mexico. Various dates. Deeds are scattered throughout Warranty Deed Books 8 and 10.

Stanley, F. *The Grafton, New Mexico Story*. N.p., 1973. He is quoting the *Black Range* newspaper of May 29, 1885.

———. *The Hillsboro, New Mexico Story.* N.p., 1964, 2.

Stein, K.S. "1890 New Mexico Tax Assessments: A Territorial Census Substitute." *New Mexico Genealogical Society* (2003): 91.

Stevens, M. *Meet Mr. Grizzly*. Albuquerque: University of New Mexico Press, 1943.

Stromberg, J.C. "Flood Flows and Population Dynamics of Arizona Sycamore (*Platanus wrightii*)." *Western North American Naturalist* 62 (2002): 170–87.

———. "The Influence of Stream Flow Regime and Temperature on Growth Rate of the Riparian Tree, *Platanus wrightii*, in Arizona." *Freshwater Biology* 46 (2001): 227–39.

Thomas, A.B. *Foregotten Frontiers*. Norman: University of Oklahoma Press, 1932.

Torres, F.R. "Frances R. Torres." In *History of Sierra County, New Mexico*, 92. Truth or Consequences, NM: Sierra County Historical Society, 1979.

Wheeler, G.M. *Geographical Surveys of the Territory of the United States West of the 100th Meridian: Annual Report of the Chief of Engineers for 1879*. Washington, D.C.: Government Printing Office, 1879.

White, J.W. *The History of Sierra County Post Offices*. N.p., 2001.

Whitham, J.D. Unpublished diary in Hillsboro Historical Society files.

Wikipedia. "Gila National Forest." en.wikipedia.org/w/index.php?title=Gila_National_Forest&oldid=64860313.

Wilkinson, T. *Last Stand: Ted Turner's Quest to Save a Troubled Planet*. Guilford, CT: Lyons Press, 2013.

Willard S. Hopewell Papers. Center for Southwest Research, University of New Mexico. Folder 6.

Wilson, J.D. "Monroe M. Faulkner." In *History of Sierra County, New Mexico*, 129. Truth or Consequences, NM: Sierra County Historical Society, 1979.

Wilson, Josephine "Daisy." Interview by Margie Ann Gibson. March 6, 2013. Williamsburg, NM.

Wilson, J.P. "Between the River and the Mountains: A History of Early Settlement in Sierra County, New Mexico." Unpublished manuscript, 1985. Provided by Black Range District, U.S. Forest Service, Gila National Forest, Truth or Consequences, NM.

Winn, F. "U.S. Forest Service Notes." 1922. On file at Arizona State Historical Society, Tucson.

Yun Feng, S.O., and P.S. Manos. "Phylogeny and Historical Biogeography of the Genus Platanus as Inferred from Nuclear and Chloroplast DNA." *Systematic Botany* 30, no. 4 (2005): 786–99.

Zamora, Luis. Recorded oral history. Ladder Ranch files.

INDEX

D

E

F

P

Q

R

S

T

U

V

W

Y

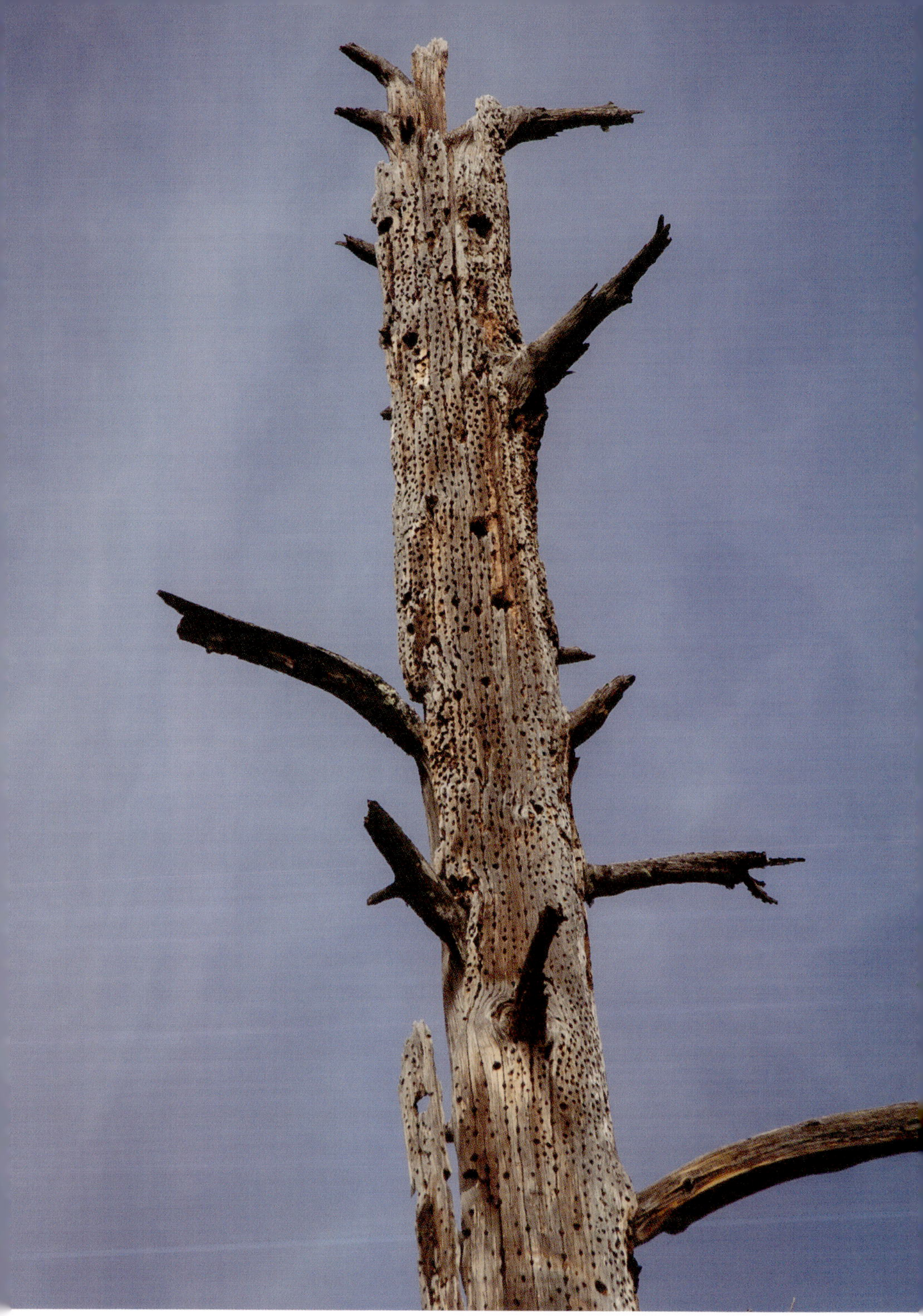

All used up. *M. Holzwarth, photographer.*

ABOUT THE AUTHORS

Charles Britton retired as associate dean of the College of Engineering at Colorado State University–Fort Collins. He became interested in New Mexico's Sierra County when his son and daughter-in-law acquired the historic Bucher House in Hillsboro. He is the author of *The Quanah Route: A Texas Short Line Railroad* and lives in Fort Collins.

David Coblentz is a deputy group leader in geophysics at Los Alamos National Laboratory. He studies solid earth geophysics and geodynamics and does tectonic stress modeling. He is also active in tectonic geomorphology, specializing in topographic fabric and its relationship to the underlying geology and biodiversity. His most recent work has focused on the common ground between plate tectonics and geoecology.

Steve Dobrott has managed the four-hundred-square-mile Ladder Ranch in southern New Mexico for over twenty-five years. Before going to work for Turner Enterprises Inc., he was a refuge biologist for the U.S. Fish and Wildlife Service working with the endangered masked bobwhite. His current position involves restoration of imperiled species like the Mexican gray wolf, bolson tortoises, Chiricahua leopard frogs, black-tailed prairie dogs and bison.

Ken Dusenberry is a retired Albuquerque police officer living in Albuquerque with his wife, Marilyn. He is president of the Artillery Company of New

Mexico, which is dedicated to preserving history through the medium of live reenactment and first-person presentations. A University of New Mexico graduate, Ken served on the Home Town Heroes Committee for the National Medal of Honor Society. This committee spent thirteen years locating the grave sites of ten Medal of Honor Recipients known to have died in New Mexico. This search led the committee to the Massacre Canyon Battle.

Art Evans (1922–2013) grew up on the family ranch north of Phoenix, Arizona. He was involved in the livestock industry most of his life. He served in the navy during World War II. After the war, he worked in the open-pit mines at Bagdad, Arizona, and as an Arizona brand inspector. In 1953, Art hired on with Tovrea Cattle Company on the Ladder Ranch. He was foreman until 1981, working for three different owners, and then became manager of several of Robert O. Anderson's ranches in New Mexico and Texas. He retired in 1991 and returned to the Ladder as a consultant for Turner Enterprises Inc.

James Ferriss (1849–1926) was an amateur shell collector who traveled widely. He made annual trips to Arizona and New Mexico between 1904 and 1919, accompanying leading conchologists of that era. He was a businessman and journalist by profession but was considered to be the foremost American land shell collector of his time.

Margie Gibson was born in Seattle and grew up exploring the Pacific Northwest. Her interest in nature led to a career in conservation and a hobby in wildlife photography. In 1979, she moved to Alaska as the field representative for Friends of the Earth and worked with native communities for habitat protection. For several years, she ran her own graphic design business but returned to conservation as executive director of Arctic Network. Margie and her husband, Mike Holloway, now live on Animas Creek in the winter and return to Alaska every summer.

Matilde Holzwarth came to fine art photography after a career in neuroscience, where technical photography was an important tool. Photography has long been Matilde's medium for expressing her artistic side. She has participated in numerous photography workshops, studying with several well-known photographers. Matilde's photographs capture unique moods in landscapes, nature, architecture and people with an eye for the beauty, intricacy and significance of each.

Gretchen Kent (Kerr) earned a BA in earth science from Dartmouth and an MS in geology/geochemistry from Michigan Technological University. Her interests focus on the volcanic evolution in the Basin and Range Province of the southwestern United States and depositions of precious metals. Her master's thesis involved the geochemistry and mineralization of the Mogollon Mining District. She was a geologist and an engineer officer in the U.S. Army. Later, while director of Strategic and Sustainability Planning at Fort Huachuca, Arizona, she helped the USGS produce a detailed geophysical survey of the Upper San Pedro Basin as part of a long-term water resource management plan. This plan led to purchases of conservation easements and changes in the county requirements for water conservation. She was also part of a team that was awarded the 2003 White House Closing the Circle Award for Sustainability and has received team-level awards from the Department of Agriculture, Department of the Interior and Arizona Chapter of the Nature Conservancy.

William Pinkney Lawson (1885–1942) joined a U.S. Forest Service timber survey team in about 1905. He published three books: *Log of a Timber Cruiser* (1915), *Lem Allen* (1923) and *Fire Woman* (1925). He served on the staff of *Harper's* magazine and wrote a column for the *Santa Fe New Mexican*. Little is known about him after he left New Mexico.

Matthew McCollister was born in Montgomery, Alabama, in 1983 and grew up hunting and fishing in Alabama, central Georgia and Florida. He attended Furman University in Greenville, South Carolina, spending summers doing fieldwork in New Mexico and Alaska. After acquiring a degree in biology, he moved to New Mexico to work with mountain lions and desert bighorn on the Ladder and Armendaris Ranches. He returned to graduate school in 2006 and completed a master's degree at the University of Tennessee, studying black bears. He has since worked on Rocky Mountain bighorn, black and grizzly bears and mountain lions. He is a wildlife biologist for the Charles M. Russell National Wildlife Refuge.

Travis Perry was raised in South Carolina. He attended Furman University for his BS and completed a PhD at the University of New Mexico. He is a professor of biology at Furman University and has carried out research on bats in Animas Creek. In 2005, he began a study of mountain lions and joined the faculty at Clemson University as an adjunct professor. Much of his mountain lion research is focused around Animas Creek.

Harley Shaw was a wildlife research biologist with Arizona Game and Fish Department from 1963 to 1990. Since retiring, he has published three books: *Soul Among Lions*, *Stalking the Big Bird* and *1200 Miles by Horse and Burro*. He has also written three previous book-length watershed-related reports: *Garden Canyon Watershed: A Vision and a Mission*, *Natural History of a Small Place: Pueblo Colorado Wash at Hubbell Trading Post* and *Wood Plenty, Grass Good, Water None: Vegetation Change on the Upper Verde River Watershed*. He is the managing editor of the *Wild Felid Monitor* and edits *Guajalotes, Zopilotes, y Paisanos*, the newsletter of the Hillsboro Historical Society. He lives in Hillsboro, New Mexico, within an easy drive of Las Animas Creek and Ladder Ranch.

Joe C. Truett (1941–2011) was a senior biologist with the Turner Endangered Species Fund, where he spearheaded restoration of prairie dogs, black-footed ferrets, bolson tortoises and Chiricahua leopard frogs. He authored many technical papers, as well as four books. Had he lived, he would have been the lead author and editor of *River of Spirits*. His kind, philosophical demeanor has been severely missed by those of us who have finished the project.

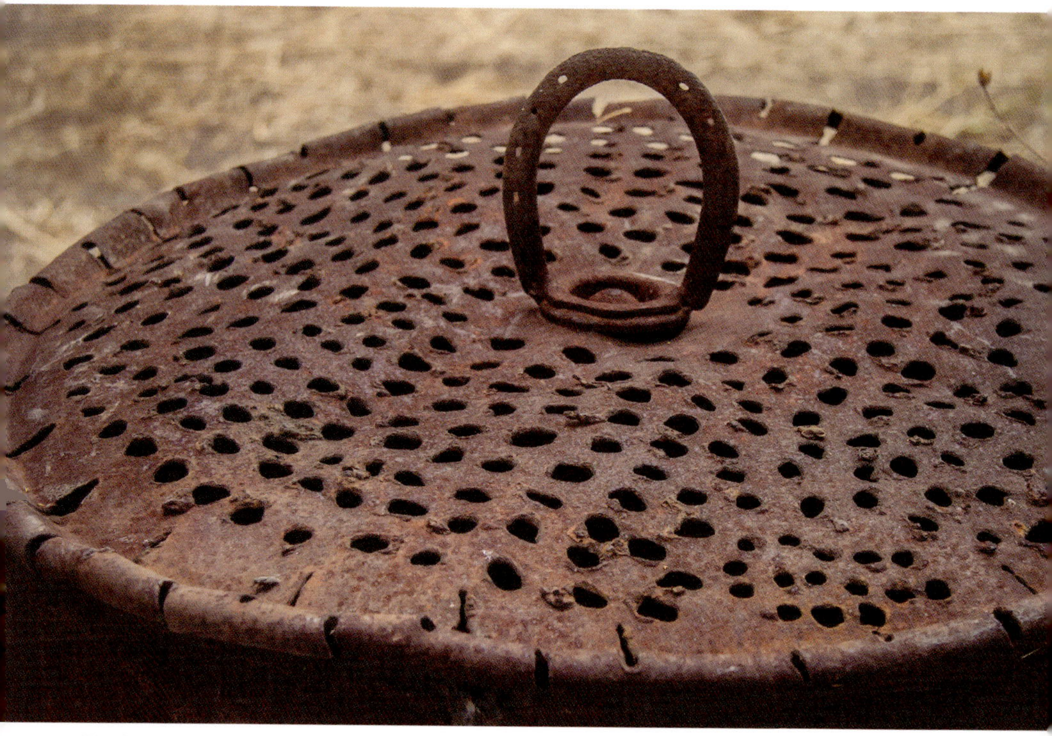

Lucky burn barrel. *M. Holzwarth, photographer.*